Shifts and Transpositions in Medieval Narrative

A Festschrift for Dr Elspeth Kennedy

The essays in this collection are in celebration of the research and teaching career of Dr Elspeth Kennedy (St Hilda's College, Oxford), whose work on the non-cyclic *Prose Lancelot* is admired by students of Arthurian literature throughout the world. The contributors to this volume (most of whom were taught or advised by Dr Kennedy) focus on the processes of innovation and transformation, and the relationship between tradition and originality in medieval literature. They consider shifts from one genre to another and their implications for audience expectations; translation and adaptation from one language and culture to another, or from one medium to another (verse to prose, lyric to romance narrative, the textual to the visual); transpositions of a theme or story within or between narratives; the process of rewriting a work in the same language and the new author's attitude to his predecessor and source. The contributors also adopt a range of different approaches, reflecting the latest research in gender studies, generic intertextuality, translation theory, psychoanalysis, anthropology, and often explaining thematic shifts and transpositions in terms of new and changing historical contexts. Several literary genres (epic, romance, didactic literature, and even the lyric and drama) are treated, and works in different languages (Latin, Old and Middle French, Middle High German, Old and Middle English) are examined, all testifying to the diversity of Elspeth Kennedy's interests and her generous encouragement of students working in all areas of medieval studies.

Elspeth Kennedy at a party held by seminar members to celebrate her retirement from St Hilda's

SHIFTS AND TRANSPOSITIONS IN MEDIEVAL NARRATIVE

A Festschrift for Dr Elspeth Kennedy

EDITED BY
KAREN PRATT

assisted by
Penny Eley, Sarah Kay, Ceridwen Lloyd-Morgan,
Jane H. M. Taylor and Jocelyn Wogan-Browne

D. S. BREWER

First published 1994
D. S. Brewer, Cambridge

ISBN 0 85991 421 6

D. S. Brewer is an imprint of Boydell & Brewer Ltd
PO Box 9, Woodbridge, Suffolk IP12 3DF, UK
and of Boydell & Brewer Inc.
PO Box 41026, Rochester, NY 14604–4126, USA

British Library Cataloguing-in-Publication Data
Shifts and Transpositions in Medieval Narrative:
Festschrift for Dr. Elspeth Kennedy
I. Pratt, Karen
809.02
ISBN 0–85991–421–6

Library of Congress Cataloging-in-Publication Data
Shifts and transpositions in medieval narrative : a festschrift for Dr. Elspeth Kennedy / edited by Karen Pratt ; assisted by Penny Eley . . . [et al.].
p. cm.
Includes bibliographical references and index.
ISBN 0–85991–421–6 (hardcover : alk. paper)
1. Literature, Medieval – History and criticism. I. Pratt, Karen. II. Eley, Penny. III. Kennedy, Elspeth.
PN681.S5 1994
809'.02–dc20 94–5305

The paper used in this publication meets the minimum requirements of American National Standard for Information Sciences – Permanence of Paper for Printed Library Materials, ANSI Z39.48–1984

Printed in Great Britain by
St Edmundsbury Press Ltd, Bury St Edmunds, Suffolk

Contents

Contributors

Professor E. BAUMGARTNER Sorbonne Nouvelle, Paris
Dr M. BOULTON University of Notre Dame, USA
Dr A. CLASSEN University of Arizona, USA
Dr P. ELEY University of Sheffield
Dr S. KAY Girton College, Cambridge
Professor D. KELLY University of Wisconsin, Madison, USA
Dr C. LLOYD-MORGAN National Library of Wales, Aberystwyth
Professor D. MADDOX University of Massachusetts, Amherst, USA
Professor S. STURM-MADDOX University of Massachusetts, Amherst, USA
Dr R. PENSOM Hertford College, Oxford
Dr J. PINDER Victoria, Australia
Dr K. PRATT King's College, London
Dr A. SAVAGE McMaster University, Ontario, Canada
Dr J. TAYLOR St Hilda's College, Oxford
Dr J. WALLACE University of Sydney, Australia
Dr N. WATSON University of Western Ontario, Ontario, Canada

Foreword

DOUGLAS KELLY

ELSPETH KENNEDY WOULD BE the first to object to the assertion that we owe the *Non-cyclic Lancelot* to her. The *Non-cyclic Lancelot*, she would gently but firmly remind us, has been there since the thirteenth century. She merely found it again and presented it to us in an impeccable edition and a masterly study.

For, to discover and identify the *Non-cyclic Lancelot* again has been Elspeth Kennedy's life work. It has been a long road, marked from time to time by major essays on different aspects of the prose romance, its manuscripts, and its relation to other twelfth- and thirteenth-century verse and prose romances, especially the *Cyclic Lancelot*. Reading those essays reminds us how the true scholar, after thorough investigation of all available evidence, acquires knowledge based on informed, well grounded conviction. As time passed, the scope of the critical text, the demands of investigation, debate, and interpretation, made us aware that here a major achievement was in the process of realization. How eagerly we awaited the results – the monumental edition, a model of the art of editing, the in-depth study. Both of which appeared, but only when they were ready.

In scholarly response to Elspeth Kennedy's presentation of the *Non-cyclic Lancelot* and her own defence of its existence and qualities, and whatever side or view one might take on the matter, two facts emerged clearly and, to my mind, irrefutably: there is a discrete entity that can be called the *Non-cyclic Lancelot* and it has been identified by a scholar whose learning, integrity, and humanity have not failed to command recognition and respect among all those who have known her.

Elspeth Kennedy's scholarship is both wide-ranging and profound. She knows the manuscripts, she knows medieval romance. Furthermore, she is open to the sensible, intelligent use of the implications of that romance for larger subjects and issues: cyclicity, intertextuality, rewriting and scribal intervention.

Elspeth Kennedy's professional standards are evident not only in her published scholarship. One finds her invited to, and busy reading papers and participating in, congresses and symposia. Indeed, she has been almost ubiquitous since retirement. She appears almost everywhere – at congresses north and south, at colloquia and symposia all over Europe and North America, visiting colleagues and students, and receiving with great hospitality visitors from Europe and North America, even from such distant sites as Wisconsin if not *ultima Thule* itself. Invited to her home, visitors enjoy her hospitality in a lovely black and white cottage surrounded by an enchanted garden teeming with animal and bird life. The rooms are full of learning, and not far is one of the finest pubs in the British Isles. The home is also near Oxford, where Elspeth Kennedy spent most of her academic life after World War II until retirement, and where she is still evident at St Hilda's at table and participating in medieval interest groups.

During the war, she continued her studies while serving. Afterwards, in the fabled courses and seminars she supervised at Oxford and the medieval discussion group she fostered there for decades and continues to animate, students and colleagues discovered the human and intellectual qualities that have made and continue to make us admire Elspeth Kennedy to this day.

To be sure, Elspeth Kennedy is English. She is an English woman in a grand, international tradition: open to the world and true to herself. And we shall always love her for it. This volume, and those who have contributed to it, is an expression of that esteem and affection.

Bibliography of Writings by Elspeth Kennedy

'The Two Versions of the False Guinevere Episode in the Old French Prose *Lancelot*', *Romania*, 77 (1956), 94–104.

'Social and Political Ideas in the French Prose *Lancelot*', *Medium Aevum*, 26 (1957), 90–106.

'King Arthur in the First Part of the Prose *Lancelot*', in *Medieval Miscellany presented to Eugène Vinaver*, ed. by F. Whitehead, A. Diverres and F. Sutcliffe (Manchester: Manchester University Press, 1965), pp. 186–95.

'The Scribe as Editor', in *Mélanges de Langue et de Littérature du Moyen Age et de la Renaissance offerts à Jean Frappier*, 2 vols (Geneva: Droz, 1970), pp. 523–31.

'The Use of *Tu* and *Vous* in the First Part of the Old French Prose *Lancelot*', in *The History and Structure of French: Essays in Honour of Professor T. B. W. Reid*, ed. by Barnett, Crow, Robson, Rothwell and Ullmann (Oxford: Blackwell, 1972), pp. 135–49.

'Un Fragment anglo-normand de la *Folie Tristan* de Berne', *Le Moyen Age*, 79 (1973), 57–72 (with Ruth J. Dean).

'The Role of the Supernatural in the First Part of the Old French Prose *Lancelot*', in *Studies in Medieval Literature and Languages in Memory of Frederick Whitehead*, ed. by W. Rothwell et al. (Manchester: Manchester University Press, 1973), pp. 173–84.

'Royal Broodings and Lovers' Trances in the First Part of the Prose *Lancelot*', in *Mélanges de philologie et de littérature romanes offerts à Jeanne Wathelet-Willem* (Liège: Marche Romane, 1978), pp. 301–14.

***Lancelot do Lac: The Non-cyclic Old French Prose Romance*, 2 vols (Oxford: Clarendon Press, 1980).**

'Le Personnage de Lancelot dans le *Lancelot* en prose', in *Lancelot*, ed. by D. Buschinger, GAG 415 (Göppingen: Kümmerle, 1984), pp. 99–106.

'Etudes sur le *Lancelot en prose*', *Romania*, 105 (1984), 34–46 and 46–62.

'Le Rôle d'Yvain et de Gauvain dans le *Lancelot* en prose (version non-cyclique)', in *Lancelot, Yvain et Gauvain: Colloque arthurien belge de Wégimont* (Paris: Nizet, 1984), pp. 19–27.

***Lancelot and the Grail: A Study of the Prose 'Lancelot'* (Oxford: Clarendon Press, 1986).**

'The Re-writing and Re-reading of a Text: The Evolution of the Prose

Lancelot', in *The Changing Face of Arthurian Romance: Essays on Arthurian Prose Romances in Memory of Cedric E. Pickford*, ed. A. Adams et al., Arthurian Studies, 16 (Cambridge: Brewer, 1986), pp. 1–9.

'Lancelot und Perceval: zwei junge unbekannte Helden', *Wolfram-Studien*, 9 (1986), 228–41.

Introduction to *Lancelot of the Lake*, trans. with notes by Corin Corley, The World's Classics (Oxford/New York: Oxford University Press, 1988).

'The Quest for Identity and The Importance of Lineage in Thirteenth-Century French Prose Romance', in *The Ideals and Practice of Medieval Knighthood II: Papers from the Third Strawberry Hill Conference*, ed. by Christopher Harper-Bill and Ruth Harvey (Cambridge: Brewer, 1988), pp. 70–86.

'Les Structures narratives et les allusions intertextuelles dans le *Tristan en prose*', in *Nouvelles Recherches sur le 'Tristan en prose'*, ed. by Jean Dufournet (Geneva: Slatkine, 1990), pp. 123–47.

'Failure in Arthurian Romance', *Medium Aevum*, 60 (1991), 16–32.

' "Lancelot li mescheans". Mischance and Individual Responsibility in the *Lancelot-Grail*', in *De ongevalliche Lanceloet: Studies over de Lancelotcompilatie*, ed. by Bart Besamusca and Frank Brandsma (Hilversum: Verloren, 1992), pp. 117–36.

'Le *Lancelot* en prose (MS 45)', in *Les Manuscrits français de la bibliothèque Parker: Parker Library, Corpus Christi College, Cambridge. Actes du colloque 24–27 mars, 1993*, ed. by Nigel Wilkins (Cambridge: Parker Library Publications, 1993), pp. 23–38.

'The Narrative Techniques Used to Give Arthurian Romance a "Historical" Flavour', in *Conjunctures: Medieval Studies in Honor of Douglas Kelly*, ed. by Keith Busby and Norris Lacy (Amsterdam-Atlanta, 1994), pp. 219–33.

Sous Presse

"The Knight as Reader of Arthurian Romance', in *Culture and the King: The Social Implications of the Arthurian Legend* (Studies in honor of Valerie Lagorio and Mildred Day), ed. by James Carley and Martin Schichtmann (Albany: Suny Press, 1994).

'Editer un bestseller médiéval: le *Lancelot* en prose', in the Proceedings of a Conference held in Liège, ed. by Janine Delcourt-Angélique.

'Chrétien de Troyes comme intertexte du *Lancelot* en prose', in *Amour et chevalerie dans les romans de Chrétien de Troyes*, ed. Danielle Quéruel (Besançon: Presses Universitaires de Besançon, 1994).

'Variations in the Patterns of Interlace in the *Lancelot-Grail*', in *The Lancelot-Grail Cycle*, ed. by William Kibler (Austin: University of Texas Press, 1994), pp. 31–50.

The Figure of Lancelot in the *Lancelot-Graal*', in *Lancelot and Guinevere: A Casebook*, ed. with an introduction by Lori Walters (New York: Garland, 1995).

Numerous reviews in scholarly journals and papers delivered at conferences.

Introduction

KAREN PRATT

'In change delight' (John Donne)

THIS COLLECTION OF ESSAYS in honour of Dr Elspeth Kennedy was conceived in 1987 just before her retirement from St Hilda's College, as a tribute to her research and teaching career in Oxford. In particular, we wanted to thank her for the generous encouragement she gave to graduate students working on a whole range of aspects of medieval studies, by welcoming them to the seminar she held at St Hilda's and providing them with a stimulating and supportive environment in which to test their ideas. Many of the contributors to this volume, some of whom are in the early stages of their academic careers, have benefited from Elspeth's inspiration, and her influence, both intellectual and humane, is now to be felt in universities as far apart as Arizona, Sydney and Cambridge.

Since her retirement, Elspeth Kennedy has been tireless in her pursuit of knowledge in the field of Old French romance; a glance at the bibliography of her published work is testimony to the great flowering of her research in the last few years. Given her enormous contribution to the field, it was only fitting that Elspeth Kennedy should be elected president of the British Branch of the International Arthurian Society and then International President, in which capacity she presided with her usual charm and diffidence over the international meeting in Durham in 1990. The well-deserved academic accolades continue to flow; our hope is that this *Festschrift*, so long in coming to fruition, will be a worthy contribution to the celebration of a great scholar and teacher.

The theme of this volume, shifts and transpositions in medieval narrative, was chosen because it is wide in scope, yet represents a fundamental aspect of medieval literature and culture. It has enabled the contributors to exploit their own areas of expertise (as indeed they were encouraged to do at Elspeth's seminars), resulting in the inclusion of a rich mixture of languages and literatures (Latin, Old and Middle French, Middle High

German, Old and Middle English), a variety of genres (epic, romance, didactic literature, lyric and theatre) and a range of approaches, which reflect the latest research in gender studies, generic intertextuality, translation theory, psychoanalysis, anthropology, narratology, and reception theory/audience response. At the same time, each essay is in some way concerned with the tension between tradition and originality so characteristic of medieval literature, and with the processes of transformation, transposition, and *translatio*, which enabled medieval authors to make their own contribution to a tradition which was constantly in the process of being rewritten.

Change in medieval literature manifested itself in various ways: most obviously in the instability of the text or its *mouvance*,[1] a phenomenon to which editors of medieval texts are at pains to do justice.[2] The text, being one manifestation/actualisation of group discourse, was considered to be the property of no-one and was therefore constantly susceptible to scribal modification, *remaniement* and plundering.[3] Within this culture, the concept of plagiarism barely existed (although Matthew of Vendôme does criticise 'ill-taught persons [. . .] who paraphrase the fables of poets word for word'),[4] and the rewriting of traditional material was actively recommended in the schools:

> Et quanto difficilius tanto laudabilius est bene tractare materiam talem, scilicet communem et usitatam, quam materiam aliam, scilicet novam et inusitatam. (Geoffrey of Vinsauf, *Documentum*, II, 3, item 132)[5]

1 See Paul Zumthor, *Essai de poétique médiévale* (Paris: Seuil, 1972), pp. 65–75 and 'Intertextualité et mouvance', *Littérature*, 41 (1981), 8–16, where he identifies *modèles* and *variations* as the two main factors in medieval text production.

2 See the special issue of *Romance Philology*, 45 (1991) on textual criticism, especially Mary Speer's survey article 'Editing Old French Texts in the Eighties: Theory and Practice', pp. 7–43, which includes interesting remarks on *la critique génétique* and a useful review of Bernard Cerquiglini's *Eloge de la variante* (Paris: Seuil, 1989).

3 See Elspeth Kennedy's publications on the evolution of the Prose *Lancelot* for an illustration of these processes of re-reading, re-writing and scribal editing.

4 See Matthew of Vendôme's *Ars versificatoria* in Edmond Faral's *Les Arts poétiques du XIIe et du XIIIe siècle: recherches et documents sur la technique littéraire du moyen âge* (Paris: Champion, 1924) and Ernest Gallo's translation 'Matthew of Vendôme: Introductory Treatise on the Art of Poetry', *Proceedings of the American Philosophical Society*, 118 (1974), 51–92 (p. 84).

5 Quoted from the edition by Faral in *Les Arts poétiques*. For a more detailed discussion of the theoretical teachings of the *artes poeticae* see my 'Medieval Attitudes to Translation and Adaptation: The Rhetorical Theory and the Poetic Practice', in *The Medieval Translator*, ed. by Roger Ellis (London: Westfield Medieval Publications, 1991), pp. 1–27.

> (And just as it is more difficult, so it is more praiseworthy to treat well such material, that is well known and familiar, than to treat the other sort of material, which is new and unfamiliar.)

That authors relished the challenge of treating such *materiam communem* is amply illustrated in this volume by the essays on the matter of Britain and of Troy. Yet, as Douglas Kelly has recently shown, even here the process of transposition remains fundamental: medieval *inventio* was defined not as the slavish imitation of models, nor as the invention of novel subject-matter, but as the new arrangement of topical material:

> First, the author has an idea or mental conception of a subject. Second, material is sought and identified through which the initial conception may find appropriate statement and elaboration. Third, the mental conception and the *materia* are meshed as the subject-matter of the work.[6]

While tradition (or Zumthor's *sub-traditions*), provided medieval culture with stability in the form of a stock of motifs to be re-used and of non-textual models to be actualised, it was not static, but a 'phenomenon of the present' and an 'agent of cultural change'.[7] The essays in this collection demonstrate that despite (or perhaps because of) medieval writers' fascination with and respect for the past, their culture constantly evolved. New genres developed and old ones were revitalised through intertextual links with the new; new modes of literary expression were introduced (notably the shift from verse to prose, with again a fruitful mixing of the two); traditional concepts were redefined (what constitutes chivalry, *courtoisie*, marriage, femininity, masculinity?) and audiences were challenged anew. In spanning much of Europe and the tenth to the fifteenth centuries, Elspeth Kennedy's *Festschrift* attempts to give us a glimpse of that 'continuity across change' (Nichols, p. 7) so characteristic of medieval culture.

To begin the collection, Emmanuèle Baumgartner surveys the shift from classical to Celtic source material, and from verse to prose in twelfth- and thirteenth-century French literature. She uses Genette's distinction between *diction* and *fiction* in order to examine how writers of romance construct an appropriate poetic language and emphasise the

6 Douglas Kelly, *The Art of Medieval French Romance* (Wisconsin: The University of Wisconsin Press, 1992), p. 38.

7 See Stephen G. Nichols, 'The New Medievalism: Tradition and Discontinuity in Medieval Culture', in *The New Medievalism*, ed. by Marina S. Brownlee, Kevin Brownlee, and Stephen G. Nichols (Baltimore: Johns Hopkins University Press, 1991), pp. 1–26 (p. 10).

fictionality of their works. The authors of the *romans antiques* concentrate on diction, their subject-matter inherited from classical sources being presented largely as history. (Penny Eley's essay later in this volume takes a rather different view of this process.) Chrétien de Troyes, on the other hand, stresses the fictionality of his works by placing the non-historical *matière de Bretagne* in a non-specific spatial and temporal context. The thirteenth-century *romanciers'* preference for prose (which, as M. Jourdain eventually discovers, is the language of common parlance, and was therefore not readily identifiable as the diction of fiction) was not motivated by a desire for authenticity. Nor, Baumgartner argues, are the references to the origins of these prose narratives in the eye-witness accounts of Arthur's knights meant to reassure us of their truth. In fact, the repetition of 'or dist li contes' (a hallmark of the prose *romancier*'s diction and indicator of his control over his story) merely draws our attention to the fact that the source of the tale's authority is fictional. A similar rejection of mimetic effect is to be found in the verse *romans réalistes* and the *Prose Tristan*, whose fictionality is marked by lyric insertions, a generic shift which Maureen Boulton analyses later in this collection.

The following two essays compare and contrast two genres: epic and romance. Donald Maddox and Sara Sturm-Maddox's discussion of the episode found in some manuscripts of the *Bataille Loquifer* in which Renoart meets King Arthur in Avalon reflects recent scholarly interest in generic intertextuality, which was particularly in evidence at the International Arthurian meeting in Bonn in 1993.[8] Indeed, an epic hero's incursion into the Otherworld associated with romance offers an excellent example of what Donald Maddox calls 'intergeneric textuality', which results in a two-way dialogue, with a *remise en question* of both genres and the audience's expectations of them.[9] This episode in the *Bataille Loquifer* challenges the Jaussian concept of the non-interchangeablity of characters from different genres. Renoart, on a quest for his lost son Maillefer, is whisked to Avalon by fairies, but instead of finding there nurture and the fulfilment of his lack, he is greeted only by antagonism, and acquires symbolic and biological sons who, under the influence of Morgan, soon prepare to betray him. The result of this mixing of genres

8 Donald Maddox's plenary lecture entitled 'Intergeneric Textuality in Arthurian Literature: The Specular Encounter' made the useful distinction between intertextuality *between* and *within* genres, and introduced the term *intergenre* into our critical vocabulary. Elspeth Kennedy's plenary paper, 'Generic Intertextuality in the *Lancelot en Prose*', considered the prose romance's relationship with epic, lyric, and chronicle traditions.

9 See Matilda Tomaryn Bruckner, 'En guise de conclusion', *Littérature*, 41 (1981), 104–08, for a useful summary of intertextuality and its effects.

is that the conventions of romance and lay are ironised, while the epic hero acquires anxieties concerning his past and future and his place in genealogy more reminiscent of a Lancelot.

Providing a companion piece for the Maddoxs' discussion of that most uncertain of states, fatherhood, Sarah Kay's essay concentrates on motherhood in the *chansons de geste*, in particular *Aiol*, *Doon de la Roche*, and *Parise la Duchesse*. Taking as her starting point Donald Maddox's identification of the Freudian model of family romance in some Old French romances and lays, she contrasts the symbolic structures and political fictions promoted by the epic and romance genres. In the *chansons de geste* the mothers' symbolic role is enhanced and they, along with fathers, are allowed to indulge in the fantasies which are mainly the preserve of sons in the romance. Moreover, while in romance paternity seems to offer a solution to the hero's quest for identity, in the epic, paternity is problematic (as it is for Renoart in the *Bataille Loquifer*) and patriarchy problematised.

Roger Pensom, like Sarah Kay, draws on psychoanalyis, anthropology and gender studies in order to analyse the thematic shifts which occurred when Adam de la Halle rewrote in dramatic form the lyric *pastourelle* in his *Jeu de Robin et Marion*.[10] Identifying a whole series of binary oppositions – nature/culture, *vilain*/*courtois*, female/male, real/ideal, literal/ metaphorical, vegetarian/carnivore – he lays bare the symbolic structures of the play, demonstrating in particular how class and gender politics are expressed through food. He rejects earlier critics' views of the play as a satire on peasant behaviour, or a 'school of love' with Marion the schoolmistress, or a utopian fantasy, arguing instead for the play's complex portrayal of class and gender, the latter being capable of transcending class boundaries. Thus Adam has invested topical material taken from the lyric with new social meanings, and, through the linking of sexuality and food, has given the modern reader an insight into his/her own unconscious desires.

The role of the lyric in the Prose *Tristan* is not as source, but as contrastive mode, emphasising the characterisation of Tristan as singer and musician, but also reinforcing the theme of doomed love, as a succession of male lovers reflect in song on their unhappy state. These *lais* of reflection, as Maureen Boulton calls them, have much in common with the specular encounters Donald Maddox has studied elsewhere.[11] For

10 Generic transposition seems to have been a feature of Adam's work, for his *Jeu de la feuillee* is a dramatic version of the lyric *Congé*.

11 See Donald Maddox, 'Specular Stories, Family Romance, and the Fictions of Courtly Culture', *Exemplaria*, 3 (1991), 299–326.

most of them are overheard by Tristan, who is thus forced to witness the pain of fated lovers who function as doubles or deputies of himself.

This group of four essays on generic shifts is followed by two discussions of *remaniement* within a given genre and language. Janice Pinder studies, via the theme of marriage in successive rewritings of the St Alexis story in Old French, 'the complex interplay of literary and social factors which governed the process of adaptation'. She shows how the growing poularity of the romance genre, with its focus on love relationships and the couple, and developments in the Church's teaching on marriage led to modifications in the saint's life, designed to suggest that Alexis leaves his wife after their wedding only with her consent. Whilst marriage is seen in the eleventh-century versions of the legend as a sign of undue attachment to worldly pleasure, later versions offer their secular audiences the model of a chaste marriage. Pinder thus locates the various *remaniements* firmly within their historical and social contexts, while anaylsing in detail some of the techniques of amplification and explicitation (especially in scenes of direct speech in the bedchamber) through which the modification of the story's message is achieved.

Nicholas Watson gives a gendered, intertextual and historicised reading of three Middle-English versions of the Troilus and Cressida story, and demonstrates that Lydgate and Henryson, rather than being in awe of their *maister* Chaucer, aimed to outdo him in their imitations of his work. Concentrating in particular on authorial pronouncements and the representation of Cressida, Watson argues that Lydgate produces a more didactic and 'historical' narrative than Chaucer, using Guido's *Historia* as his main source, but relies more heavily on Chaucer for the structure of his *Troy Book* and for his portrayal of the heroine. Thus, while appearing to flatter Chaucer through imitation, he in fact associates him with female deceit, implying that his master's sympathetic narrative is as seductive and morally dubious as Cressida herself. Henryson's *Testament*, on the other hand, provides non-historical, fictional closure for Chaucer's work, thereby increasing the ambiguity of the model's moral authority and drawing our attention to the pleasure taken by successive male recreators of Cressida as object of desire.

Albrecht Classen, like Maureen Boulton, provides us with a further example of the specular encounter, this time in the form of a dream. Various heroes and heroines from Middle High German literature (the *Nibelungenlied*, Wolfram's *Parzival*, Gottfried's *Tristan*, Hartmann's *Iwein*, *Morîz von Craûn*, *Helmbrecht*) are confronted with dreams which frequently convey a deeper insight into the reality of their situation than they themselves possess. The protagonists are often incapable of interpreting their dreams correctly, thus implying a degree of self-deception, and it is the discrepancy between their perception of reality and the truth as portrayed by their dreams which creates much of the dramatic irony in these works and encourages greater awareness in their readers.

The problem of interpretation is also raised by Anne Savage as she analyses the many stories told within the *Beowulf* narrative. She draws our attention to the shifting perspectives of audiences both within and outside the work, showing how the meaning of narratives changes over time, and how the present for the intra-diegetic audience and storyteller is already a past for the extra-diegetic audience of *Beowulf*, who have the benefits of hindsight and Christianity with which to contemplate the past. She reassesses the exemplary nature of these stories, pointing out that what might be received as tales in celebration of heroic values by the internal audience, might become elegaic tales of a lost, and perhaps misguided, era for listeners outside the poem. These stories not only underline the fragile nature of opening and closure, but also the limitations and impermanence of human understanding of history.

Time and history are also the subjects of Penny Eley's essay on the *Roman de Troie*, the first of several contributions to treat the transposition of material from one language and culture to another.[12] By comparing the internal chronology of Benoît de Sainte-Maure's romance with that of its main source, Dares' *Historia*, Eley shows that while Dares exploits the apparent precision of a spurious overall time-frame in order to give his work the illusion of historicity, Benoît employs time affectively, concentrating on the symbolic effects of indications of time within individual episodes, rather than on the overall chronology of his adaptation. This, Eley argues, is a feature of romance composition, which distinguishes Benoît's work from the historical writing of Wace. Thus even minor modifications made to the presentation of the source material can reveal an author's perception of his subject-matter and the type of reaction he was soliciting from his new audience.

No *Festschrift* for Elspeth Kennedy would be complete without mention of Lancelot, the subject of the next two essays. Joy Wallace's contribution centres on the transposition of the phrase 'emprendre l'aventure' and its cognates from their French context in Chrétien's *Charrete*, the Prose *Lancelot* and the Prose *Tristan* to Malory's *Morte Darthur*. She analyses the phrase's semantic shifts, its structural function and its role within the adaptation's ideological and ethical framework. During the process of adaptation, Malory, like many a German adaptor of

[12] For a bibliography on medieval translation, see *Medieval Translators and their Craft*, ed. by Jeanette Beer, Studies in Medieval Culture, 25 (Kalamazoo, Michigan: Medieval Institute Publications, 1989), pp. 373–410.

French material, included details taken from a source he was not ostensibly working from at that point in the narrative.[13] Thus he transferred the concept of taking the adventure from the Prose *Tristan* and relocated it in the *Morte*, associating it positively with the Fair Unknown-type narratives of Gareth and La Cote Male Tayle, but introducing negative overtones when applying it to the more mature Balin and Launcelot, who are characterised as reckless because of the meaning the motif has acquired in Malory's text.

Progressing from the transposition of a motif to the transplanting of a character, we find Ceridwen Lloyd-Morgan investigating the references to Lancelot in Welsh literature, and demonstrating that he is not an indigenous, Celtic figure, but an import from French romance. The texts in which his name appears, the Triads and Welsh poetry, all seem to post-date the late 14th-century *Y Seint Greal*, which was a translation of the *Queste* and the *Perlesvaus*, and seems to have been responsible for introducing Welsh writers and audiences to Lancelot. There is some evidence, however, that the French Prose *Lancelot* was also known in Wales by the 15th century, and this leads the author to speculate on why no fully-fledged Lancelot story was ever produced in Welsh. The situation mirrors that of Tristan in Wales, and the answer may lie in a Welsh distaste for stories involving the adultery of the king's wife, or even a preference for tales about chivalric exploits rather than love-affairs. Lancelot, Lloyd-Morgan concludes, may owe his brief appearance in Welsh literature simply to the fact that he is Galahad's father.

In a final essay on medieval *translatio* Jane Taylor uses modern translation theory to explain the process by which Lydgate adapted the French *danse macabré*, investing it with a new meaning of his own. She concentrates on the lexeme *danse(r)* and shows how the translator develops the vehicle of the metaphor in a way which suggests that in adapting his written source he was influenced by the images which accompanied the verses on the wall of the Innocents' cemetery in Paris. For in Lydgate's version the individual *Morts* are replaced by a personified abstraction *Dethe*, whose dance the living are unwilling to join, not merely because it signifies death, but because the dance-steps are so alien and unattractive to them. By changing small details in his model, Lydgate has succeeded in his English *Dance of Death* in producing a translation of his French source which incorporates his own commentary on it.

13 See my *Meister Otte's* Eraclius *as an Adaptation of* Eracle *by Gautier d'Arras*, GAG, 382 (Göppingen: Kümmerle, 1987), chapter 12, on *transmutatio*.

It remains for me to thank all those involved in the production of this book: the contributors, for their diligence and patience; my assistant editors Penny Eley (for her painstaking copy-editing), Ceridwen Lloyd-Morgan (for her help with references and financial matters), Jocelyn Wogan-Browne (for the editing of English contributions), Jane Taylor and Sarah Kay (for their careful reading of some of the essays); Linda Gowans, for producing the index; Richard Barber at Boydell and Brewer, for his encouragement and practical help; and the Vinaver Trust and St Hilda's College, Oxford, for their generous financial support.

Vers, prose et fiction narrative (1150–1240)

EMMANUÈLE BAUMGARTNER

RAPPELER L'AMBIGUÏTÉ, au moyen âge, du mot 'roman', d'un mot qui désigne aussi bien la langue usuelle de la communication qu'une langue devenue très tôt langue littéraire par la grâce de quelques écrivains, est un lieu commun des études qui cherchent à cerner la naissance du 'roman' au sens moderne du terme. En dédiant ces quelques pages à Elspeth Kennedy, qui a contribué de manière si décisive à notre connaissance de l'un des textes fondateurs du genre romanesque, le *Lancelot* en prose, mon intention n'est donc pas de revenir une fois encore sur cette ambiguïté. Mais en prenant comme point d'ancrage la distinction que propose G. Genette entre 'diction' et 'fiction' – serait 'littérature de fiction celle qui s'impose essentiellement par le caractère imaginaire de ses objets, littérature de diction, celle qui s'impose essentiellement par ses caractéristiques formelles – encore une fois sans préjudice d'amalgame et de mixité'[1] – je voudrais plutôt tenter de voir comment les textes médiévaux auxquels la critique moderne confère le statut de roman, au sens du mot anglais *novel*, construisent leur fictionnalité et comment ils inventent, à partir de ces formes non marquées que sont le vers narratif puis la prose, leur 'diction' propre, se présentant ainsi comme objet esthétique.

Je ne m'attarderai pas sur les plus anciens de ces textes, l'ensemble formé par *Thèbes*, *Enéas* et *Troie*.[2] Je rappellerai simplement, à la suite de plusieurs études fort suggestives,[3] que ces oeuvres, qui restent plutôt

1 Voir Gérard Genette, *Fiction et diction* (Paris: Editions du Seuil, 1991), p. 31.

2 Il faudrait également prendre en compte les différentes versions du *Roman d'Alexandre*, coulées dans le moule formel de la chanson de geste, et dont le statut exact est encore plus difficile à cerner.

3 On se reportera, pour les romans antiques, au travail d'Aimé Petit, *Naissances du roman:*

dépendantes, au plan narratif, de leurs sources, créent en revanche en langue vulgaire une 'diction' propre en transposant savamment et en adaptant en 'roman' des techniques d'ornement et d'amplification reprises à la littérature latine et médio-latine. Les auteurs de *Thèbes* et surtout d'*Enéas* et de *Troie* exploitent ainsi jusqu'à la limite, et parfois dans l'excès, toutes les ressources de la rhétorique, à travers l'efflorescence des portraits, la surcharge des descriptions ou la riche diversité des monologues dans lesquels la parole amoureuse prend une place prépondérante. Mais même s'ils insistent, comme le fait surtout Benoît, sur le travail de l'écrivain, artisan du langage comme le sculpteur l'est de la pierre – l'image est récurrente et présente de multiples et intéressantes variantes – les auteurs des romans antiques ne semblent pas être allés jusqu'au bout de l'aventure de la fiction. La trame narrative de ces trois romans, les personnages et leur destin sont historiques, ou du moins perçus, reçus comme tels par les écrivains et par leur public. On peut supposer que Benoît, par exemple, est persuadé de la vérité de ce qu'il lit dans ses sources médio-latines, le pseudo-Darés ou le pseudo-Dictys, et il est exact, comme il l'affirme dans son prologue, qu'il suit fidèlement la matière que lui fournissent ces textes. En revanche, lorsqu'il précise tout aussitôt qu'il ne se fera pas faute d'ajouter quelques 'bons dits',[4] on peut voir dans cette formule, au reste assez énigmatique, l'annonce d'une pratique qui recouperait assez bien le concept de diction proposé par Genette: l'intervention, encore ponctuelle, d'une diction propre, au sein d'une oeuvre qui hésite par ailleurs entre l'histoire, la chanson de geste et le récit de fiction, et qui se manifeste notamment par un mode d'écrire fondé sur l'ornementation comme sur la répétition, l'emploi systématique des synonymes, la recherche très sensible de la 'copia', etc.

Reste que le caractère fictionnel de ces oeuvres est quelque peu brouillé non seulement par leur rapport à l'Histoire mais aussi par leur orientation didactique, par le souci que manifestent leurs auteurs de faire du 'roman', ici entendu au sens de langue, un nouvel espace de savoir à l'usage des laïcs. Ainsi des 'images du monde' que proposent aussi bien la description de la tente du roi Adraste et celle du char d'Amphiaraüs dans

les techniques littéraires dans les romans antiques du XIIe siècle (Paris: Champion; Genève: Slatkine, 1985), et pour une étude d'ensemble sur le roman médiéval, au récent ouvrage de Douglas Kelly, *The Art of Medieval French Romance* (Madison: University of Wisconsin Press, 1992).

4 Thomas fait également allusion, à la fin de son *Tristan*, v. 3135, aux 'diz' et aux 'vers' qu'il a 'retrait' (éd. Félix Lecoy, Classiques Français du Moyen Age (Paris: Champion, 1992)), une formule qui rappelle celle de Benoît (Le *Roman de Troie*, éd. L. Constans, SATF, 6 vol. (Paris: Firmin-Didot, 1904–12), vv. 142–43): 'Ne di mie qu'aucun bon dit/ n'i mete, se faire le sai'.

Thèbes que la 'descriptio mundi' ou la digression sur les moeurs des Amazones chez Benoît; ainsi de l'inventaire du savoir médiéval ciselé, dans *Thèbes*, sur le char d'Amphiaraüs; ainsi encore de l'importance des discours et de la réflexion politiques dans *Enéas* et dans *Troie*. Même la parole amoureuse des monologues, qui pourrait paraître signer l'avènement du roman, laisse autant percer, dans l'excès et la minutie de ses interrogations, l'intention de produire des fragments, voire la totalité (chez Benoît), d'un discours sur l'amour que de suivre les flamboiements et les incertitudes des passions individuelles.

Tout change avec Chrétien de Troyes, même si la révolution ne passe pas par l'invention d'une forme neuve. Comme ses prédécesseurs, voire ses presque contemporains, Chrétien utilise la forme neutre, non marquée, du couplet d'octosyllabes à rimes plates, une forme qui est aussi bien celle de l'hagiographie (des Vies de saints anglo-normandes, du *Voyage de saint Brendan*), du discours scientifique (des Bestiaires) ou de la chronique historique (du *Roman de Brut*, du *Roman de Rou*, etc.), et ce n'est guère que dans la pratique généralisée de la brisure du couplet qu'il innove sur le plan purement formel. Une rupture autrement importante est en revanche le rejet de la matière antique, même légendarisée, au profit de la matière de Bretagne, et le traitement que lui fait subir d'entrée de jeu Chrétien, à partir du texte fondateur, *Erec et Enide*. Le début de la narration, dans *Erec et Enide*, extrait en effet brutalement l'espace-temps arthurien du temps chronique, historique, dans lequel l'avaient inscrit Geoffroy de Monmouth puis Wace, et le prive de tout ancrage temporel et même spatial: le royaume de Logres n'est exactement ni l'Angleterre ni la Grande-Bretagne. Les premiers vers posent sans aucun préavis et comme autant d''existants', Arthur, son royaume, ses chevaliers, et leur occupation aussi essentielle qu'apparemment dérisoire, la chasse au blanc cerf, la quête de l'aventure merveilleuse dans la forêt périlleuse. Que l'on relise ce début dans une écoute neuve:

> Au jor de Pasque, au tans novel,
> a Quaradigan, son chastel,
> ot li rois Artus cort tenue (27–29)[5]

et l'on est aussitôt frappé par l'immanence de ce monde, surgi tout constitué sur fond d'absence, né, semble-t-il, du seul bon plaisir de l'écrivain. Coup de force et coup de génie que reproduira Chrétien au terme de sa carrière en présentant de manière tout aussi abrupte un graal et une

5 Voir Chrétien de Troyes, *Erec et Enide*, éd. M. Roques, Classiques Français du Moyen Age (Paris: Champion, 1973).

lance qui saigne sous les yeux fascinés de Perceval comme du lecteur/auditeur du *Conte du Graal*.

A cet espace-temps coupé de ses amarres et de ses repères correspond une structure temporelle qui est celle du fragment, du 'vecteur libre' arbitrairement prélevé sur le temps chronique, et par laquelle s'affirme la toute-puissance de l'écrivain à débuter et à clore à son gré, à son rythme, le temps du récit. Les premiers héros de Chrétien, il est vrai, ont encore des pères, un lignage, un passé, qui pourraient renvoyer à quelque prétexte: Erec est 'le fiz Lac'; Yvain, 'le fiz Urien', est cité à plusieurs reprises ainsi que son père dans le *Brut* de Wace. Mais à leur entrée en texte, ils sont sevrés de ce passé, présents depuis toujours, semble-t-il, à la cour d'Arthur, assis autour de la Table Ronde, personnages en quête d'auteur et d'aventures, et nous ne saurons rien de leur genèse, de leur formation, de leur passé. Erec sans doute fait retour pour s'y perdre, à la fin du récit, au royaume du père. Mais Yvain 'oublie' auprès de Laudine et le père et le royaume. Lancelot n'est plus que Lancelot du Lac, l'enfant de la féerie. Perceval n'apprendra jamais, dans le *Conte du Graal*, quel fut le lignage de son père et le lecteur, ignorant de l'origine des héros, ne saura jamais, s'il ne lit que Chrétien, quel sera leur devenir et quelle sera leur fin.

Cette coupe arbitraire faite dans le temps chronique prend tout son sens si on la compare aux structures antérieures fondées sur le déroulement sans faille des lignages, comme dans la chronique historique selon Wace ou selon le roman antique, qui tous deux remontent systématiquement aux origines d'une ville, d'une race, d'un héros, qui s'arrêtent à leur mort ou à leur ruine ou dans l'épuisement du chroniqueur, tandis que, au sein même de la matière de Bretagne, les récits sur Tristan s'articulent eux aussi sur la biographie de leur héros.[6]

Dans le déroulement même de la narration, Chrétien suit sans doute, globalement, l'ordre chronologique, mais d'une certaine manière il soustrait cet ordre au temps pour, autre rupture, l'incarner dans l'espace. Le devenir et le destin des héros de Chrétien se jouent d'abord au long du chemin parcouru (Lancelot hésite deux pas et non deux anachroniques secondes avant de monter dans la charrette) et à la densité des aventures qui suspendent leur quête, c'est-à-dire leur déplacement dans l'espace. On sait surtout comment Chrétien double la forme signifiante de la quête, forme qu'il invente en 'roman' et lègue à la fiction occidentale, d'une autre forme signifiante, la 'conjointure'. Le terme est obscur et il a été abondamment étudié, mais l'on peut penser qu'il marque la volonté de Chrétien de croiser la structure chronologique, trop facile et trop

[6] Chrétien cependant reprend dans *Cligés*, le moins arthurien, il est vrai, de ses romans, une structure biographique bipartite, très proche de celle des *Tristan*.

ouverte aux tentations de la mimésis, avec des structures artificielles, et exhibées comme telles, d'organisation du matériau romanesque. On citera ainsi, sans s'arrêter au détail, car il s'agit juste d'une mise en perspective et les faits sont bien connus, la structure bipartite d'*Erec et Enide* et du *Chevalier au Lion*, la création de liens entre le *Chevalier au Lion* et le *Chevalier de la Charrete* dans le va-et-vient de Gauvain d'un récit à l'autre, et, enfin, l'alternance concertée des héros dans le *Conte du Graal*; tous procédés par lesquels l'écrivain signifie sa présence dans le texte, les pleins pouvoirs qu'il s'octroie sur la disposition du récit et la marche des aventures et que reprendront assidûment ses successeurs.

La mise en place, à partir d'*Erec et Enide*, d'un univers fondé sur la coutume et sa stricte observance a fait l'objet de bien des études, des articles d'E. Köhler au dernier livre de D. Maddox,[7] et je n'ai nullement l'intention de sous-estimer l'intérêt et la pertinence de ces travaux. Je constate cependant que nombre de coutumes introduites par Chrétien dans le 'roman' – la chasse au blanc cerf, la pratique du don contraignant, la coutume de la charrette, celle du 'conduit' des demoiselles, le 'cri' du héraut d'armes, la coutume de la fontaine au Pin, etc. – se caractérisent par leur aspect insolite, arbitraire, et semblent fonctionner à rebours des us et coutumes du monde réel. Je me demande donc si l'une des raisons d'être de ces coutumes, qui vont ensuite définir un 'droit coutumier' spécifique du texte/du monde arthurien en vers puis en prose, n'est pas aussi de signaler le caractère totalement fictif, inventé, et gratuitement inventé, de l'espace-temps arthurien tel que le dispose Chrétien et que le remploient ses épigones.

Sans doute conviendrait-il d'intégrer également au nombre des coutumes à rebours le recours au merveilleux tel que le pratique Chrétien, par petites touches, en contraste concerté avec le caractère réaliste de certaines scènes et la fréquence des effets de réel. L'intrusion du merveilleux, qui déconstruit comme à plaisir la vraisemblance du récit, montrerait ainsi combien cet univers possède ses loix propres de fonctionnement, différentes de celles de l'univers réel, et signalerait, souvent sur le mode de l'ironie, les coups de pouce que l'écrivain de fiction, l'auteur de 'roman', se permet de donner dans l'image du monde qu'il redessine.

On sait enfin comment, dans le roman en vers ultérieur, le retour du monde et des personnages disposés par Chrétien suffit à indiquer l'entrée en fiction. Qu'un écrivain débute ainsi son récit: A la Pentecôte/ à l'Ascension/ à Pâques, le roi Arthur tint une grande fête . . . et le lecteur, l'auditeur sait aussitôt qu'il va pénétrer une nouvelle fois dans le monde

7 Voir Donald Maddox, *The Arthurian Romances of Chrétien de Troyes: Once and Future Fictions* (Cambridge: Cambridge University Press, 1991).

de la fiction arthurienne, tout comme la formule magique 'il était une fois' signe l'entrée dans l'univers du conte de fées.

Deux traits majeurs caractérisent, au début du XIIIe siècle, l'évolution du roman: l'apparition de la prose littéraire, en étroite liaison avec le motif du Graal et de sa quête; l'apparition, dans le même temps, de récits qui, 'ignorant' la matière de Bretagne, se déroulent dans un monde proche de leur premier public et que l'on a qualifiés un peu vite de romans réalistes. Faute de pouvoir prendre en compte tous ces récits et leur diversité, de Jean Renart à Philippe de Rémi, je me contenterai d'évoquer rapidement quelques-uns des procédés par lesquels ils construisent – ou non – leur fictionnalité et comment ils s'inventent, en rupture avec les textes précédents, une diction autre, qui démarque par exemple la prose du *Lancelot-Graal* de la 'commune parleüre', de la langue usuelle de la communication, ou le récit 'réaliste' des platitudes de la mimésis. Je note, pour n'y plus revenir, qu'un trait commun à ces oeuvres, si différentes par ailleurs, est les liens privilégiés qu'elles tissent avec des référents littéraires: la poésie lyrique, dans le cas du roman dit réaliste, l'ensemble du pré-texte arthurien, pour le *Lancelot* en prose, le *Tristan* en prose et les textes apparentés.

On a souvent assimilé, et les écrivains du XIIIe siècle eux-mêmes, le choix de la prose comme langue littéraire, en remplacement du vers et de ses contraintes, à la quête d'une plus grande vérité. Prose et relation exacte des faits, notamment des faits historiques, seraient liées. Faut-il en conclure que le choix de la prose par un très grand nombre d'écrivains du Graal, au XIIIe siècle, signifierait leur intention de nier ou de masquer le statut fictionnel du texte produit, de s'opposer ainsi, comme le prétend par exemple l'auteur du *Perceval* en prose, aux mensonges des 'troveor' (de ceux qui écrivent en vers), et de faire passer la fiction du Graal sur les rives du discours historique, de la chronique? Il se peut, si l'on considère les premiers d'entre eux. Un texte comme le *Merlin*, par exemple, adopte, comme les romans antiques, et comme le *Brut*, de sa source immédiate, le rythme et le cadre de la chronique historique et dispense également, comme l'a montré A. Micha,[8] un enseignement politique, moral et religieux. Le *Lancelot* en prose reprend au reste cette tradition dans l'abondance du discours didactique qu'il tient sur la chevalerie, sur l'exercice du pouvoir, sur le droit féodal, etc.

Mais l'on sait aussi combien ces récits en prose sont également hantés par un imaginaire de la mise en écrit, de la transformation de la parole parlée, celle de Merlin ou celle des chevaliers de la cour d'Arthur, en

8 Alexandre Micha, *Etude sur le 'Merlin' de Robert de Boron: roman du XIIe siècle* (Genève: Droz, 1980).

'parole écrite', fixée par l'écrivain aux pages du livre, et comment ils miment les conditions de leur production en un milieu qui est précisément le milieu arthurien, alors devenu le lieu même où prend naissance la fiction. Le retour insistant sur la genèse de l'écrit peut sans doute se lire comme garantie de l'authenticité du texte, produit au contact même de l'événement. Mais il peut être aussi le moyen de souligner la circularité d'une écriture qui n'a d'autre source que l'univers généré par les textes eux-mêmes. Plus décisif encore paraît être, dans cette perspective, l'usage constant que font les récits en prose, à partir du *Lancelot*, de la formule 'or dist li contes' et de la technique de l'entrelacement. L'amorce de cette formule et de cette technique apparaît en fait dès le *Conte du Graal*,[9] au moment où l'écrivain, se retranchant derrière l'autorité du 'conte', cesse de s'occuper de Gauvain pour revenir à Perceval, et exhibe ainsi la liberté avec laquelle il manipule le devenir de ses héros en pratiquant une coupe arbitraire dans le temps du récit et le développement des aventures:

> De mon seignor Gauvain se test
> li contes ici a estal,
> si parlerons de Perceval (6006–08)

A partir du *Lancelot* en prose, la formule 'or dist li contes' se systématise en liaison étroite avec la technique de l'entrelacement dont elle jalonne les tours et les détours. Elle assure ainsi dans les textes en prose une fonction généralement dévolue ailleurs au narrateur: l'organisation et la gestion du récit. On a pu voir dans cette formule un procédé destiné à masquer la présence de l'écrivain dans la narration, à dissimuler toutes traces d'une intervention qui paraîtrait truquer l'éminente 'vérité' de la prose, l'adéquation à la source ou au référent. Elle peut être aussi, comme le suggère G. Genette, 'l'esquisse d'un alibi hypertextuel' ou 'un désaveu plaisamment hypocrite'.[10] Mais ne serait-ce pas également un moyen efficace sinon habile (le roman en prose aurait eu intérêt, au regard d'un lecteur moderne, à soigner et à diversifier ses transitions) de mettre en évidence la manière dont l'écrivain travaille à son gré souverain le déroulement du récit et entrelace, suspend et reprend comme il l'entend, en son 'point', comme dit si fréquemment le narrateur du *Tristan* en prose, les aventures des personnages? La formule 'or dist li contes', associée à la technique de l'entrelacement, cette 'taille' que l'écrivain impose à la pierre brute du matériau pour en multiplier les facettes et lui donner tout

9 Voir Chrétien de Troyes, *Le Conte del Graal*, éd. F. Lecoy, Classiques Français du Moyen Age, 2 vols (Paris: Champion, 1975 et 78).

10 Voir G. Genette, p. 80, note 1.

son éclat, serait alors, comme la 'conjointure' de Chrétien de Troyes, la marque spécifique, la 'diction' propre de la prose arthurienne, et signerait à son tour l'entrée en fiction. Et peut-être est-ce l'un des aspects majeurs de l'art et de la technique des prosateurs du Graal que d'avoir ainsi réinventé un 'ordo artificialis' généralisé, qui démarque la prose arthurienne de la 'commune parleüre', et en signifie la littérarité.[11]

Si l'on cherche toutefois dans la littérature narrative du XIIIe siècle des exemples nets d'une diction spécifique du 'roman', le texte qui s'impose d'abord est le *Roman de la Rose* de Jean Renart et sa pratique neuve des insertions lyriques qui interrompent une narration de type réaliste. Inutile de rappeler l'intérêt archéologique de ces insertions qui nous ont conservé une sorte d'anthologie de la poésie lyrique de la fin du XIIe siècle et du début du XIIIe. Mais on notera également l'extrême artifice et la nouveauté d'un procédé qui substitue par exemple au traditionnel monologue amoureux ou aux commentaires du narrateur, procédés bien intégrés à l'écriture du roman au début du XIIIe siècle, un mode d'expression doublement marqué, et par l'intervention d'une 'diction' autre, la strophe lyrique, et par la présence du chant, de la voix vive, du temps de la performance musicale, voire de la danse.

Dans le roman de Jean Renart, texte narratif et texte lyrique restent encore distincts. Ils ne seront amoureusement réunis que dans l'autre *Roman de la Rose*, celui de Guillaume de Lorris. Dans le roman de Jean Renart, le texte lyrique est encore, selon l'écrivain lui-même, broderie, parure ajoutée au tissu narratif, plutôt que travail sur le tissu même, qui en métamorphoserait la texture. On soulignera également, à la suite, encore, de Jean Renart, l'adéquation entre les sentiments prêtés aux personnages, les situations dans lesquelles ils évoluent, et les poèmes lyriques qu'ils interprètent. Mais le procédé de l'insertion montre aussi comment l'écrivain prend le risque délibéré d'introduire dans un récit qui se présente comme 'réaliste', et qui abonde de fait en 'effets de réel', la forme médiévale la plus codée qui soit: la strophe lyrique. L'effet de rupture, de discordance que produisent ces insertions, ne serait-il pas alors un autre moyen de miner la dimension réaliste et de reconduire le récit à son statut d'objet littéraire?

Le dernier texte que je prendrai brièvement en compte est le *Tristan* en prose, l'un des exemples les plus élaborés, pour le XIIIe siècle, d'un récit

[11] Il va de soi que cette remarque n'épuise pas, loin de là, les fonctions et les incidences de la technique de l'entrelacement dans les romans en prose en général et dans le *Lancelot* en prose en particulier. Voir Elspeth Kennedy, *Lancelot and the Grail: A Study of the Prose Lancelot* (Oxford: Clarendon Press, 1986), Ch. VII, 'The Tale and the Interlace' et Ch. VIII, 'Repetition and Other Linking Devices'.

en quête de sa littérarité. Le montre déjà l'image complexe que forgent d'eux-mêmes les 'auteurs' du *Tristan*. Entre Luce à Hélie, les deux 'noms' qui prennent en charge le récit, sont en effet présentes en texte la plupart des figures de l'écrivain médiéval: l'instance énonciative, le je d'un narrateur très présent dès le prologue puis dans le cours du texte; la fonction de translateur et de scripteur, illustrée par le texte du prologue et de l'épilogue comme par l'enluminure du folio initial de plusieurs manuscrits; avec Hélie de Boron s'impose enfin la figure dominante du compilateur, celui qui trie, dispose, harmonise, complète, supplémente les textes précédents, en quête d'une impossible clôture du récit.

L'un des signes distinctifs des romans antiques puis du *Lancelot* en prose est sans doute la coexistence de modes d'expression spécifiquement littéraires et d'un discours didactique, politique, etc. qui tire souvent le récit hors de la sphère de la fiction. L'option choisie par le *Tristan* semble différente. Elle serait plutôt de faire co-exister, ou mieux encore de générer par le récit toutes les ressources formelles de la prose et du vers. J'en prendrai comme exemple la parole amoureuse, qui décline dans ce texte toutes les modalités possibles du discours littéraire: narration et description, des effets de l'amour par exemple; procédé traditionnel du monologue; passages enfin où la prose tend vers le mode lyrique jusqu'au moment où se produit sous les yeux du lecteur l'alchimie qui transmute l'énoncé prosaïque dans la diction lyrique du lai ou de la lettre en vers. Et pourtant . . . Ni le *Lancelot* ni le *Tristan* ne se définissent comme 'roman'. C'est le terme de 'livre', 'livre de Lancelot', 'livre de Tristan', qu'emploient de préférence narrateurs et copistes, comme si leur ambition ultime était de rivaliser avec les modèles latins, avec une image sacralisée et/ou savante de l'écrit, ou bien d'achever enfin ce produit fini, autonome, à la fois contenu et contenant, que désigne dans la plurivocité de ses sens le terme de 'livre', écorce et moelle confondues, pour paraphraser librement Isidore de Séville.

Dès les romans antiques, l'écrivain médiéval insiste sur son travail, sur la forme neuve qu'il donne au matériau hérité. Ce travail emprunte des voies diverses. J'ai tenté ici d'en suivre quelques-unes. Au delà des différences de thématique (antique, arthurienne, réaliste) et des différences formelles, du choix du vers ou de la prose, l'intention semble cependant identique: effacer, à chaque fois qu'elles deviennent trop présentes, les traces de l'illusion mimétique, que la mimésis porte sur un texte source, sur le référent littéraire ou sur le référent réel, présenter le texte comme le produit d'une écriture créative et assurer, dans la quête renouvelée d'une diction propre au récit de fiction, sa dimension esthétique, sa littérarité.

Renoart in Avalon: Generic Shift in the *Bataille Loquifer*

SARA STURM-MADDOX and DONALD MADDOX

IF WITHIN THE CORPUS OF medieval French epics Renoart is an uncommon hero, beginning his career as something of a comic giant and later wielding not a sword but a massive 'tinel', in certain manuscripts of the thirteenth-century *Bataille Loquifer* he becomes the first epic hero to visit the fairy otherworld of Avalon. This episode, not found in the Arsenal/Boulogne manuscripts, comprises most of the third part of a textual triptych in the majority of manuscripts of the so-called 'Vulgate' version of the poem.[1] Introduced into a work concerning which critical pronouncements have not been favourable (it is 'de valeur littéraire assez piètre',[2] the *chanson* 'la plus médiocre du cycle assurément',[3] a poem 'plutôt fastidieux'[4]), it has attracted a modest amount of attention, in part because its innovation was not to remain without sequel.[5] It merits

[1] The Arsenal/Boulogne version (Paris, Bibl. de l'Arsenal 6562, fols 119–66, Boulogne sur Mer, Bibl. Municipale, ancien fonds St Bertin 192, fols 142–58) was edited by H. J. Runeberg, *La Bataille de Loquifer*, Acta Soc. Scient. Fennicae, XXXVIII, 2 (Helsinki: Imprimerie de la Société de littérature finnoise, 1913). All citations herein are from an edition whose base manuscript, Paris, BN, fr. 1448, fols 272–97, represents the Vulgate version: *La Bataille Loquifer*, ed. by Monica Barnett, Medium Aevum Monographs, New Series, VI (Oxford: Blackwell, 1975). For a discussion of the Vulgate manuscripts, see pp. 3–29.

[2] Jeanne Wathelet-Willem, 'La fée Morgain dans la chanson de geste', *Cahiers de Civilisation Médiévale*, 13 (1970), 209–19 (p. 217). She thinks the episode set in Avalon is probably an interpolation (p. 218).

[3] Madeleine Tyssens, *La geste de Guillaume d'Orange dans les manuscrits cycliques* (Paris: Les Belles Lettres, 1967), p. 265. In her opinion, the Breton episode was not part of the 'chanson primitive' (p. 273).

[4] Marguerite Rossi, 'Sur Picolet et Auberon dans la *Bataille Loquifer*', in *Mélanges de philologie et de littérature romanes offerts à Jeanne Wathelet-Willem* (Liège: Marche Romane, 1978), pp. 569–91 (p. 569).

[5] For a discussion of *Loquifer* and its epic legacy, see François Suard, 'La *Bataille Loquifer* et

more, as Jeanne Wathelet-Willem suggests.[6] In a seminal essay on 'Littérature médiévale et théorie des genres', Hans Robert Jauss cited as an indicator of generic affiliation 'la non-interchangeabilité des personnages de la chanson de geste et du roman courtois', observing that heroes from the two traditions 'ne furent jamais transférés d'un genre à l'autre dans la tradition française, malgré l'assimilation progressive de l'épopée au roman chevaleresque'.[7] Yet here is Renoart in King Arthur's court. What is an epic hero doing in Avalon? To put the question another way: what modification of meaning might have obtained in the manuscripts that attest this generic shift in the third panel of the triptych?

Epic convention largely prevails in part one, in which Renoart slays the Saracen warrior Loquifer after a monumental struggle, and in part two, wherein Guillaume d'Orange does mortal battle with Desramé, the archenemy of Christendom. Part three, set against an epic backdrop of competing religions and familial enmity (we recall that Renoart, like Guillaume's spouse, is the apostate offspring of Desramé), grows from the Saracens' abduction of Renoart's infant son Maillefer, and it is during the hero's solitary quest for his son that part three shifts abruptly into the mode of romance and lay. Having vowed to rescue Maillefer, Renoart falls asleep at a seaside dune and is spirited straightaway to Avalon by three fairies, one of them the Morgue well known in Arthurian tradition.

The prologue of the poem, as Wathelet-Willem ('La *Bataille Loquifer*', pp. 235–36) observes, anticipates the introduction of extraordinary events in its announcement of a 'mervaillose chançon', and the remarkable change of venue to Avalon relatively late in the poem is anticipated by various minor infractions of generic expectations.[8] For example, in the eponymous epic combat that sets Renoart against Loquifer in the principal action of the poem, a 'baume magique' with resuscitative power

la pratique de l'intertextualité au début du XIIIe siècle', in *VIII Congreso de la Société Rencesvals* (Pamplona: Institucion Principe de Viana, 1981), pp. 497–501.

6 'La *Bataille Loquifer* dans la version D: une "mervaillose chanson" ', in *Studies in Medieval French Language and Literature presented to Brian Woledge*, ed. by Sally Burch North (Geneva: Droz, 1988), pp. 235–52 (p. 251); see also Emmanuèle Baumgartner's review of Barnett's edition, *Romance Philology*, 31 (1977), 455.

7 *Poétique*, 1 (1970), 79–101 (p. 84).

8 These are not without analogues in other *chansons de geste*. For an inventory of occurrences of the *merveilleux* in a select corpus of epic poems, see Adolphe-Jacques Dickman, *Le Rôle du surnaturel dans les chansons de geste* (Geneva: Slatkine Reprints, 1974), pp. 79–105, and his 'Index', pp. 169–84. Of particular interest for comparison with the Avalon episode of the *Bataille Loquifer* is a late poem in the cycle of Renaut de Montauban, *Mabrien*, in which the hero confronts supernatural forces, seeks the favours of a fairy, and visits Arthur in an island court.

figures prominently.[9] Or again, the Saracen messenger Picolet is endowed with extraordinary abilities of a very fairy-like nature.[10] With the arrival of the fairies, however, the generic confrontation is inescapable. Now they transform the trappings of the epic hero into properties more evocative of the *matière de Bretagne*:

> sa mace font müer en .I. falcon,
> et son hauberc .I. jugleor gascon
> qui lor viole clerement a cler ton,
> et son vert hiame müer en .I. Breton
> qui dolcement harpe lou loi Gorehon,
> et de s'espee refirent .I. garsçon;
> si l'anvoierent tout droit a Avalon. (3654–61)

These elements function exclusively to alert the reader to the transition from one literary world to another, disappearing with the ending of the enchantment; when Renoart awakes, startled, it is to seize, not a falcon, but his familiar mace.

Because of the explicit signal of generic interface in the mention here of a Breton who sweetly plays a lay, one might seek a primary model for the episode in that genre, citing for example *Lanval*, in which a fairy, enamoured of the hero, takes him to the otherworld.[11] The fit between model and episode, however, is problematic: there is no indication that Renoart is drawn to the otherworld by a fairy, nor that the fairies who transport him, introduced abruptly with the epic formula 'es vos', come to seek him, although they do recognize him as he lies sleeping; that he is magically transported unwittingly into Avalon is an emphasis repeated in the text (ll. 3652–53, 3654, 3671–72).

One is reminded, on the other hand, of the conventional opening of numerous Arthurian romances, beginning with those of Chrétien de Troyes, in which a hero whose prominence is achieved or recognized at court soon becomes involved in a conflict that will take him far afield.[12]

9 ll. 1797–98. Such a substance is one of the motifs cited by Jauss as 'constitutifs du roman d'Arthur [. . .] qui seraient une entorse à l'une des règles du genre' (p. 84).

10 On this character, who eludes the epic opposition Christian/Saracen, good/evil, see Rossi, esp. pp. 577–81.

11 See Suard, p. 499, who adds that 'tout se passe [. . .] comme si l'élection venue de l'autre monde apparaissait à l'auteur de geste comme le moyen privilégié d'apporter à son héros la consécration suprême' (p. 501).

12 Nelly Andrieux examines this passage as a 'séquence arthurienne' in 'Arthur et Charlemagne réunis en Avalon: la *Bataille Loquifer* ou l'accomplissement d'une parole', in *Essor et fortune de la chanson de geste dans l'Europe et l'Orient latin*, Actes du IXe Congrès de la Société Rencesvals pour l'Etude des Epopées Romanes (Modena: Mucchi, 1984), II, 425–34.

The episode, moreover, has evident affinities with romances in which at some remote locus the hero confronts his supreme challenge in the form of a *merveille* that only he, the chivalric *élu*, is destined to conquer. Like the inhabitants of the Grail Castle before Perceval's arrival, for example, the community at Avalon in this poem has long awaited the coming of Renoart; it is he alone, as we shall see, anticipated as the 'mellor chanpïon/ c'onques portast ne escut ne baston' (ll. 3816–17), who can remedy the bodily affliction of one among them. Yet again differences are striking. Here the Arthurian court and the otherworld, spatially poles apart in lay and romance, are eclectically blended into a single supernatural dimension. Hence, with regard to the hero's experience, another innovation: combined here are two loci of values and potential judgement traditionally distinct in texts such as *Lanval*.

Awakening in Avalon, Renoart finds himself in King Arthur's court, in the company not only of king and queen, of Gauvain, Yvain, and Perceval, but also of Roland; hence a generically hybrid anterior order of heroes past, assembled at the court of a monarch whose renowned temporal realm has already passed from the scene. And Renoart's introduction into this august assembly is in part a means of measuring his mettle on an heroic scale which is intergeneric: Arthur and his courtiers will evaluate the qualities of a converted Saracen and latter-day Carolingian. Renoart's arrival occasions curiosity: is he really as good as his reputation?

> Avent en vienent celle gent faerie,
> esprover volent sa grande baronie;
> S'an Renoart a tel chevalerie
> con an on dit, ja sera essaïe. (3718–21)

Arthur too desires to test this hero whose epic reputation has preceded him:

> 'An prise molt cel vasal chanpïon;
> talant m'est pris c'orendroit l'esaon'. (3736–37)

More is at issue, however, than satisfaction of curiosity by means of a test. A unique *épreuve* is foreseen, one in which Renoart will be obliged to do single combat against a very unusual foe: Arthur sends for 'Chapalu le felon,' an exceedingly ugly, monstrous creature with cat's head, dragon's feet, horse's body, lion's tail (ll. 3811–12), to 'try' Renoart: 'Une bataille d'ous dous esgarderon' (l. 3740).

In the course of their fierce confrontation we learn that the grotesque physical form of Chapalu is central to Arthur's motivation in calling for the battle. Because Chapalu's birth resulted from the rape of his fairy mother by a *luiton*, a traditionally demonic creature, she had caused her son, at birth an exceedingly beautiful infant, to assume this monstrous form; it can be ended only if he drinks blood from the heel of the great warrior Renoart. Her revenge for the sexual violence she sustained was apparently twofold: first to commemorate the father's monstrous deed by assigning the fruit of this unholy union to a perverted state, then ultimately to have this creature transformed, 'reborn' as it were, through material access to an heroic 'bloodline', a surrogate 'paternity' afforded by the literal ingestion of Renoart's blood. The narrator affirms that Arthur's motive in promoting this combat is not a frivolous thirst for entertainment but his desire that this transformation be effected:

> Li rois Artus por cestai ochoson
> laissoit conbatre Chapalu au baron.
> Molt volantiers müeroit sa façon;
> por cest se met Chapalu a bandon. (3819–22)

Thus the feudal juridical institution represented by Arthur is intent upon redressing an injustice born of sexual violence.[13] This he will do by authorizing the foreordained process requiring the heroic intervention of the epic hero.

At the same time, while injecting its own feudal 'real' world back into the otherworld, the poem undermines the purity of the appropriated *matière*. Far from providing the conventional kinds of *évasion*, abundance, and succour of the hero in need that one often finds in works based on Breton *materia remota*, the generic shift toward lay and romance ushers a new cultural dimension into the previously-dominant epic conventionality of the *Bataille Loquifer*, and it does so by ironizing the very conventions that it appropriates from a genre foreign to the medieval French epic. Arthur, for example, instead of offering welcome or reassurance to the disorientated hero, makes of him almost an object of sport, reacting with amusement to Renoart's terror as he confronts his monstrous adversary: 'Artus l'entent, si s'an rist et gaba'; 'Arthus l'antent, si a

[13] We are reminded that in Chrétien's *Chevalier de la charrete* and *Conte du graal* the custom that bears the name of Arthur's realm, the 'coutume de Logres', prescribes a harsh penalty for rape. See the *Charrete*, ed. M. Roques, Classiques Français du Moyen Age, 86 (Paris: Champion, 1958), ll. 1302–16; and *Conte du graal*, ed. Roach, Textes Littéraires Français, 71 (Geneva: Droz, 1959), ll. 7118–31. See also Donald Maddox, *The Arthurian Romances of Chrétien de Troyes: Once and Future Fictions* (Cambridge: Cambridge University Press, 1991), pp. 36–48; 104–08; 124–29; Kathryn Gravdal, *Ravishing Maidens: Rape in Medieval French Literature and Law* (Philadelphia: University of Pennsylvania Press, 1991).

.I. ris geté./ "Renoars est," dist li rois, "efraé" ' (ll. 3785; 3845–46). One has only to compare this confrontation with Yvain's combat against demonic adversaries to see that Renoart is not faced here with an *épreuve* in the tradition of romance and lay. In fact, the hero's role here conforms more closely to a sacrificial than to an heroic model; while the bloodshed Renoart is forced to undergo for the transformation of Chapalu is not fatal, the outcome of the struggle is nonetheless a victory, not for him, but for his adversary.

Despite these disquieting elements, the outcome of Renoart's ordeal initially appears positive. Through the sanguinary nourishment attained from the hero's vulnerable heel, Chapalu is transformed from a composite monster into a composite of curly-haired Aucassin and broad-chested Lancelot:

> Lou poil ot blont, menu recercelé,
> les iolz ot vars et lou vis coloré,
> gros fut par pis, graille par lou baldré. (3867–69)

In a truly intergeneric transformation, an epic transfusion thus infuses new life into a figure reminiscent of *chantefable* and prose romance.[14]

This resolution would seem to cast a positive light over the entire episode, justifying Arthur's enthusiasm. Between the main epic narrative and the lay-like interlude, moreover, we recognize the kind of complementarity that often typifies the relation between the 'real' world of the hero and the frequently compensatory otherworld of the lay: in the latter, the hero often finds precisely the object or quality of which he had been bereft in the 'real' world, as for example in Marie's *Guigemar* and *Lanval*. Likewise Renoart: in his epic quest he had been seeking his son Maillefer, and now the transformed Chapalu, in gratitude, informs him of the well-being of the son whose abduction had occasioned his grief, and offers to take him to the place where the infant is held:

> 'Servirai toi tout a ta volanté,
> si t'en menrai, se il te vient a gré,
> en Odïerne ou tes filz est porté.' (3874–76)

In this light, in seemingly compensatory fashion, the Avalon episode would appear to provide the hero with a means of liquidating his primary lack, that of his firstborn son: by effecting the 'rebirth' of Chapalu, the

[14] Cf. *Aucassin et Nicolette*, ed. M. Roques, Classiques Français du Moyen Age, 41 (Paris: Champion, 1968), p. 2 *et passim*; and *Lancelot do Lac: The Non-Cyclic Old French Prose Romance*, ed. by Elspeth Kennedy, 2 vols (Oxford: Clarendon Press, 1980), p. 40, ll. 14–24.

son born of a nefarious supernatural union, he gains the helper who will presumably lead him to the son awaiting him at the end of his epic quest. As his main quest involves rescue of a son, so too is his acquisition of an adjuvant in Avalon accomplished by the rescue of a son, according to the foreordained ritual of heroic *agon*. Accordingly, his fright now turns to joy: 'Renoars l'ot, si a .I. ris geté;/ por son fil l'a dolcement acolé' (ll. 3881–82).

Yet Renoart's adventures in Avalon have not ended, and now the Arthurian court, having witnessed his demonstration of chivalric prowess, yields to Morgue. In *Lanval*, we recall, the fairy mistress who has chosen the eponymous hero rescues him from victimization by an erroneous judgement emanating from within the Arthurian court; here, as Badel points out, 'un "Autre-Monde" [. . .] juge la société des hommes: est-elle capable de s'ouvrir à l'inconnu, à un univers plus beau, plus juste, où les êtres sont unis par une confiance mutuelle spontanée et par une totale disponibilité à l'autre?'[15] In *Loquifer* however, as we observed, there is no election of the hero by the supernatural creature. Although two of the fairies who transported Renoart to Avalon had desired, one avowedly, the other silently, to make of him her 'ami' (ll. 3646–51), the liaison between Renoart and Morgue is instigated by the hero himself, and seconded by Arthur's amused approbation:

> Dist Renoars cant i l'ot escouté:
> 'Je volroie or, par sainte charité,
> que je l'aüsse sanpres a mon costé!'
> Artus l'antent, si ait .I. ris geté.
> 'Renoars, freire, savriés me vos greit?'
> Dist Renoars: 'Oïl, sire, o non Dé!' (3909–14)

Now, with Morgue, Renoart demonstrates his sexual aptitude: 'Morgue la nuit fut a lui a bandon;/ toute la nuit fist Renoars son bon' (ll. 3920–21).

The new paternity resulting from this encounter affords a provisional answer to the question of what, precisely, Renoart is doing in Avalon. It suggests as well that we read the entire episode in a new light. In search of a son, the hero is characterized through two successive encounters, one combative, the other amorous. In the first, Chapalu is 'reborn' by his blood; in the second, he engenders a son. Avalon is thus the locus of an emblematic opposition of sons linked to the hero, one in symbolic, the other in biological paternity.

In this episodic shift out of the epic mode and into the realm of Breton

[15] Pierre-Yves Badel, *Introduction à la vie littéraire du Moyen Age* (Paris: Bordas, 1984), pp. 32–33.

conventions, Avalon serves as decor for the dramatization of a preoccupation widespread in feudal culture, one having to do with rights of succession. When Morgue informs Renoart that their nocturnal tryst will bear fruit, he exclaims:

> 'Dex an soit aorés.
> Cant il iert grans, si lou me trametrés;
> je li querrai terrë et erités.
> Por Deu vos prie que vos nel retenés.' (3933–36)

Is this son Corbon then to be an epic analogue of Gauvain's son in *Le Bel Inconnu*, raised in isolation by a fairy mother before making his entry into the paternal sphere of chivalric heroism and assuming, finally, a seigneurial role in the feudal world? The motif occurs in another epic text in which the *merveilleux* is not only prominent but central to the epic action, *Huon de Bordeaux*, in which we learn that the magician Maugis had been taken from his family at birth and raised by a fairy, who later reveals his origins; he then sets out in search of his own lineage.

The singularity of the *Bataille Loquifer* in this regard lies in the fact that here the fairy otherworld is an ominous, threatening environment, overshadowed by the spectre of failure. The thematic specularity based on the motif of son-rescue that relates the epic intrigue and the Avalon interlude is as disquieting as is the encounter of the hero with the monstrous Chapalu, for central to this reflexivity is violence and evil. Chapalu, the son born of sexual aggression, is 'reborn' from the bloodshed of battle; Maillefer was wrested with an iron implement from the womb of his dying mother (ll. 782–90).[16] And Corbon, Renoart's son to be born of Morgue, is identified with evil even before his birth: 'icelle nuit anjandra il Corbon,/ .I. vif diable; ans ne fist se mal non' (ll. 3920–23).

In fact, the reiteration of the filial motif results not in the fruition but in the miscarriage of the heroic intrigue. Having declared his intent to provide 'terre et erités' for Morgue's son 'cant il iert grans,' Renoart determines to resume the quest for his *other* son, and Morgue at once enjoins Chapalu to sabotage the effort. This portrayal of a perfidious Morgue, while reminiscent of the fairy who bears that name in Arthurian tradition, is highly unusual in the tradition of the *chanson de geste*: Wathelet-Willem points out that of the dozen epic poems in which she studies the figure of Morgue, this is the only text in which the fairy plays

[16] A recent study examines the medieval significance of this practice: Renate Blumenfeld-Kosinski, *Not of Woman Born: Representations of Caesarean Birth in Medieval and Renaissance Culture* (Ithaca and London: Cornell University Press, 1990).

a maleficent role.[17] Here her treachery underlines the question of succession: fearful that Renoart might ultimately succeed in his attempt to rescue Maillefer, she seeks to ensure an auspicious future for Corbon, the son *she* will bear in Renoart's lineage:

> 'et se il puet Maillefer conquester,
> Corbans mes fil ne poroit riens clamer
> a Porpaillart, n'a Tolose sor Mer.' (3953–55)

Her action is motivated by reasons similar to those that underlie Ganelon's betrayal in the Oxford *Roland*: the elimination of Roland, the son by a previous marriage of Charlemagne's sister, Ganelon's wife, would considerably enhance the prospects of succession of Ganelon's own son Baldewin.[18] Likewise, if Maillefer is never found and perishes at the hands of the Saracens, Corbon's claim to Renoart's fiefs of Tolose and Porpaillart would be immeasurably strengthened. The Avalon episode thus brings into prominence a not uncommon anxiety in feudal culture, one having to do with the complexities of succession and the asperities, rivalries, even treasons, that this issue could occasion within a feudal clan.

When Morgue appropriates Chapalu to thwart his search for Maillefer, Renoart loses the essential accessory to his quest for his epic firstborn. In sum, our hero's second, sexual encounter cancels the benefits that might have accrued from his first, heroic one. Moreover, by involving him in this awkward situation of transgeneric paternity, it renews and prolongs the tensions of the father-son opposition that had set the apostate Renoart against his Saracen father Desramé. Wathelet-Willem ('La *Bataille Loquifer*', p. 250) has argued that the Avalon episode is 'un hors d'oeuvre' because in her view it is unrelated to the main theme of the poem, which she takes to be founded on that struggle. Our reading suggests instead that the episode emphatically renews the father-son theme, again in relation to the question of inheritance and to the contradictions between generations, thus tightly integrating the Avalon episode into the thematic concerns of the poem as a whole.

It becomes apparent that the locus of Renoart's otherworld adventure is something quite other than the compensatory and idyllic land of abundance often suggested in lay and romance, and equally distant from

17 Wathelet-Willem, 'La fée Morgain', p. 218, note 42.
18 See Donald Maddox, ' "E Baldewin mun filz": la parenté dans la *Chanson de Roland*', in *VII Congreso de la Société Rencesvals* (Pamplona: Institucion Principe de Viana, 1981), pp. 299–304.

the sporadic occurrences of the *merveilleux* in other epic poems.[19] Its opening does indeed carefully set the stage for a representation of the otherworld as a nurturant realm: the objects borne by the fairies provide an abundance of food and drink; there are trees and flowering meadows and delightful garments and illumination of the world upon command. The wish-fulfilment aspect of this Avalon itself, moreover, is fully evident in its description: 'Molt seroit riches qui avroit sou conquis', the narrator tells us of this enchanted place, 'puis an fut sires Renoars .XV. dis' (ll. 3621–22). On the other hand, who indeed inhabits Avalon, that place that the fairies call 'nostre cité vaillant' (l. 3634)? While Morgue and her companions are identified as fairies and those who come forward to observe Renoart on his arrival are 'celle gent faerie' (l. 3718), Arthur tells Renoart that Avalon is home to those enchanted, and those dead: 'ce sont la gent faé/ et de cest sicle venu et trespassé' (ll. 3900–01).[20] Chapalu, even following his transformation, remains a being who is 'faés', as Morgue reminds him in urging that he contrive the shipwreck: 'tu es faés, ne poras riens douter./ A ton voloir t'en poras eschaper' (ll. 3958–59). The felicitous outcome of Renoart's combat, moreover, will be subverted, like our generic expectations, because the physical transformation of Chapalu from a monstrous into a beautiful creature is not paralleled by a transformation of character. He is obedient to Morgue: ' "Dame", dist il, "je ne vos puis veer!" ' (l. 3960). In epic terms, the narrator also identifies him as a traitor:

> vers Renoart a traïsson pansee
> par lou covent que il ot a la fee;
> jamais si grande ne sera porpansee. (4145–47)

Contriving Renoart's shipwreck as they journey to seek Maillefer, when the hero is plunged into the sea and in danger of drowning, he taunts him by recalling their combat, provoking Renoart's renewed attempt to destroy him.

The treachery to which Renoart falls victim in Avalon is particularly telling in the light of two other episodes in the poem. He escapes drowning only with the aid of sirens, one of whom he had pitied when she was captured at his behest; she now, unlike Chapalu 'le felon', enacts her gratitude by coming to the rescue of her benefactor. In contrast with the

19 As Dickman observes, the 'merveilleux moyen littéraire' serves epic poets most often 'pour exprimer quelque chose de beau et agréable aux sens [. . .] surtout comme ornement' (*Le Rôle du surnaturel*, pp. 101–02).

20 The inhabitants are repeatedly characterized as 'faee'; see ll. 3639, 3664, 3701, 3706, 3718, 3725, 3741, 3886, 3915.

conniving fairies who had transported the sleeping Renoart to Avalon, these benevolent creatures put him to sleep now with their sweet music and transport him safely 'home', to the shore from which he had unwittingly departed. Even more telling is the depiction of the hideous giant Loquifer, the eponymous adversary in the epic action of the poem. Although his appearance is almost equal in monstrosity to that of Chapalu (see ll. 1010–25), he first shares his magical healing unguent with Renoart when both are grievously wounded in their combat, then invites him to spend a restorative night aboard his own ship before resuming the struggle, and fights at his side against the Saracen forces who dare attack the adversary to whom he has given his word. This depiction of the Saracen archenemy as an opponent who can be trusted to adhere to a chivalric code contrasts starkly with the experience of Renoart in Avalon.[21]

Thus Renoart's sojourn in Avalon leads to near-disaster. It brings him no nearer to closure of his epic adventure: rescued from the sea by sirens, he awakens on the same shore where the fairies had found him. While audiences familiar with the parameters of lay and romance might have been susceptible to the humour of the hero's leaving the otherworld with more woes than when he arrived, at the poem's end we find a grief-stricken Renoart who returns empty-handed to his fief at Porpaillart, having failed to achieve his objective of reunion with his son Maillefer. This son remains under the protection of Picolet, Loquifer's messenger, who had abducted the infant but then used his magical powers to save him from death (ll. 4073–106). The separation between the feudal father and the son raised in the milieu of the *merveilleux* might again suggest less an epic sequel than a romance like *Le Bel Inconnu*, in which the son is in time to forsake the maternal sphere of fairydom and discover the chivalric father. Yet now Renoart has another son as well, and, like Maillefer, the newborn Corbon remains in a nurturant realm of enchantment, with his mother Morgue in Avalon.

The potential rivalry between these two sons suggests that generic rivalry has yielded in the end to conflicts emblematic of a much larger cultural sphere. In late medieval texts, chivalry's ambition to found its nobility on the material wealth and prestige afforded by a distinguished genealogy is sometimes alloyed with the superhuman and the supernatural.[22] Other texts, including *Esclarmonde*, which also places Arthur in

21 Wathelet-Willem comments on the 'opposition curieuse, qui doit être voulue', between these examples of courteous behaviour and the violence of the combats leading to Renoart's conquest of the famous *loque* ('La *Bataille Loquifer*', p. 249).

22 See Georges Duby, 'Structures de parenté et noblesse dans la France du nord aux XIe et

Avalon along with epic heroes, would attempt to Christianize the fairy otherworld to blend its function into accounts of heroic adventure.[23] Here, however, the anxiety concerning the representation of the otherworld, along with the subversion of its status as purveyor of knowledge and power and as arbiter of values and judgment, affords no reassuring recourse for the destabilized institutions of the feudal world.

On the contrary: as a result of the generic shift, the robust optimism, zeal, and unicity typical of early feudal epic yields in this text to the uncertainties and anxieties often evident in more courtly types of narrative. While early epic convention locates the warrior-hero within the immediate concerns of a militant Christian community united against the infidel, the situation in which Renoart finds himself at the end of the *Bataille Loquifer* is more akin to that of the principal hero of the *Lancelot-Grail* cycle. Both are preoccupied on the one hand with their not uncomplicated status as regards the antecedent order of father and forbears, on the other with the legacy each will bequeath to the offspring from whose nurturance, under the aegis of some type of supernatural agency, they are exceedingly remote. In the course of this work, Renoart becomes a hero for whom the mandates of the past and anticipation of the future outweigh current events. In the wake of the generic shift, he moves away from the profile of the epic hero, and closer to that of a Lancelot.

XIIe siècles', in his *Hommes et structures du moyen âge* (Paris and The Hague: Mouton, 1973), pp. 267–85; R. Howard Bloch, *Etymologies and Genealogies: A Literary Anthropology of the French Middle Ages* (Chicago and London: University of Chicago Press, 1983), pp. 79–87, 203–17.

23 See Wathelet-Willem, who cites the similar movement in Geoffrey of Monmouth's *Vita Merlini* ('La fée Morgain', p. 217).

Motherhood. The Case of the Epic Family Romance

SARAH KAY

A RECENT PAPER EXPLORES the psychotherapeutic exchange of transference and countertransference as a model for the relations between supervisor and supervisee.[1] It is at great pains to avoid seeing them in Oedipal terms, although the author is an ex-student of the person he is attacking. The academic 'father' is indeed a familiar figure, benign or sinister according to where you stand (on appointments committees, for instance). I was fortunate to be taught almost entirely by women, among them Elspeth Kennedy. This paper, dedicated to her, takes motherhood as its subject at least in part because I think 'mothering' is a better model for the relation between teachers and taught than either 'fathering' or 'therapy'. The Old French word *norrir* has meanings that range from nursing and feeding, through receiving into one's house and rearing, to training and educating. It is not only mothers who do these things; but they are among those that do, and so did Elspeth.

I can think of four ways of becoming a mother in OF narratives: pregnancy, fostering (especially breastfeeding), becoming a stepmother, or a godmother. Of these the first appears least 'symbolic' or resulting from cultural construction (and has concomitantly the most obvious biological basis) whereas the last is most symbolic and least biological; the others fall on a cline between them. It is striking that only the first is commonly depicted in literary texts;[2] this contrasts with paternity,

My thanks go to Karen Pratt for her pertinent criticisms of an earlier draft of this paper.

1 Rod Giblett, 'The Desire for Disciples', *Paragraph*, 15 (1992), 136–55.

2 Doris Desclais Berkvam, *Enfance et maternité dans la littérature française des XIIe et XIIIe siècles* (Paris: Champion, 1981) (henceforth Berkvam), is concerned almost solely with maternity resulting from pregnancy, though she discusses fostering and breastfeeding (pp. 46–54).

represented not only by biological fathers but by stepfathers[3] and godfathers,[4] not to mention the many figures who act as symbolic fathers (assisting the hero, making him an heir, giving him land, finding him a bride, raising troops for him).[5] This contrast is not particularly surprising. It reflects the old tag whereby 'pater semper incertus est, mater certissima' which, for Freud and others, serves as a prop to the generally masculine bias of symbolism(s), and to the idea that whilst 'nature' may be gendered feminine, 'culture' is masculine.[6] Does that leave an opening for women to be symbolic mothers, and transmitters of symbolic values? Proverbially a mother's place is in the wrong,[7] but less so, I think, in the *chansons de geste* than in romances.

The critical framework of this paper is provided by 'family romances', a term used by Freud as the title of a short essay describing childhood fantasies.[8] Their commonest form occurs when the child, having reached an age where he understands the role of the father in conception, and no longer feeling for the person he is assured is his father the same degree of reverence that he felt for him in infancy, imagines that this man is not, after all, his father, and that he was begotten by someone far grander. The fantasy expresses ambivalence towards the real father, since on the one hand it rejects him, but on the other invests in the fantasy father the love the child feels or felt for the real one. The very young child experiments with replacing the mother in the same way as the father, but when he has developed understanding of the mother's biological role he

3 Bueve de Hantone, Esmeré and Milon (in *Florence de Rome*), and Auberi (in *Auberi le Bourgoing*) all have unpleasant stepfathers; Ganelon is of course the best known example.

4 Julien in *Raoul de Cambrai* has the count of Saint-Gilles as his godfather; Roland stands godfather to Beton in *Daurel et Beton*; Hugon, King of Hungary, becomes Huguet's godfather in *Parise la Duchesse*; no description of a Saracen baptism is complete without the mention of Frankish godfathers.

5 For a remarkable example of symbolic fatherhood, see Sturm-Maddox and Maddox, this volume. Symbolic motherhood is sometimes exercised by queens or noblewomen towards young ladies and knights, whom they assist in love and general courtly advancement, as Guinevere does with Erec and Enide, or Soredamors and Alexander. Iseut in Beroul's *Tristran* and Guinevere in *Lancelot* are also expected to help younger ladies to find husbands, but are prevented by their own love affairs from doing so.

6 See especially Freud's late essays 'Civilization and its Discontents' and 'Moses and Monotheism', both in the standard edition of Freud's works, *The Complete Psychological Works of Sigmund Freud*, trans. by James Strachey, 24 vols (London: Institute of Psycho-Analysis and The Hogarth Press, 1953–74) (henceforth *SE*), XXI (1961), 59–145 and XXIII (1964), 3–137.

7 Berkvam, p. 107: 'Une mère peut conseiller ses fils, surtout s'ils le sollicitent, mais elle n'a pas le droit d'agir directement, son influence ne peut se manifester que verbalement. Il est vrai que, dans les romans, les mères interviennent presque toujours malencontreusement [. . .]'.

8 *SE*, IX (1959), 237–41.

concentrates instead on fantasizing her in irregular sexual predicaments. The different treatments accorded to father and mother reflect the more 'symbolic' role of the former.

An interesting article by Donald Maddox identifies a number of courtly examples of 'family romances': Marie de France's *Yonec*, the anonymous lai *Tydorel*, *Li Biaus Desconneüs* and *Li Conte del graal*.[9] He notes that the protagonist of each of these texts is confronted by the narration of his own family background, and that this narration is a 'specular' reflection of the fantasy those texts inscribe. The article is full of new insights, though it inevitably sacrifices certain aspects of individual texts for the sake of clarity of pattern, most notably perhaps in the case of the *Conte del graal*. Even so, I am struck by the fact that only the first two works conform closely to Freud's model. Both Yonec and Tydorel learn that the man in whose household they have been reared is not their progenitor. The 'real' father, in both cases, has fairy attributes: this confirms the 'family romance' framework, whereby the father fantasized as authentic is superior to the previously accepted father. The narrators' endorsement of the second father as 'real' indicates their complicity with the filial fantasy. Both *lais* are therefore prepared to admit the bastardy of their protagonists – though apparently not to discuss it – whereas the other two texts are not. They either announce legitimacy (the Fair Unknown goes from being fatherless to 'discovering' that he is Gawain's son) or supplement it with additional father-figures (Perceval, whose own father has died, learns of his relationship to the Fisher King and to the hermit, and is taught to acknowledge his dependency on God; though this analysis is not unproblematic).[10] The relationship to the father is not conflictual, except in *Yonec*, where the son, learning the identity of his 'true' father, kills his mother's husband. Furthermore, in all four of Maddox's texts the election of the father (in Perceval's case the 'fathers', though again this reading could be contested) entails abandoning the mother, who is killed off by the plot

[9] Donald Maddox, 'Specular Stories, Family Romance, and the Fictions of Courtly Culture', *Exemplaria*, 3 (1991), 299–326.

[10] Maddox underplays here the fact that these significant male figures are all maternal relatives, and that the father's tradition of secular knighthood is negated, or transcended, by maternal kin whose lives are peaceable and whose concerns revolve around such 'feminine' themes as lack of fecundity (the waste land) and the provision of food. Yet when Perceval and Gawain set out on their independent quests, Gawain, who is looking for the lance, finds himself involved with his elderly female relatives, and has adventures that alternate between the burlesque and the sinister. Perceval, by contrast, meets a male relative (the hermit) who tells him of his other male kin, and addresses his spiritual needs. This contrast suggests that the significant opposition here is between female and male kin, rather than between mother's and father's kin.

(*Yonec*, *Graal*), left and never seen again (*Tydorel*), or just forgotten (*Li Biaus Desconneüs*). They thus describe a passage from the régime of the mother to that of the father. This is not effected without loss; the Fair Unknown, learning that he is Gawain's son, can never fulfil his love for the Pucele as Blanches Mains, who recalls his fairy mother, and is instead married by the fatherly régime of Arthur's court to Blonde Esmérée. As he embarks on a career of knighthood in imitation of his dead father, Perceval's first duty is to unlearn his mother's instructions, overlaying them with those of his (fatherly) mentor Gornemant, and this leads to errors which he seems unable to resolve. Nevertheless, the death or abandonment of the mother in all these romance texts indicates her expendability as the hero moves away from her into a 'symbolic' world where men predominate. Yonec acquires his father's sword, Perceval progresses to the mysteries of the grail,[11] the Fair Unknown becomes enmeshed in the Arthurian world and Tydorel combats insomnia with endless story-telling: all of them, in so doing, acquire a history and identity stressing their relationships to men. Such family violence as these stories contain is expressed more from son to mother than between father and son.

A study of family romances in the *chansons de geste* points up important differences between them and Maddox's corpus:

(1) the child has to negotiate the problems of having two (or more) parents simultaneously;
(2) the chief axis of conflict is father-son;
(3) the issue of illegitimacy is explicitly raised in this context.

These three features are thoroughly Oedipal and in conformity with Freudian thought.

(4) The 'epic' family romance articulates not only fantasies of the son experimenting with his parents but also those of the parents, i.e. it adopts several subject positions simultaneously. Of Maddox's examples, only *Yonec* offers an account of the fantasy of the mother, an aspect of the *lai* which Maddox does not explore.
(5) The mother's role may emerge as the most 'symbolic' of the triad.

The first of these latter two features is a development which the Freudian account half allows for,[12] the second an important departure. I

11 Although the inexhaustible nurturing power of the grail could assign it to the 'feminine', especially by contrast with the lance, the fact that it carries the host also aligns it with the Father.

12 'Family Romances' was first published as the preface to Otto Rank's *Myth of the Birth of the Hero*, i.e. in association with group psychology; and the ideas it contains are also

shall briefly illustrate these points using three *chansons de geste* of the later twelfth century (and so roughly contemporary with Maddox's texts): *Aiol*, *Doon de la Roche*, and *Parise la Duchesse*.[13]

The first part of *Aiol* tells how the hero, equipped only with his father's old armour and horse, travels incognito to the royal court to regain his father's fief, lost through the treachery of Macaire. Although at first everyone derides the youth, he eventually demonstrates his merits and reveals his identity. Mancini has read the poem as ideologically ambiguous between Aiol's 'obstination patrilinéaire' (p. 308) and occasional 'régression' into the clan (p. 307), an ambiguity he relates to historians' accounts of the decline of the clan in favour of an agnatic conception of lineage devolving through the father.[14] In my view, however, the ambivalence is not between 'clan' and 'lineage' but between mother and father; I see the episodes with Aiol's two cousins in an entirely different way from him. Gilebert, Count of Bourges, is Aiol's father's sister's son. He has become a bandit in his efforts to win back the same fief as Aiol. Aiol fights him along with other bandits in his service of the king; only after taking him prisoner does he realize who his adversary was. Lusiane, conversely, is his mother's sister's daughter, and Aiol narrowly avoids being seduced by her when he receives hospitality from his aunt, only discovering the next morning how close he came to the crime of incest (ll. 2270–76). For Mancini, both cousins represent the cognatic family or clan. The episode with Gilebert is therefore 'progressive', since Aiol opposes him, unlike the meeting with Aiol's maternal aunt, 'regressive' insofar as he accepts assistance from her. What I find striking about these encounters, however, is that their combination recalls the Oedipal fantasy of killing the father and sleeping with the mother: each of these two acts is displaced on to a first cousin, and neither is fully realized.[15] Unlike

drawn upon by Freud in writings on social psychology such as 'The Future of an Illusion', (*SE*, XXI (1961), 3–36), 'Group Psychology', (*SE*, XVIII (1955), 67–143), and 'Moses and Monotheism' (see note 6).

13 *Aiol*, ed. by Jacques Normand and Gaston Raynaud, SATF (Paris: Firmin Didot, 1877); *Doon de la Roche*, ed. by Paul Meyer and Gédéon Huet, SATF (Paris: Champion, 1921); *Parise la Duchesse. Edition et commentaires*, ed. by May Plouzeau, 2 vols (= *Senefiance* 17, 18) (Aix-en-Provence: Publications du CUERMA, 1986). The earlier editors of *Parise la Duchesse* date it around 1200, 'plutôt en avant qu'en arrière': see the edition by F. Guessard and L. Larchey, *Anciens Poètes de la France* (Paris: Vieweg, 1860), p. xiii. The later dating proposed by Plouzeau is on the basis of its relation to *Gaydon*, which I am not certain I find convincing. See vol. I, pp. 143–49 of her edition and note 22 below.

14 Mario Mancini, 'Aiol et l'ombre du père', in *VIII Congreso de la Société Rencesvals* (Pamplona: Institución Principe de Viana, 1981), pp. 305–11.

15 Interestingly it is the memory of his father which prevents Aiol succumbing to the seductions of Lusiane (ll. 1408–11). Subsequently, Aiol will cause two squires from the household of his father's brother to be imprisoned because he sends them back to Louis

the romance protagonists discussed by Maddox, Aiol, in these two scenes, is negotiating Oedipal relations with *both* his parents. The poem's opening scene, which presents him living with his father, his mother, his father's lance,[16] and a hermit, in a series of little huts in the forest, is indeed bizarrely reminiscent of key elements in the *Perceval.* In Chrétien's romance they are dispersed over thousands of lines; in the *chanson de geste*, they seem as it were to have been shuffled and dealt out all at once, giving the hero the cards with which he must play.

In this game the father provides a framework but not a content. Aiol's arms, deriving from his father, denote a knighthood which, in the absence of wealth, is an empty sign earning only derision. During the period when Aiol is incognito he gives his father's name as Gautier de Pont Elie (ll. 2088, 3504). 'Elie' thus identifies land, the object of Aiol's quest, not his linear origin. This use of the name of the father to designate a lack and a symbolic space confirms the assignation of the paternal to the symbolic found in the courtly 'family romance', but differs in its recognition that the symbolic designation is a fiction, an absence. Indeed, the text is full of men who have lost their lands and status. Gilebert has been reduced to banditry, and twelve thieves have become so because, although formerly knights, 'il sont de lor terre bani et essillié' (l. 6658); Hunbaut's wife's father 'sold' her into marriage because he had been ruined (ll. 7111–20). Even when Elie's fief is regained, it is not named until Aiol and Mirabel return there at the very end of the poem (l. 9560), and even then is not explictly identified as his. It is as though Elie and his fief have only one name between them, and the restoration of the name 'Elie' to the father, with its meaning completed by the fief, displaces the absence back onto the land. The symbolic world of the father remains lacunary.

Content comes rather from the mother. The nobility Aiol inherits from her is recognizable to the king (l. 3833) and the people of Orleans (ll. 4371–74). Assistance also comes primarily from the mother's side. For Mancini, Louis, as a Capetian royal, represents the agnatic imperative given that it was the royal family which set the pattern of father-son descent (p. 308). Mancini underplays his role as maternal uncle: 'Si l'on regarde de près, l'on trouvera également un rapport avunculaire entre Louis et Aiol' (p. 308). But there is no need to 'look closely' to see this: it is heavily underlined from the start, when Elie charges Aiol with his

in circumstances which make them appear traitors, l. 5105ff. He does, however, get help from another paternal cousin, Geraume, l. 6442ff.

16 His father's hauberk and shield also appear to have little huts to themselves.

mission. He recommends Aiol to ask Gilebert's help and join with him to recapture their land, to which Aiol replies:

> 'Sire,' che dist Aiol, 'c'est por noiant;
> ains en irai a mon oncle u France apent,
> de lui terai me tere, mon casement;
> je ne querrai ja autre en mon vivent
> jusques j'orai de lui le covenent,
> car chou est li plus riches de mes parens.' (341–46)

Louis allows Aiol unlimited credit in Orleans, and his maternal aunt is one of the few people he encounters who recognizes his noble quality and gives him lodging. Indeed, the fief which is usually referred to as Elie's (ll. 508, 812, 880, etc.) is also identified as the mother's (l. 1509).[17]

Thus whilst the poem insistently uses 'Aiols li fieus Elie' as a first hemistich formula, it problematizes this view of descent by stressing the violence and lack which inhere on the father's side and by counterposing the values, as well as the dangers, transmitted by the mother's. The mother's brother acts as a point of synthesis in the dialectic.[18] After capturing Gilebert, Aiol unwittingly also takes the king prisoner; this enables him to trade Louis's release for Gilebert's safety. The mother's brother thus seems to be the means by which the hero escapes the Oedipal impasse; he can devote himself to the king's service, and avoid family violence. In Aiol's big scene, when he finally reveals his identity to Louis, he starts by demanding the whole of his realm: the king, by listening to Macaire's deceptions, had aligned himself with fictions and deficiency, but through his role as maternal uncle he is also able to replenish these lacks and restore content:

> Jel vous ai demandé, si dirai le raison
> por coi l'ai demandé, comment et comment non.
> Mes pere(s) a non Elie a la clere fachon,
> ma mere ert vostre seur, fille le roi Charlon,
> de Franche le cachastes par .i. malvais glouton,
> par le concel Makaire et des autres larons:
> Damelde[x] lor en renge ains la mort gueredon! (8097–103)

The same scene witnesses Mirabel's baptism and betrothal to Aiol. Louis,

[17] Cf. Berkvam, p. 127: '[Aiol] va reconquérir les terres paternelles et l'héritage maternel'.

[18] The status of the avunculate is a vexed question which I cannot go into here. For a survey of epic texts contending that the child is closer to his maternal uncle than to his father, see William Oliver Farnsworth, *Father and Uncle in the 'chansons de geste'* (New York: University of Columbia Press, 1913).

as Mirabel's godfather (l. 8156), can give her to Aiol and so enable him, by his marriage to a royal princess, to replicate his father's career and introduce a second royal mother into the text. The mother's brother can fulfil the nurturing and empowering role of the mother, and reverse the lack on the side of the father, whilst also permanently solving the 'problem' of incest.

Aiol has obvious similarities with romances such as the *Perceval* and *Li Biaus Desconneüs*, since it relates the *enfances* of a young and untried knight in quest of social status.[19] But whereas the protagonists of these texts experience parental figures in succession, Aiol must negotiate the complexities of family existence with both parents at once, just as he will later come to accept the responsibilites of having a wife and children himself.

In other *chansons de geste* the mother as a representative of inherent value stands out even more clearly against the deficiencies of a symbolic world associated with the father. In *Doon de la Roche* the mother, framed as an adulteress by having a *garçon* introduced by traitors into her bed while she sleeps, is maltreated by her husband, who is the traitors' dupe, whilst their child is denounced as a bastard. Olive tells, with the help of her son and a variety of other figures, a counter-narrative of her innocence that is repressed by figures of authority – her husband Doon, most of his barons, his overlord king Pepin (who is also her brother) – who combine to protest her guilt.[20] Father and mother tell different stories, but ultimately the mother's prevails. Even as he agrees to marry the traitor's daughter, Doon admits that she could never be 'de sens si bien garnie' as Olive (l. 570).

Olive also transmits nobility. As the king's sister, she is of far higher rank than Doon, and her child Landri is a hero whereas Doon's second marriage to the traitor's daughter (a rare example of a literary stepmother) produces the treacherous son Malingre (ll. 940–41). The differences between the two sons, who both have the same father, manifestly derive from their respective mothers:

> Ce dit sainte Escripture, si [com] savez bien tuit,
> que ja de mauvais arbre ne issera bon fruiz.
> Or norrissiez .j. lop tant qu'il soit parcreüz,

[19] See the studies cited by Mancini and, more recently, Steven M. Taylor, 'Comic Incongruity in Medieval French *enfances*', *Romance Quarterly*, 35 (1988), 3–10.

[20] For the term 'counter-narrative', see my 'Compagnonnage, désordre social et hétérotextualité dans *Daurel et Beton*', in *Actes du XIe Congrès International de la Société Rencesvals*, = Memorias de la Real Academia de Buenas Letras de Barcelona, XX (Barcelona, 1990), 353–67.

quant vos l'avrez nori, gardé et bien peü,
toz tens sera il lous: cuidiez qu'il desnaturt? (870–74)

The tree metaphor inevitably privileges the motherhood of Olive, named after the fruit of the olive tree, over that of the treacherous Audegours. When Landri leaves his father's house as the result of the traitors' death-threats, he tells Olive that last year he planted '.j. douz aubre': it and he will die in the same year, but so long as it flourishes Olive will know he is safe (ll. 1273–80). Mother and son are thus fruit (seed) and tree; they are on the side not only of truth but also of nature, and the two reinforce each other, such that 'truth' is 'natural' and 'nature' 'true'. The knights of Pepin's court may contend that her adultery is likewise 'natural' – 's'ele a fait son pechié, c'est a fame nature' (l. 459) – but this idea of woman's 'natural' lechery is subordinated to the natural fruitfulness of motherhood. Thus ideologically buoyed up, mother and son are bound to triumph over deceit and contrivance.

What Olive chiefly represents in the eyes of the other characters is, however, not 'nature' but 'property'. On her marriage she brings to Doon the duchy of Lorraine and lordship over Cologne. Doon identifies her as a piece of land when he complains of her adultery to Pepin:

il [sc. Pepin] me dona .j. don, genz fu et honorez:
ce fu un pan de terre que molt fait a loer.
.I. hom la me chalonge, qui est d'autre regné;
ma terre en est enfraite et ses bans trespassez.
Or viengne en Loeroigne por sa terre aquiter. (313–17).

The messenger interprets this correctly: 'de putage la rete' (l. 340). Pepin responds by judging that Lorraine should be given outright to Doon and that Olive should be repudiated; this is 'droiz et mesure' (l. 464). For Olive and Landri, conversely, it is Doon who is identified with territory: he is Doon *de la Roche*, the 'rock' being the terrain on which they should both be allowed to grow, since it was settled on Olive as her dower and should be given to Landri (ll. 1027–28); both Olive and Landri will fight for its return, Landri adopts it as his battle cry (l. 1106ff.), and they eventually win it back. Thus whilst the characters of the dominant narrative equate Olive with sexual territory, and jockey for control of her lands with deceit and bribery, for the protagonists of the counter-narrative Olive is identified as 'mother' and the father becomes the passive space where her fertility should flourish.

Doon is a far from impressive figure – less a rock than a broken reed. His authority is renounced by Landri, who turns up at Doon's marriage to Audegours to denounce his father's injustice (ll. 677–87). Later, Landri prepares to leave christendom since his father is 'fel et traïtre' and fails to protect him (ll. 1237–40); he fights with his father, and later goes to war against him. By contrast, he promises not to forget his mother for another woman (l. 1300). The father is present only as violence and deficiency. Pepin, having become an accessory of the traitors, does nothing to make good this lack. In these circumstances, legitimate birth is of doubtful value. It is best defended by Malingre, the offspring of Doon's union with the traitor Audegours, in a complaint to Doon that he shows more favour to Landri than to himself:

> je sui li vostre filz et ma mere est leals.
> Ci illuec me honi[st] chascun jor .j. bastarz. (1006–07)

Ironically it is Malingre himself whose legitimacy is in doubt, since Doon's marriage to his mother is bigamous. To the emperor of Constantinople, whose daughter has fallen in love with Landri, the significant question is not whether Landri is legitimate, but whether he is truly related to Pepin (ll. 1463–68). Presumably, it is the transmission of royalty through the *mother* which is most valued by this king, whose wealth puts France in the shade (l. 1390).

The end of the text shows the admission by the traitors of their deceptions and the reunion of Doon and Olive. The separated family is at last reunited with the 'patriarch'. The mother-son dyad is valued, but incomplete without him. Olive's fidelity is what guarantees all along the rightness of her cause, and Landri is truly his son. The father's world ultimately assures legitimacy, then; and yet its symbolic fabric of law (injustice), power (cruelty and bribery), and representation (lies and pretence) has been irremediably impaired. As a 'family romance', *Doon de la Roche* has succeeded in balancing the two terms of a contradiction, both requiring and undermining the paternal function. It likewise illustrates contradictory thinking about the mother, playing with the idea of compromising her sexually,[21] but disavowing this fantasy by turning it into a traitors' plot. Negative impulses towards the mother are directed towards the evil stepmother, Audegours, who is then eliminated, whereas the 'good' mother, who had been driven out, makes a triumphant return. In the end, the poem concludes both that motherhood is 'truer' than fatherhood and meaningless without it. *Aiol*'s work of synthesis is countered in this poem by patriarchy's deconstruction.

[21] 'The child, having learned about sexual processes, tends to picture to himself erotic situations and relations, the motive force behind this being his desire to bring his mother (who is the subject of the most intense sexual curiosity) into situations of secret infidelities and secret love affairs', Freud, 'Family Romances', *SE*, IX, 239.

Although both *Aiol* and *Doon de la Roche* voice the claims of mother and father in the family group, they privilege the position of the son, who experiments with the roles of both his parents and ultimately resolves family tensions to his own satisfaction. *Parise la Duchesse*, however, whilst giving a voice to the child and the father, and depicting their opposition, is primarily focused on the mother, who, expelled from one family, gathers a surrogate one around herself; motherhood is thereby articulated as a symbolic relation.

The reason for Parise's exile is that she is convicted of the murder of her brother-in-law, having misguidedly given him a poisoned apple with which the traitors intended to kill her. She disposes of the body, but of course it turns up again as fictional bodies tend to do; one of the traitors then claims to have overheard her confessing the murder to the pope, and she is put on trial. The traitor Milon pretends to undertake her defence, though with the intention of losing the judicial duel and so ensuring her conviction. To this end he boobytraps his own weapons by breaking and reassembling them with wax, and is consequently defeated with ease. However, his friends' plot also backfires: they had intended to ransom his safety, but Raimont puts him to death and banishes Parise.

This plot, which is also found in the *chanson de geste Gaydon*, is here more reminiscent of *La Mort Artu* where Guinevere kills Gaheris with a poisoned fruit intended for Gawain.[22] Everyone is convinced of her guilt, but Lancelot's defence leads to acquittal. The *Mort* episode is deeply ambiguous. Guinevere is 'innocent' in the sense that she had no intent to kill (which is presumably why Lancelot is allowed to win); however, the act of handing a poisoned fruit to a man recalls Eve's seduction of Adam, and the biblical intertext undermines Guinevere's 'innocence' by suggesting that she is also 'guilty' of corrupting the courtly world by her sexuality. Thus although the court is 'wrong' to condemn her for the results, rather than the motives, of her action, it is also 'right' to view her as a threat. In the *chanson de geste*, the naming of the fruit as an apple invokes the biblical model if anything more strongly than the episode in the *Mort*; yet although Parise is convicted, and indeed confesses her part in Bueves' death (ll. 668–70), it is hard to discern any imputation of guilt to her. Violence and cupidity are instead ascribed to the traitors, who want to kill her before she discovers that they killed her father, and wish

[22] See *La Mort le roi Artu*, ed. by J. Frappier, 3rd edn, TLF (Geneva-Paris: Droz, 1964) §§ 62–85. Yolande de Pontfarcy, 'Source et structure de l'épisode de l'empoisonnement dans *La Mort Artu*', *Romania*, 99 (1978), 246–55, considers the *Mort* version to be closer to the *Vita Merlini*, and groups the two epic redactions together, but she does not pick up the sexual subtext present in all three of the *Vita*, the *Mort* and *Parise*. See also Plouzeau's edition of *Parise*, vol. I, 143–50.

to persuade Raimont to marry one of their daughters, so that they can have access to Parise's estates. The discrepancy between intention and outcome, so important in the prose romance, is not an issue here. At the end of the poem Raimont accepts her back without question and puts the traitors to death.

The traitors choose dangerous ground on which to make their stand. The bogus confession which Aumaugin claims to have heard explains that Parise killed Bueves from anxiety lest Raimont repudiate her for being childless and make his brother his heir (ll. 230–37). But the traitors have miscalculated: though childlessness may turn a woman into a murderer, Parise is pregnant, and as a result the death sentence against her is commuted to exile (l. 619ff.). This part of the poem recalls hagiographic texts where successive attempts to martyr a saint all fail: not sanctity, but motherhood protects Parise from the death the traitors intend for her, and which instead slips sideways on to others.[23] Whereas Guinevere's relation to a crime of violence is ambivalent because some blame can be attached to her sexual conduct, Parise seems to be innocent of the death she caused because she is expecting a child.

This child is of course her husband's child, and a son. But the weakness of the patriarchal framework is far more marked in this text than in *Doon*. Not only does Raimont make all the same mistakes as Doon by driving away his wife and marrying the daughter of traitors, he is also displaced from the lives of both of them. Parise's infant son Huguet, born in the forest, has a 'family romance' career, since he is given by thieves to be reared by the Hungarian king, his godfather. The possibility that he may be a bastard is viewed by him with equanimity: 'se je sui bastarz, ne sui mie mauvés' (l. 1500). By the end of the poem, having fought and been reconciled with Raimont, he has acquired two high-ranking fathers and inherits from both of them. Parise, for her part, is taken into the household of the count of Cologne as foster-mother to his son Antoine. Although socially degrading, this role provides her too with a surrogate family; Antoine and Huguet accept each other as brothers (l. 1548ff.), the count of Cologne provides an army to help oust the traitors from Parise's lands (l. 1572), and Antoine plays a prominent role in the campaign, accusing Raimont of bigamy on his 'mother's' behalf (l. 2526). After Raimont, defeated, has apologized (ll. 2784–85), he asks the count of Cologne to let him have Parise back, and Antoine with her:

> Sire, je veil ma feme, se vous plait, ramener,
> et mon fil et lo voutre, s'il ne vos doit peser,

[23] See also Berkvam, pp. 13–14 on the potentially redemptive value of motherhood.

> car tant s'aiment andui ne püent desevrer.
> J'an donrai votre fil grant part de mon regné. (2810–13)

Through Parise, Antoine has likewise acquired two noble fathers from whom he can inherit. Parise, for her part, has two sons:

> Premiers baisa son fil qu'en ses flancs ot porté,
> et après baisa l'autre que ot nori söé. (2765–66)

These last words are echoed by Antoine when he agrees to go with them: 'Ma dame m'a nori doucement et söé' (l. 2817). The generous impulse to feed, which went so disastrously wrong at the start of the poem, has proved its worth.

The botanical images of *Doon de la Roche* relegate maternity to 'nature' as against the 'culture' of the father in conformity with Freudian thought, except that their valuation is reversed.[24] The symbolic processes required to construe paternity, which can be seen positively as evidence of cultural achievement, become negative when associated with the fabrications of traitors. In *Parise la Duchesse*, however, motherhood is also 'symbolic' since it is transferable. The text ends with two pseudo-families – Huguet and the Hungarian royal family, Parise and Antoine – each surpassing the biological family of Raimont, which has no real existence (Huguet having been born after Parise's banishment) until it can be formed on the model of the other two. Thus whereas we might think of the biological family as the 'original' and surrogate families as secondary, in *Parise* it is the other way round. Symbolic motherhood is put at the service of biological paternity. The pattern of the 'family romance' in the romance texts discussed by Maddox has undergone a radical reversal.

To conclude: the psychic fantasies identified by Freud as the 'family romance' undergo significantly different shifts and transformations in epic and romance. Whilst the masculine component in courtly texts may be somewhat overemphasized in Maddox's account, it remains that a conspicuously greater prominence is accorded to the mother in the *chansons de geste* considered here, than in the romance exemplars. The experiments with family structure which are played out in these epic poems permit each of the three positions of father, mother and son to form the focus of a narrative, and several such narratives may be run against each

[24] Fatherhood is often a source of *nature* in OF texts, insofar as the father imprints his nobility on the child, a pattern registered by texts as dissimilar as *Les Enfances Vivien* and *Guillaume d'Angleterre*. This confidence that one's son is unmistakably one's own is, indeed, the commonest contribution from the subject position of the father to the medieval 'family romance'; a fact which makes its absence from *Doon de la Roche* the more remarkable.

other within a single poem. The family, birthplace of violence and sexual tensions, imposes contradictions on all its members which they must do their best to negotiate. In the last resort the father's importance is always recognized, despite the frequently negative evaluation of the 'symbolic' world he represents. But whereas in the romance texts paternity has the air of a solution to the protagonist's search for an identity, in the *chansons de geste* it is rather a problem which no amount of conflict can permanently resolve. Moreover, motherhood can be promoted as itself a symbolic structure. Sadly, this does not lead to the representation of significant mother-daughter relationships.[25] Epic women, unlike Elspeth, seem not to feed, rear, and train other women. But we should not look to establish a matriarchy: only to keep questioning the pretensions to hegemony and self-sufficiency of the patriarchy.

[25] See also Berkvam, p. 101.

From Lyric to Play: Thematic Structure and Social Structure in *Le Jeu de Robin et Marion*

ROGER PENSOM

AS KEVIN BROWNLEE MOST RECENTLY reminds us, Adam's play is a sophisticated transposition of lyric forms and themes, its shape deriving from a conflation of the 'pastourelle' and the 'pastourelle-bergerie'.[1] An example of the 'pastourelle' will set out the raw materials from which Adam made his play: here is one by Jean de Braine from the first half of the thirteenth century:

Par dessoz l'ombre d'un bois
Trovai pastore a mon chois.
Contre iver ert bien garnie
La tosete o les crins blois.
Quant la vi senz compagnie,
Mon chemin lais, vers li vois.
Aé!

La tose n'ot compaignon
Fors son chien et son baston;
Por le froit en sa chapete
Se tapist lez un buisson;
En sa fleüte regrete
Garinet et Robeçon.

Quant la vi sotainement,
Vers li tor et si descent;
Si li dis: 'Pastore, amie,
De bon cuer a vos me rent:

1 See K. Brownlee, 'Transformations of the Couple: Genre and Language in the *Jeu de Robin et Marion*', *French Forum*, 14 (1989), 419–33 (p. 419).

Faisons de fueille cortine,
S'amerons mignotement.'

'Sire, traiez vos en la,
Car tel plait oï je ja.
Ne sui pas abandonée
A chascun qui dit: 'Vien ça.'
Ja por vo sele dorée
Garinez rien n'y perdra.'

– Pastorele, s'il t'est bel,
Dame seras d'un chastel.
Desfuble chape grisete,
S'afuble cest vair mantel;
Si sembleras la rosete
Qui n'espanit de novel.'

– Sire, ci a grant covent;
Mais mout est fole qui prent
D'ome estrange en tel maniere
Mantel vair ne garniment,
Se ne li fait sa proiere
Et ses bons ne li consent.'

– Pastorele, en moie foi,
Por ce que bele te voi,
Cointe dame, noble et fiere,
Se tu vueus, ferai de toi:
Laisse l'amor garçonniere,
Si te tien del tot a moi.'

– Sire, or pais, je vos en pri:
N'ai pas le cuer si failli;
Que j'aim mieuz povre desserte
Soz la fueille o mon ami
Que dame en chambre coverte,
Si n'ait on cure de mi.'[2]

The subject of 'pastoral', from the *Idylls* of Theocritus to the country stories of Chekhov, is the opposition of the urban and the rustic, with the implied superior 'naturalness' of the latter. Mazouer has written on the 'naïveté et naturel' in Adam's play, while Duvignaud and Brusegan have insisted on the conventional ideality of this example of the pastoral theme.[3] De Braine's text shows the tensions at work, the erotic/ludic

[2] From *Anthologie poétique française: Moyen Age 1*, ed. by A. Mary (Paris: Garnier, 1967), pp. 436–39.

[3] See C. Mazouer, 'Naïveté et naturel dans le *Jeu de Robin et Marion*', *Romania*, 73 (1972),

disposition of the narrator running into the cold weather of the shepherd's life. Although the shepherdess has the 'crins blois' of romance heroines, her cloak serves to protect her from the cold and she is crouching under a bush. The register alternation of 'crins blois' and 'se tapist lez un buisson' is continued in 'faisons de fueille cortine' where the 'natural' is expropriated by the cultural, recalling the 'sotz ram /dins cortina' pair of the troubadour lyric. The 'vair mantel' offered in exchange for the 'chape grisete' overlays the 'town/country' opposition with the opposition 'Desire/Need', the functional dress of the countrydweller opposed to the disseminating metaphor of warmth, fur and flowering roses. The shepherdess's refusal is a refusal to trade the wild for the cultural, the real for the metaphorical, thereby attaching a positive value to the first of each of these pairs of terms. The implication is that the rustic scheme of things is marked by a degree zero of the metaphorical. This is a world in which a sheep is a sheep and whose simple ideality depends on a theory of the linguistic sign which does not imply an alienation from the Real. The shepherdess has her dog, stick and cape and is not drawn into the pattern of fugitive meanings suggested by the knight's castle, gilded saddle and fur-lined cloak.

Adam's play begins with such a meeting between knight and shepherdess, but Marion's opening song problematizes her rustic status with mention of the 'souskanie', a high-waisted fashion garment that Robin has given her. Brusegan (p. 120) sees evidence of the 'bourgeois' in this evocation of country life, whereas Varty reminds us[4] that sung texts such as this one may have pre-existed the play and thus may have already been known to Adam's audience.[5] The possibility of a tension between sung and spoken may then be part of the text's strategy of generic transformation and this is a question to which we must later return. The ensuing conversation with the knight follows the pattern set in de Braine's 'pastourelle' in that the *malentendus* centre on the confrontation of the metaphorical and the 'real'. The knight's relationship with the natural is dominated by codes through which the 'natural' signifies the 'cultural'. The class of birds he is hunting – represented by his use of the

378–93; J. Duvignaud, *Les Ombres collectives: sociologie du théâtre* (Paris: PUF, 1973), p. 124; R. Brusegan, '*Le Jeu de Robin et Marion* et l'ambiguïté du symbolisme champêtre', in *The Theater in the Middle Ages*, ed. by H. Braet, J. Nowé and G. Tournoy (Leuven: Leuven University Press, 1985), pp. 119–29.

4 Adam de la Halle, *Le Jeu de Robin et Marion*, ed. by K. Varty (London: Harrap, 1959), p. 14.

5 See J. Dufournet, 'Complexité et ambiguïté du *Jeu de Robin et Marion*. L'ouverture de la pièce et le portrait des paysans', in *Études de philologie romane et d'histoire littéraire offertes à Jules Horrent*, ed. by J-M. d'Heur and N. Cherubini (Liège: [n. pub.], 1980), pp. 145–59.

word 'oisel' – is a class the lower orders are forbidden to hunt and eat. The same word denotes for Marion a class of birds that sing: 'Qui mout cantent joliement' (l. 30),[6] since it is inserted into a code which for political reasons does not cover the edible (Brusegan, p. 122). However playful Marion's language may appear, it is still true that the paronomasia centres on words which are highly charged through their membership of a code whose existence implies the cultural expropriation of the 'natural' and the subjugation of agrarian workers through their exclusion from the enjoyment of certain classes of the natural. Thus the wild duck – a 'natural' comestible which defines the aristocratic status of the person who eats it – is replaced in Marion's punning reply by a beast of burden (connoting the productive life of the *laboratores*), while the heron is replaced by the herring – a rare Lenten treat for these country vegetarians. The knight playfully admits that Marion has the better of him: 'Par foi! Or sui-jou esbaubis!' (l. 45), but the political implications of the text's codes could tell another story. Marion enquires about the hawk on the knight's arm:

> Quele beste est-che seur vo main?
> LI CHEVALIERS
> C'est uns faucons.
> MARIONS
> Mangüe-il pain?
> LI CHEVALIERS
> Non, mais bonne char. (48–50)

Back again to the socialised taxonomy of birds. The falcon – a metaphor of the chivalric aristocrat – is precisely not a vegetarian or breadeater. He is a carnivore and a raptor just like his master. Nature is mapped by the codes of aristocratic hunting – the war against animals, 'deduit de bois et de riviere' – each with its special apparatus of weapons and trained animals, dedicated to maintaining the flow of animal protein to the warrior's table and to differentiating his caste from that of the *laboratores*. The question of meat is, as we shall see, a central one in the world of the play.

Marion breaks off to speak of Robin and his bagpipe playing, thus assimilating him through music to the world of birds (some of whom are the knight's prey) and their natural music, but the knight is not interested and asks for her love. She tells him to back off and how she loves only Robin, who visits her daily bringing presents of cheese and bread:

6 All references are to *Le Jeu de Robin et Marion*, ed. by K. Varty.

Encore en ai-je en mon sain,
Et une grant pieche de pain (66–67)

The knight invites her to go off with him on his palfrey. Marion talks of Robin's work-horse, which is more docile, as she, Marion, follows the plough. Again the animal whose function is to furnish pleasure and confer prestige upon its rider is counterpointed by an animal dedicated to production. The animal-for-man symbolism of the knight's horse mediates the menace of the aristocrat, whose world is perceived as strange and threatening:

Aimi! sire, ostés vo cheval!
A poi que il ne m'a blechie. (73–74)

Soon the knight leaves her and Robin comes on stage. As in de Braine's 'pastourelle' the theme of 'cold' arises:

J'ai desvestu,
Pour che qu'i fait froit, men jupel,
S'ai pris me cote de burel.
Et si t'aport des pommes. Tien! (112–15)

As the *chevalier* was associated with meat, so Robin brings apples. Marion recounts to him the knight's attempted seduction and in her version the knight's glove becomes ' une moufle' – a hedging glove – and his hawk 'un escoufle' – a kite. This second misprision is significant in that the kite, while belonging to the family of raptors, is excluded from the emblematic élite to which the 'faucons' belongs, probably because of its liking for carrion and refuse. By citing it, Marion's language creates the possibility that those competent in the relevant code will perceive this as a judgement on the knight as well as on the naïveté of the speaker.

Once the excitement is over, the lovers settle down to a picnic. Since Robin has come empty-handed, Marion provides the food and, to the reader/spectator, much besides:

Ne t'en chaut, Robin; encore ai-je
Du froumage, chi, en mon sain,
Et une grant pieche de pain, (142–44)

This is the second time that Marion has mentioned where she keeps her cheese (see ll. 66–67). Dufournet (p. 152) analyses the structural function of such repetition, but it must also have an affective one.[7] Possibly

[7] See K. Varty, 'Le Mariage, la courtoisie, et l'ironie comique dans *Le Jeu de Robin et Marion*', *Marche Romane*, 30 (1980), 287–92 (p. 288).

on the first mention and certainly at the second (l. 143) Marion gestures towards her breast at the mention of the cheese, marking it metaphorically and metonymically with her body. She takes the cheese from her bosom and as they eat Robin exclaims: 'Diex! que chis froumages est cras!' (l. 146). After they have drunk some water from a jug, Robin falls into a gastric reverie:

> Diex! qui ore eüst du bacon
> Te taiien, bien venist à point! (150–51)

Again the text goes back to animal protein, so abundant in the world of the knight and so hard to come by in that of the peasant. Domesticated bacon is opposed to the game hunted by the knight. Marion is revealed as a kind of social policeman who suppresses illicit longing for meat:

> Robinet, nous n'en arons point,
> Car trop haut pent as quieverons.
> Faisons de che que nous avons . . . (152–54)

– a longing for the Other of carnivorous plenty. The bacon is doubly 'out of reach', inaccessible through its scarcity and its remoteness hanging from the rafters. At the end of the picnic, Marion puts away the bread and cheese:

> Dont metrai-je arrier
> Che pain, che froumage *en mon sain*
> Dusqu'à ja que nous arons fain?
> ROBINS
> Ains le met en te panetiere! (163–66)

Here the insistent identification of 'froumage' with 'sain' is interrupted by Robin's reminder that she is not using the basket that he had given her. This interjection may be more significant than it appears. Dufournet (p. 148) sees in it Robin reproving Marion's rustic manners. It should also be remembered that the social function of food-giving is often tied into power structures and the breaking of the metonymic-metaphoric relation between Marion and the food, which is implied by the move from *her* bosom to Robin's basket, may not be as trivial as it appears.

There follows a scene of songs and dances between the lovers during which we learn more of the symbolic and material organization of their lives. Women wear hats whereas men do not (l. 180, see also l. 500). Robin has the wrong kind of haircut to do what is probably an aristocratic dance (l. 206) and when it comes to leading the 'treske' the ground is too soft and his boots are leaking. Here we see recurring the thematic opposition 'ideality/reality' that we encountered in de Braine's 'pastourelle'. Here the alternation between play and reality is marked by the alternation sung/spoken which exploits the tension discussed earlier between the idealised Marion of her opening song and the rustic Marion of the first scene with the knight. The mud and the leaky boots are here the reality outside the song.

Robin leaves to find friends and relatives for a party, and Marion, left alone, is again visited by the knight. He is looking for his lost falcon. Marion urges him to leave but he persists:

> Certes, de l'oisel ne me caille
> S'une si bele amie avoie. (287–88)

The desired substitution of a metaphorical hunt for the real one casts the knight as the raptor and Marion as the quarry. She resists, asking to be left to look after her sheep. He is about to leave when he meets Robin, who is manhandling the knight's falcon. The knight, furious, punches him under the chin and cuffs him when he howls, manhandling Robin just as Robin has manhandled the falcon. Robin's relation with the aristocratic bird – perhaps he is holding it by the legs like a fowl – strips it of its metaphoric significance and it may be that the knight's anger shows that he feels that his aristocratic identity, partly invested in his metaphorical equivalence with the falcon, is under attack. This tightly managed visual-thematic patterning is completed by the knight-raptor carrying off the shepherdess-bird on his horse. The effect of this poetic strategy is again to segregate the lovers in the world of the 'natural' as natural quarries of the knight's violence and sexual appetite. When the knight has left with Marion, Robin relates the adventure to his friends as a hunt:

> Taisiés! Il nous couroit ja seure
> S'il en i avoit .iiii. chens! (347–48)

again with him and Marion as the quarry. The rustics take refuge behind a tree and hear the last conversation between Marion and the knight.

He woos her with presents of game, which she refuses:

> J'ai plus chier mon froumage cras [. . .]
> Que vostre oisel à tout les plumes. (369–71)

The knight impatiently leaves her with the words:

> Certes, voirement sui-je beste
> Quant à ceste beste m'areste. (378–79)

Dufournet remarks 'Il demeure que les paysans sont assimilés peu ou prou à des êtres qui échappent à l'humanité' (p. 157) and argues that the rural world of the play is a carnivalesque caricature of rustic fools. The picture which is emerging from this analysis is of a more complex reality. As Marion is a 'beste' for the knight, he is for her a predator and a carnivore. It is not the case that the play is laughing with the aristocracy at the peasants; we have a double perspective and when that of the knight is removed in the second part of the play, it invites our participation in the life of the rustics.

As Brownlee suggests 'in broad structural terms, the *Jeu* involves two equal halves in which the central female figure, Marion, interacts in sequence with two very different lover figures' (p. 421). The second half, whose subject matter derives from the 'pastourelle-bergerie', consists of a series of games which are constantly menaced by the disruptive influence of violence and the *bas corporel*. But I hope to show that Dufournet (p. 156) goes too far in seeing a stereotype of the *monde à l'envers* in this rustic society. The shepherds and shepherdesses collectively police behaviour to deal with these irruptions as they occur. The first violation of social protocol occurs when Robin kisses Marion after she has invited him to embrace her:

> MARIONS
> Vien donques cha, acole-moi.
> ROBINS
> Volentiers, suer, puis qu'il t'est bel.
> MARIONS
> Esgarde de cest sosterel
> Qui me baise devant le gent. (387–90)

Clearly the distinction between 'acoler' and 'baisier' is a critical one for Marion. Varty ('Mariage', p. 289) argues that the representation of sexual behaviour implied by the text is very explicit indeed and that kissing and genital sexual activity can both be signified by 'baisier'. Another possibility is raised in a recent discussion of the iconography of medieval kissing by Camille.[8] Although he does not discuss the distinction between embracing and kissing as such, his illustrations suggest a possible classification. 'Lecherous kisses' have both parties in profile, with mouths together (pp. 153–55), whereas nuptial or ceremonial kisses show one party in profile and the other three-quarter face (pp. 159–61). Given

8 See M. Camille, 'Gothic Signs and the Surplus: the Kiss on the Cathedral', in *Contexts: Style and Values in Medieval Art and Literature*, ed. by D. Poirion and N. Freeman Regalado (New Haven: Yale French Studies Special Issue, 1991), pp. 151–70.

that 'acoler' in its etymological sense involves only encirclement with the arms,

> Je vos an jur seint Pol
> Et les braz, don vos *acol*. (*Guillaume d'Angleterre*, l. 2660)
>
> Maint arbre . . .
> Que trois granz hommes *acollet*
> N'eüissent . . . (*Mesquief de Tournai*, ll. 181–83).

while 'baisier' involves oral contact with something else which may be another mouth:

> En la bouche la *baixai*
> Et sor l'herbe la getai.
> (*Altfranzösische Romanzen und Pastourellen*, II,11,50.)
>
> Lo vis et lo nes et la face
> Li a plus de mil foiz *baisié*.
> (*Folie Tristan de Berne*, ll. 553–54)[9]

the available spectrum of possibilities from the formal to the sexual would thus go:

1. Encirclement with arms without oral contact.
2. Encirclement with arms with oral contact.
3. Encirclement with arms with mutual oral contact.

Camille (p. 161) also mentions the power structures implied by the giving and taking of kisses. In his illustrations of men kissing women in the 'non-lecherous' mode, it is in both cases the woman's face which is averted to receive the kiss (this suggests the ethological parallel of throat-offering). When Marion says 'Acole-moi', she is probably expecting a hug (1 above or perhaps 2), which would express her submission to Robin's authority, but what she gets is probably 3 with its sexual connotations. This mild violation of social rules parallels the knight's earlier forcing of Marion and reminds us that sex and aggression are closely related whatever the social register.

The game that the shepherds play next is another test of self-control. The victim has to offer a present to the Saint – probably while all the others are making faces at him – without laughing. If he laughs, he's 'it'. Gautier is first and laughs. But he cheerfully owns up and takes Robin's place as Saint. Marion is next and does not laugh. Next comes Baudon who laughs and grumbles. Last comes Huart who gets quarrelsome when

[9] All examples are taken from Tobler-Lommatzsch.

he has to pay the forfeit. He is vigorously reprimanded by Gautier and knuckles under. It is clear that the thematic significance of the game in the play is to show that self-control is something women do better than men. This points to an interesting paradox in the play's picture of social structure: women are the focus of the erotic and hence the cause of social disruption, but it is also a woman who is foregrounded as the guardian of social order and exemplar of self-control (see Brownlee's description of Marion as an 'educator', p. 425). Huart's outburst leads to Marion's call for an end to the game: 'chis jeus est trop lais.' (l. 462) and Peronnele's rejoinder:

> Et sachiés que bien *apartient*
> Que fachons autres festeletes –
> Nous sommes chi .ii. baisseletes
> Et vous estes entre vous .iiii. (464–67)

expresses the idea of sexual difference as fundamental to social order, with the impersonal verb 'apartient' referring to an objectified standard of conduct which in this instance implies the avoidance of conflict. Gautier, who had represented the law in reproving Huart, now violates it by suggesting a farting contest. This time it is Robin who whips him in:

> Dehait ait par mi le musel
> A cui il plaist ne il est bel! (473–74)

'Musel' assimilates Gautier to the non-human animal and the text continues the idea of a social Law which exists collectively for the men in the play, but which is never integrally expressed through any one of them, each of the men being guilty of dereliction at some point in the play. This Law finds its constant expression only in the persons of the women. The counting game that follows shows the women sticking together:

> HUARS
> Conte apres, Marot, sans debatre.
> (The women must be gossiping)
> MARIONS
> Trop volentiers. Et .v.
> PERONNELE.
> Et .vi. (492–93)

As in l. 181, a woman gives her hat to a man, this time to crown the King. Now the game and Baudon's questions centre on sexual matters. Gautier's reply, which jokingly equates a dog with a man (Brusegan, p.

126), stresses the potentially non-human dimension of sexuality, just as the *bas corporel* theme of the proposed farting contest stresses the animality of the body. Robin and Marion are both outraged at a question about sexing newborn animals, but Robin has to pay a forfeit:

> LI ROIS
> Va, s'acole dont Marion
> Si douchement que il li plaise. (528–29)

But again Robin breaks the rules and kisses her, this time on the face:

> MARIONS
> Esgardés!
> Je cuit que mors m'a ou visage. (532–33)

This love-bite is followed by Robin's words:

> Je cuidai tenir .i. froumage
> Si te senti-je tenre et mole! (534–35)

The idea of love as eating is very near the surface of the text at this point and mobilises our awareness of the 'food/sex' theme from earlier in the play. Here the metaphoric/metonymic equivalence established earlier is 'cashed in' with Robin taking a bite out of her cheek. Marion's insistence on law and order here again paradoxically intersects with her identity as an erotic comestible. Woman is defined as the locus of temptation *and* prohibition. Robin's transgression involves the opposition 'acoler/baisier' in the sense discussed above rather than the opposition 'baisier/foutre' as proposed by Varty ('Mariage', p. 289). As we have already seen, it is the woman, whose erotic allure destabilises social equilibrium, whom the play presents as the policeman of social order. The equivalence 'sex = food', so prominent in the play's representation of woman as the *symbolic* provider, furthermore identifies male sexuality as oral/infantile, thus suggesting the man's subordinate and dependent status.

After all this talk about sex, it is no surprise that Baudon's question to Huart is about – food. Baudon asks him what he likes to eat best and he replies:

> Bon fons de porc, pesant et cras,
> Certes j'en mengai l'autre fois
> Tant que j'en euch le menison. (548, 550–51)

Here Huart's excesses with fat meat from the back end of a pig give him the runs. The theme of much-desired animal meat, which begins with the knight's offer of game to Marion, surfaces here in a daydream of oral plenitude. The idea of the *bas corporel* raised by Gautier's proposed farting match is here repeated and given thematic status by 'fons' and 'menison'. This rudeness is sharply juxtaposed with Perronele's account of her wholly proper meeting with her lover in the fields: 'Lès mes brebis, sans vilenie' (l. 564). Marion is close behind in confessing her love for Robin, who is more to her even than a ewe which has lambed. The picture of men here is one of beings who are both law-abiding and submissive.

Just then, Gautier raises the alarm; a wolf has carried off one of Marion's ewes! As Brownlee observes, 'We have what appears to be a replay, entirely in the 'shepherd register' of the *chevalier's* attempt to carry off Marion' (p. 427), and this reading is amply vindicated by striking parallels. But as is often the case in this text, less obvious but perhaps telling thematic traces cut across this stronger articulation. It may be significant for our understanding of this scene that the last occurrence of 'brebis' – five lines before – is one in which Robin is assimilated to a ewe in Marion's confession of love. Later Marion's words to Robin: 'Et comment tiens-tu chele beste?' (l. 591) echo the knight's words to him in reproof of his mishandling of the falcon:[10]

> Et comment a-il atiré
> Mon faucon? (328–29)

The text seems, through these structures of thematized repetition, to be simultaneously suggesting Robin's prowess *and* his subordinate status. By placing the key repetition of the knight's reproof to Robin in the mouth of Marion, the text once again identifies her as an authority-figure. Similarly, Robin's warning that the ewe might bite Marion (joke? Has anyone ever been bitten by a ewe?) recalls Marion's words of l. 533: 'Je cuit que mors m'a ou visage', again reinforcing the equivalence (Robin —> bite) = (ewe —> bite): Robin = ewe!

Baudon then suggests that Robin take hold of Marion, with his and Gautier's permission. Although this time Robin holds back from kissing her, Marion complains about being hugged too hard, while the three remaining men try to get off with Perronele. Gautier evokes his own prosperous peasant status but the bar to a union is the threat of violence between her brother and Gautier: 'S'en porroit tost venir bataille' (l. 637).

They all settle down for a picnic and Huart enquires of Perronele: 'Di-moi, c'as-tu chi en ches boches?' (l. 640). The structure of previous similar moments might lead a director to have Huart feel Perronele's

10 See Brownlee, p. 427, who notes but does not interpret this.

bosom at this point – a further intersection of 'food' and 'sex' (cf. l. 650). Other delights are proposed to Huart by Gautier: 'Et qui veut deus gambons salés?' (l. 648). Now this is a dramatic crux in that salted hams at a peasant picnic are, as our text has shown, a dietary *impossibilium*. When I have directed this playtext, discussion with actors has thrown up the solution of having Gautier turn his back on the audience and baring his buttocks as he delivers the line: 'Vés-les chi, tous pres'(l. 649). This reading is in keeping with the *bas corporel* theme that marks Gautier's dialogue throughout the play. If it is plausible, its interest is that it produces a further intersection of the themes of 'carnivore' and 'bas corporel', repeating the structure in ll. 548 ff., in which Huart details the consequences of a surfeit of fat pork. Marion's earlier refusal of the knight's game inaugurates a scheme in which the women are contentedly vegetarian while the men constantly long for animal protein. The other major characteristic which marks men off from women is the pre-occupation of the former with sex and bodily functions. The role of the women includes the responsibility for suppressing any mention of sex or the lower body. Moments like Gautier's joke about the salted hams are points at which the 'carnivore' and 'bas corporel' themes intersect and characterise male gender identity. In the context of this reading, the fact that Gautier's joke about the two salted hams is followed by Perronele's line: 'Et jou ai deus froumages fres' (l. 650) is significant. As male buttocks have stood in for hams, so thematically cheeses represent the female breasts. The opposition/parallel is heightened by the isotopic recurrence of 'deus' – two of each. The thematic oppositions here are multiple; male/female, scatological/erotic, carnivore/vegetarian, lower body/upper body, preserved/raw, opposing Gautier and Perronele as exemplars of the gender role opposition within the play. It may even be that the incident in which Marion claims to have been bitten by Robin fleetingly creates a paradigmatic grouping of predatory carnivores crossing the thresholds of caste and species, of which Robin, the other men, the knight and, later, the wolf are all members. The vegetarian shepherdesses are identified with the vegetarian sheep.

Now when Robin leaves Marion and the picnickers in l. 681, he has been singing about the pasty and roast fowl he will bring back to share with Marion. When he does return in l. 700, he certainly brings two musicians with him, but it is difficult to find in the text any evidence that he brings the promised food. He says:

> Marote, je sui venus. Tien.
> Or di; m'aimes-tu de bon cuer? (700–01)

This might imply that he hands her the promised food, but it is unlikely.

Such dainties would surely have provoked comment from the other male picnickers. It is a notable feature of the sung interludes between Robin and Marion, that they represent an idealised view of the lovers' life. At the outset, Marion sings of the gifts she has received from Robin, among which the 'souskanie' seems an unlikely present for a shepherd to give his mistress. So here, the fact that the edible dainties are promised in a song may indicate their virtuality. He arrives dancing to the music of the two musicians and his 'Tien' probably refers to them. He has brought music not animal protein, and the music ends a thematic sequence which began with the

> Cardonnereuls et pinçons
> Qui mout cantent joliement. (29–30)

and which continued with Robin's 'musete' (l. 56) and Huart's 'chievrete' (l. 517). Music, as we noted first in the flute of de Braine's shepherdess, evokes the ideality and the playfulness of country life but even music falls victim to corporality in Gautier's famous one line epic recital: ' "Audigier dist Raimberge, bouse vous di . . ." ' (l. 729). Here, the 'ideal' theme of music intersects with that of the 'bas corporel' which makes this moment in the text something more than Gautier being predictably obscene; the corporality of the body (*bouse/menaison*, *cul/gambons*, etc.) naturalises the bodiless ideality of music. This is not necessarily destructive. Just as in the epithalamion for Robert d'Estouteville in Villon's *Testament* where we are surprised by the 'agriculturalization' of courtly themes, the move in Adam's play is towards the deletion of 'oppositional' conceptions of the human real in favour of a conception in which the 'serious' is seen as interdependent with the 'comic', the 'immaterial' with the 'material', the sacred with the 'obscene'.[11] Although Gautier's art is decried, the play finishes in the harmony of the dance, led by Robin, encouraged by a decent hug from Marion.

The play as I have described it is less tidy than some critics might wish. Dufournet (p. 156) sees it as a satire on rustic life, in which the knight, the shepherdesses and Robin express the author's condemnation of its excesses; Brownlee (p. 431) sees it as a kind of 'school of love' in which Marion – a diegetic avatar of the authorial *je* – instructs Robin in the niceties of peasant courtliness, while Brusegan sees in it an escape into 'un espace utopique alimenté par des motifs folkloriques qui se prêtent au procès idéalisant du discours' (p. 129). All these readings identify literary

[11] See A. Gurevich, *Historical Anthropology of the Middle Ages*, ed. by J. Howlett (Cambridge: Polity Press, 1992), p. 162.

creation as a 'monological' process in which outcomes are recognisably re-expressible in terms which are ideologically familiar: the shepherds are rustic fools deserving of reproof, the 'pastoral' is a means of literary escape, the shepherds imitate their courtly betters under the author's tutelage. As I may have shown, another view is possible. The generic transformation from 'pastourelle' to play creates a representation which escapes the power to define of the original generic given. The idea of Desire as it arises in the lyric text in the knight's evocation of the world of the courtly, ramifies into and structures the rustic world as well, deleting its status as a transcendent domain where language and the Real coincide. The rustic world is defined by its own characteristic symbolic forms. The metaphorical process through which the hunt for meat becomes the hunt of love (game = Marion) in the encounter between the knight and Marion, creates in the 'bergerie' of the play an identity between a vegetarian comestible and the female love-object. The 'comestible' is defined *against* the flesh of animals which is the illicit object of male desire, progressively associated with the 'indecent' body, the *bas corporel*. Socialised male desire in this rustic society is oriented towards a vegetarian female love-object. Thus the themes of 'edible' and 'love-object' are redistributed in ways that give rise to outcomes that are unpredicted within the frames of historical or generic expectation. The complex thematic of our text resolves into a multifacetted model of a society's symbolic structure. As we have seen, the role of women as creators of social order in rustic society is tied in with their being abstainers from animal flesh and thus structurally disjoined from the aristocratic world. Males on the other hand are grouped together thematically in ways that transcend social class. The knight and the shepherds are one in their desire for animal flesh and for Marion, and their propensity for violence. The text also establishes equivalences between the human and the non-human worlds through the metaphoric series knight = Robin = wolf (carnivores), and shepherdesses = sheep (vegetarians). Its metaphoric strategy exposes unexpected relationships between the social orders of *bellatores* and *laboratores* and between those orders and that of the natural.

The aim of this argument has been to show that the complexity and richness of Adam's playtext lies in its power to represent the role of sexual difference in the ordering of social reality through the creation of new meaning from topical material existing in another genre. This is yet another dreary abstraction. It is from the historical and symbolic specificity of the text that the excitement comes. For example, though everyone eats, the structure of what is eaten will vary as a function of economic and symbolic determinants. In the world of our text, the structure of the 'edible' is determined economically by scarcity, and symbolically by caste-privilege and by the creation within the text of a food-code which expresses the ordering of power relations and gender in terms of what is eaten. The emotional investment that we have in orality is our point of contact with the 'edible' theme of the play, and its transformations will resonate with our own unconscious organisation of the relationship between eating and sexuality. What we recognise in the text is a possible transformation of our own picture of the role of sexual difference in social life realised in terms of a historical reality which is strange to us but to which we are affectively drawn, finding in it unexpected opportunities for self-discovery.

Tristan and his Doubles as Singers of *Lais*: Love and Music in the Prose *Roman de Tristan*

MAUREEN BOULTON

TRISTAN IS ONE OF VERY FEW romance heroes known as much for his musical talent as for his prowess: his skill on the harp was mentioned by Eilhart as a distinctive trait, and was woven into the texture of the story in the versions by Thomas d'Angleterre, Gottfried von Straßburg, and Marie de France. But it was only the anonymous author of the thirteenth-century prose romance who sought to portray his hero as a poet-lover by attributing songs to him and quoting them in the prose text. This talent is not confined to Tristan in the prose romance, however, for his friends and rivals also compose *lais* in episodes that serve to unify the romance and to comment on the protagonists' love affair.

If the *lais* inserted in the prose *Tristan* are a late innovation in the legend, they represent an early technical innovation in the genre. The literary device of inserting lyrics into works of narrative fiction was first popularized, if not actually invented, by Jean Renart in his *Roman de la Rose* (which we now call *Guillaume de Dole*), early in the thirteenth century.[1] Jean quoted, at least in part, *rondets de carole*, stanzas of *chansons* by *trouvères* and troubadours, *pastourelles*, and *chansons de toile*, and used these quotations not only to embellish the description of court life, but to replace interior monologues, and to influence the sequence of events. This device proved both popular and versatile, for it is to be found in at least seventy works composed in some dialect of French over the next two centuries, and served a growing variety of literary functions. In addition to the functions demonstrated by Jean Renart in his seminal

[1] The romance has been variously dated between 1200 and 1228, but there is agreement on placing it after *Galeran de Bretagne*, which contains a single *refrain*.

romance, later authors used lyrics as vehicles of communication both in dialogue and in correspondence, and, on occasion, to mark the formal division of a work.[2] The *Roman de Tristan* appeared early in the tradition of works containing inserted lyrics – only *Galeran de Bretagne*, *Guillaume de Dole*, the *Roman de la Violette*, and the *Lai d'Aristote* certainly predate it[3] – and its use of inserted lyrics is therefore of special interest in the history of the device as a whole, as well as in the context of studies concerned more particularly with the romance itself, in any of its surviving redactions.[4]

The prose *Tristan*, as preserved in the 'Vulgate' form, contains no fewer than twenty-one lyric insertions: fifteen *lais* and six *lettres en forme de lai*.[5] There is in addition one *lai* omitted from the more common version, but included in Paris, B.N. f. fr. 757.[6] The insertion of these lyric

2 For studies of the lyric insertion device, there are two unpublished dissertations, Anne Preston Ladd, 'Lyric Insertions in Thirteenth-Century French Narrative' (Yale University, 1977); and Helen Solterer, ' "Acorder li chans au dit": The Lyric Voice in French Medieval Narrative 1220–1320' (University of Toronto, 1986); and my *The Song in the Story: Lyric Insertions in Medieval French Narrative, 1200–1400* (Philadelphia: Univ. of Pennsylvania Press, 1993).

3 Eugène Vinaver, *Etudes sur le Tristan en prose. Les sources, les manuscrits, bibliographie critique* (Paris: Champion, 1925), p. 23, suggested 1225–30 as the original date of composition; Emmanuèle Baumgartner, *Le* Tristan *en prose: Essai d'interprétation d'un roman médiéval* (Geneva: Droz, 1975), pp. 62, 85–87, gave 1240 as the earliest possible date for the compilation of any of the extant versions. The first quarter of the text has been edited by Renée L. Curtis, *Le Roman de Tristan en prose*, 3 vols (Cambridge: Brewer, 1985). The edition is being continued under the direction of Philippe Ménard, who has chosen as his base a manuscript of the 'Vulgate' version: *Le Roman de Tristan en prose*, I, ed. by Philippe Ménard (Geneva: Droz, 1987); II, ed. by Marie-Luce Chênerie and Thierry Delcourt (1990); III, ed. by Gilles Roussineau (1991). Volumes IV, ed. by Jean-Claude Faucon (1991), V, ed. by Denis Lalande and Thierry Delcourt (1992), and VI, ed. by Emmanuèle Baumgartner and Michele Szkilnik (1993) were inaccessible to me until after this article was written; they contain no significant variants from the passages quoted from Paris, B.N. f. fr. 335–36, which I used for parts of the romance then unedited.

4 On the different versions, see E. Löseth, *Le Roman en prose de Tristan, le roman de Palamède et la compilation de Rusticien de Pise: Analyse critique d'après les mss de Paris* (Paris: Bouillon, 1890–91; repr. New York: Burt Franklin, 1970), pp. xii–xiii; Baumgartner, pp. 29–87; and Renée L. Curtis, 'Les Deux versions du *Tristan* en prose: examen de la théorie de Löseth', *Romania*, 84 (1963), 390–98.

5 Baumgartner, *Le* Tristan *en prose*, pp. 298–300, lists twenty-six lyric insertions, including six riddles, which I have not considered. Seventeen *lais* with notation in Vienna, N.B. ms. 2542 have been published by Tatiana Fotitch and Ruth Steiner, *Les Lais du roman de Tristan en prose* (Munich: Fink, 1974). See also Jean Maillard, *Evolution et esthétique du lai lyrique des origines à la fin du XIVe siècle* (Paris: Univ. de Paris, 1963); 'Le Lai lyrique et les légendes arthuriennes', *BBSIA*, 9 (1957), 124–27; and 'Lais avec notation dans le *Tristan en prose*', in *Mélanges [. . .] Rita Lejeune*, 2 vols (Gembloux: Duclot, 1969), II, 1347–64.

6 This is the episode of the Knight of the Red Shield (Löseth, § 453); it occurs after

compositions into the narrative does not begin until after Tristan's marriage to Iseut of the White Hands, that is, after most of the events of the traditional love affair have been recounted. Some of the characteristic features of this affair – the love potion, for example – are recalled in *lais* that are said to have been composed at the time of the events, but even these are performed (and quoted) much later in the romance, and no mention was made of them at the (supposed) moment of composition. In analysing this and other contrasts between the first two volumes of her edition and the third, Renée Curtis suggested that they reflect the change in authorship, and that the idea of inserting songs into the work is attributable to Hélie de Boron, the continuator of the romance begun by Luce del Gat.[7]

The use of lyric insertions in the prose *Tristan* involved a number of technical innovations. All four of the earlier works containing inserted lyrics are in octosyllabic verse, and their insertions consist, for the most part, of *refrains*, *rondeaux*, and partial quotations of courtly *chansons*. Since some of these citations are attested elsewhere – indeed Jean Renart actually named some of the *trouvères* in his romance – it has, at least until recently, been assumed that virtually all of the quotations in these works were borrowed from the lyric repertoire rather than composed by the authors of the narratives.[8] The *Tristan*, on the other hand, is a prose romance, and its insertions consist exclusively of complete songs which were probably composed for their narrative contexts.[9] If the contrast between prose and song was even greater than that between narrative and lyric verse, the songs occur in the contexts for which they were written, which eliminated the possibility of discrepancies between song and narrative. The *lais* in the prose *Tristan*, furthermore, are all presented as the compositions of the characters who sing them (or, in a few cases, entrust them to minstrels). In this they differ from the insertions in the earlier works, which were often consciously appropriated by the singers. The diversity of the singers to whom the *lais* are attributed is another striking feature of the device in this romance. In both *Guillaume de Dole*

insertion No. 23 in Baumgartner's list (p. 300). As Ménard has used this manuscript to supply *lacunae* in his base, I have felt obliged to consider it.

7 Curtis, III, pp. xxvi–xxviii; and 'Who Wrote the *Prose Tristan*? A New Look at an Old Problem', *Neophilologus*, 67 (1983), 35–41.

8 Songs unknown from other sources may, of course, have been composed directly for the narrative, but this is difficult to establish.

9 Jeanne Lods, 'Les Parties lyriques du *Tristan en prose*', *BBSIA*, 7 (1955), 73–78 (p. 78); Curtis, III, p. xxvii. Maillard (*Esthétique*, p. 85) suggested that the *lais* circulated independently of the romance, a view accepted by Pierre Bec, *La Lyrique française au moyen âge (XIIe–XIIIe siècles). Contribution à une typologie des genres poétiques médiévaux. Etudes et textes*, 2 vols (Paris: Picard, 1977–78), I, 208–09.

and the *Roman de la Violette*, although many characters sing briefly, there is a tendency to restrict songs of emotional expression to the hero.[10] In the prose *Tristan*, by contrast, the talent of composing songs seems widespread, and most *lais* are used for emotional expression.

Of the total number of twenty-two *lais*, fewer than half are composed and/or sung by the protagonists: Tristan sings four *lais*, sends two *lettres en forme de lai*, and listens to a performance of another of his *lais* by a female minstrel. Iseut composes only three *lais* in the romance: her *lai mortel* composed and sung before her attempted suicide, a sung rejection of Kahedin's suit, and a lyric letter to Tristan. She is the only female character to compose *lais;* female minstrels are common in the romance, but they are performers only. With the exception of Iseut's reply to Kahedin, and Tristan's letters to Arthur and Lancelot, these *lais* are all songs of amorous meditation.

The remaining twelve *lais* and verse letters are composed by a group of secondary and even minor characters: Mark, Dinadan, Arthur, Lancelot, Kahedin, Lamorat, Palamedes, Helys, the Knight of the Red Shield, and an anonymous visitor to Arthur's court. Mark's *lai* is a verse letter to Guinevere describing her relationship with Lancelot in insulting terms,[11] while Dinadan's song is pure invective directed at Mark in retaliation for his attack upon Guinevere.[12] The verse letters from Arthur and Lancelot form a group with Tristan's letters, and serve to demonstrate in lyric and epistolary form Tristan's acceptance in Arthurian circles. In contrast to the verse letters and Dinadan's invective, the remaining *lais* by secondary characters are all – like those of the protagonists – meditative love songs. The *lais* by Kahedin, Lamorat, Palamedes, Helys, and the two anonymous knights, are inspired by doomed love affairs. These unhappy lovers are echoes of the hero: some are rivals (Kahedin and Palamedes) in love with Iseut; another is in the same predicament (Lamorat), while yet another sings for love and dies a violent death (the anonymous knight).

Prior to the insertion of the first *lai*, the references to Tristan's musicianship in the prose *Tristan* are infrequent.[13] The lyrical expression of

[10] In *Guillaume de Dole*, Conrad sings a series of stanzas of the *grand chant courtois* that reflect his growing love, while the heroine sings only *chansons de toile* that do not express her sentiments. In the *Roman de la Violette*, however, both hero and heroine sing stanzas from the *grand chant courtois*, although the hero's songs are more numerous.

[11] The musical form of the *lai* is meant to suggest that this view of their affair is in public circulation, as Elspeth Kennedy observed, in the paper 'The Role of Lyrics in the Narrative Structure of the Prose *Tristan*', read at the conference 'Music and Narrative in Medieval Romance: The Poetics of Lyric Insertions', Chicago, Newberry Library, 4–5 October, 1991.

[12] See my *The Song in the Story*, chapter 3, p. 114.

[13] Only two occasions stand out: first, when suffering from the Morholt's poisoned wound,

love assumes its full importance in the romance only after the lovers' passion has been discovered and they are obliged to part. The periodic insertion of songs in the remainder of the romance evokes the love theme in a form that distinguishes it from the forest of chivalric adventures that might otherwise engulf it. Each *lai* recalls the others and commemorates the pair of lovers whose *lais mortels* introduce this lyricism into the romance.

It is in this light that I shall consider the songs of the hero and his fellow lovers – his doubles in the romance.[14] The multiplicity and sporadic appearance of singing voices – who, with the exception of Kahedin, perform only once – raise the question of their function in the romance. I shall argue that the *lais* performed by Kahedin, Lamorat, Helys, Palamedes, and the two unnamed knights resonate with and thus reinforce the love affair that is both the frame and the centre of the romance. For that reason their resemblance to Tristan's compositions, and the manner in which they comment on his love affair, will be of particular interest.

The first insertion in the romance, Tristan's *lai mortel*, sets a pattern for many of the later insertions.[15] When he discovers a kind letter from Iseut to Kahedin, who has fallen violently in love with the queen, Tristan explodes in a paroxysm of jealous despair, and flees to the forest. Virtually out of his mind with grief, he sheds his armour and meditates ceaselessly on his torment. After days of fasting, his concentration is interrupted by a female minstrel, who seeks to distract him from his thoughts and thus save his life. She does so by playing some of his own songs, accompanying herself on the harp. There follows a literary discussion of his compositions, and the girl extracts a promise from Tristan

Tristan takes with him his harp and other instruments out in the boat that carries him to Ireland (Curtis, I, §§ 308, 311). See Emmanuèle Baumgartner, *La Harpe et l'épée. Tradition et renouvellement dans le* Tristan *en prose*. (Paris: SEDES, 1990), pp. 108–10. Second, when Tristan finds that his marriage to Iseut of the White Hands has only intensified his longing for Iseut of Cornwall, he pours out his woe in song (Curtis, II, § 579).

[14] On doubles of the hero, see Elspeth Kennedy's discussion of the device in the *Prose Lancelot* in *Lancelot and the Grail: A Study of the Prose 'Lancelot'* (Oxford: Clarendon Press, 1986), pp. 218–35.

[15] This *lai* is discussed in more detail by Renée L. Curtis, 'Tristan Forsené: The Episode of the Hero's Madness in the *Prose Tristan*', in *The Changing Face of Arthurian Romance. Essays on Arthurian Prose Romances in Memory of Cedric E. Pickford*, ed. by Alison Adams, Armel Diverres, Karen Stern and Kenneth Varty, Arthurian Studies, 16 (Cambridge: Brewer, 1986), pp. 10–22; Baumgartner, *La Harpe et l'épée*, pp. 114–18; Kennedy, 'The Lyrics in the Narrative Structure'; and my *The Song in the Story*, chapter 2, pp. 47–50.

that he will sing in turn. When she returns the next day, Tristan is ready with his composition:

> . . . ele vient a monseignor Tristan, qui encores estoit devant la fontaine ensi com il soloit. [. . .] Et il prent maintenant la harpe et la comence a acorder si bien et si bel com il le savoit faire. Et quant il l'a tant bien acordee com il vit qu'il estoit besoig au chant qu'il voloit dire, il dist a la demoisele: 'Demoisele, oïstes vos onques parler dou Lai Mortal?' 'Sire, je non, fait ele; se m'eïst Diex, onques mes parler n'en oï.' 'Ce n'est mie merveille, ma demoisele, fait il, quant il ne fu onques chantez se de moi non. Je l'ai fait anuit tot novel de la moie dolor et de ma mort. Et por ce que je l'ai fait encontre mon definement, l'ai je apelé Lai Mortel; de la chose li trai le non.'
>
> (Curtis, III, § 870)

There are several elements in this passage that will recur in the discussion of other *lais*. The setting, with the hero in (relative) isolation in the forest, resting near a spring, is a feature of most of the insertions that interest us here, as is the insistence upon the immediate inspiration for the song, and the fact that it is a new composition. At the same time, other parts of this scene are distinctive, and serve to set Tristan off from all other singers. The most important of these is the mention of instrumental accompaniment for the song. While all of the other *lais* (as opposed to *lettres en vers*) are shown in the text as sung, only one other singer is portrayed playing an instrument. Also without parallel in the romance is the extreme nature of the sufferings described. No other hero suffers for such a long period of time, nor derives so little comfort from his song.

Kahedin, the brother of Tristan's wife, Iseut of the White Hands, is the only character besides the protagonists to sing more than once in the romance. He came to Cornwall with Tristan out of curiosity to see Iseut la blonde. At his first glimpse of her he fell hopelessly and violently in love with her, and declared himself in a letter. Iseut's attempt to treat Tristan's friend with kindness caused the episode of Tristan's madness just described, and the near death of both protagonists. It is only after Iseut's attempt at suicide that Kahedin composes his two *lais*. The pair are important because they link the opening *lais mortels* – that of Tristan and that of Iseut – with the following series of songs by supporting characters.

In his first *lai*, Kahedin repeats his declaration of love to Iseut, but since he uses it as a message, it is quoted at the moment of its performance rather than of its composition. As a result of its placement, it is the reception of the *lai* that is stressed. The circumstances could hardly be less favourable, for Iseut is singing when the minstrel arrives: '[elle]

harpoit adonc le lay qu'ele avoit fait pour l'amour de monseigneur Tristan, a celui point que elle se vouloit occire' (Ménard, I, § 153). This reference to Iseut's *lai mortel* recalls her despair for Tristan, and forms the context for Kahedin's song, which describes his own torment. Although he arranges for the song to be performed before the queen, he addresses himself only to Love, whom he asks to intercede with Iseut to prevent his death:

> Pour chou, Amours, ne soufrés riens
> Ma mort. Mais ma tres douce dame,
> Ki a mon esperit et m'ame,
> Proiiés que Kahedin ne laist
> Ensi morir se il li plaist. (Ménard, I, § 154, 20–24)

These references to dying are a commonplace of courtly poetry, and are meant to convince the recipient both of the dire consequences of her indifference, and of the singer's sincerity. In the case of Kahedin, however, his claims are validated by the narrative. When he receives Iseut's brusque reply 'Folie n'est pas vaselage' (§ 158), he composes one final song, and then dies for love.

In his despair, Kahedin – like Tristan before him in similar circumstances – withdraws to the forest and finds refuge near a spring. Where Tristan's isolation was interrupted by a minstrel who urged him to compose a *lai*, Kahedin has brought a minstrel with him to witness the song that he has already composed, and to carry it and the news of his death to Iseut. Both the setting and the symptoms of love-sick despair that are the context of Kahedin's *lai*, resemble those of Tristan's *lai mortel*. For three days Kahedin sits by the spring absorbed by his grief, and unable to eat or drink. On the fourth he breaks his silence: 'Hui en cest jour me verras tu morir sans doute, se tu ne pars de cest lieu. Je connois bien tout apertement que li cuers me faut: ma mors aproce durement. Veschi le brief que tu porteras a ma dame Yseut' (Ménard, I, § 162). Thereupon he unfolds the written text of the *lai* and performs it in order to teach the melody to the minstrel. The *lai* announces his death in the opening line 'En morant de si douche mort' (§ 163), stresses it in the repetition of the rhyme of the first stanza, and repeats it throughout the song (ll. 12, 16, 17, 23, 39, 46, 53, 90, 105, 117, 125). This death, because it is caused by love, is as sweet as it is painful: 'Douche mort, souef odourant' (l. 25), 'mortel confort' (l. 84). In addressing himself to Iseut, Kahedin nevertheless refrains from reproaching her: it is Love who bears the blame for his destruction: 'Hé! Amours vous m'avés trahi / Morteument m'avés envahi' (ll. 57–58). Singing the *lai* is Kahedin's final act of love: he folds the letter, gives it to the minstrel, and falls dead at once.

The 'douche mort' that runs through this *lai*, the result of a love both fated and doomed, is a clear anticipation of the lovers' end. That Kahedin loves Iseut only makes more obvious his status as a double for Tristan. The song itself, moreover, contains nothing that could not have been sung by Tristan in his own despair, and nothing that is not ultimately true of the lovers, whose happiness is never more than temporary. These *lais* by Kahedin are closely connected to the story of the protagonists: he is Tristan's brother-in-law, and he loves the same woman. The Kahedin-Iseut-Tristan triangle replicates the initial one. The death of this unhappy lover, so closely associated with the hero, anticipates the death of Tristan and Iseut at the end of the romance. Kahedin's doomed passion broadens the treatment of the love theme, and prepares for other doublings of the hero by Lamorat and Palamedes. The episodes in which these characters and others sing *lais* allow the author of the romance to elaborate the love theme and, as we shall see, to comment indirectly on the central story.

The *lai* of Lamorat is the sixth to be included, and the first purely meditative lyric in the romance. Lamorat's song is disinterested in the sense that he does not intend it to win his lady's favour. In this respect it differs from Kahedin's first *lai*, and anticipates two *lais* of Tristan performed and apparently composed quite late in the romance.[16] Lamorat de Galles is a notable knight of the Round Table, the son of King Pellinor of Listenois, and a brother of Perceval. His *amie*, and the inspiration of his song, is the Lady of Orcanie, a widow who is the half-sister of Arthur and the mother of several sons, including Gawain and Gaheriet. This passion is disapproved of by her sons in the romance: Gaheriet will finally kill his mother when he finds her in bed with Lamorat. Lamorat will eventually avenge her, only to be killed in his turn by Gawain.

As evening falls, Lamorat arrives alone at a spring at the edge of the forest; thinking himself unobserved, he relaxes his reserve and allows himself to reflect on his love. What he does not know is that King Mark, pursuing Tristan with murderous intent, has arrived before him and is hidden in the brush. The unsuspecting Lamorat falls into a state of sorrowful meditation punctuated only with sighs. At last he reproaches Love: 'Amours, fait il, en grant paine me faictes tous mes fais user; vous me faictes a douleur vivre. Ma vie si est tout adés grevee de plours et de larmes; se je ay bien ou joie de vous, je l'achate si chierement comme vous meismes le savés' (B.N., f. fr. 335, f. 367r). This brief speech announces the *lai*:

[16] Fotitch and Steiner, Nos. 13 and 17, the former sung by Tristan while engaged in the Grail quest, the latter during an interlude just prior to his final reunion with Iseut.

Sans cuer sui et sans cuer remain,
Je n'ai membre ne pié ne main,
Sans amour en amour me main,
Tel que mort et vif me demain.[17] (Ménard, IV, § 13, 1–4)

The themes of deprivation and constancy introduced in the opening stanza – characteristic of the courtly *chanson* – are developed in the succeeding stanzas, which explore the paradoxes associated with love. Other typical themes woven into the song are those of dying of love ('morant d'amours', II), love's wound, (here a 'double plaie', VI), the pleas for mercy, and his not daring to approach his lady. Lamorat complains of the fickleness of Love (IV), who promises great boons, but inflicts undeserved pain on his creatures. The lover's sense of betrayal by Love is explored in the metaphor of the tender plant:

Amours, ja sui je vostre plante,
Vostre force en grant prise me plante;
Voiiés, ki sa plante desplante
Soi meïsmes ocist et sousplante.
Se je, ki par vous sui plantés,
Em pris en honour, em bontés,
Sui aprés par vous desplantés,
Vostre pris en iert sousplantés. (41–48)

The *annominatio* of the metaphor at the rhyme emphasizes it, but the fact that the syllable occurs so often in words of negative meaning drives home the idea of the fragility of the plant, in danger of uprooting and destruction.

The themes of the courtly lyric are rendered effectively in Lamorat's *lai*, but are not individualized in any way. Lamorat does not name himself or his lady, nor does he describe her beauty or recall any past moments in their love affair. This anonymity is in marked contrast to the *lais* sung by Tristan and Iseut, who both identify themselves and evoke the principal turning points in their legendary affair. The reason for the lack of specific personal reference in Lamorat's song becomes clear when we examine its final stanza and the narrative setting of the song.

In the penultimate stanza, Lamorat states that he does not dare to send his *lai* to his *dame*. Although this appears to be a commonplace expression of the lover's timidity before his lady, Lamorat is more probably

[17] Except where noted, the remaining quotations from the *lais* refer to the Ménard edition. References in Roman numerals identify the stanzas.

afraid of compromising the Queen of Orcanie, who is under close surveillance by Gaheriet. In his closing lines, Lamorat makes what seems a surprising decision:

> Au boin Tristan, au preu, au sage,
> Qui passe tout l'umain lingnage
> De bonté et de vasselage,
> Le manderai par mon message. (69–72)

Tristan's professional interest in *lais* will be discussed later in the context of the *lai* of Palamedes, and this is certainly one explanation for Lamorat's decision. The passage following Lamorat's *lai*, however, supplies another, more significant motive for his action. The narrative following the insertion reveals all the specific references that were missing from the *lai*. Lamorat identifies his beloved and the obstacles to their love – chiefly the hostility of Gaheriet and his brothers, who feel themselves dishonoured by their mother's passion. He goes on to compare himself to Tristan:

> . . . Cil [Gaheriet] me fait autretel bonté conme ne fait le roy March a monseigneur Tristan, car tout autressi conme le roy March eslonge monseigneur Tristan de ses amours tout autressy fait moy Gaheriet le bon chevalier. Cil m'eslongne de toute joie et de toute bonne aventure; cil m'occit bien sans coup de glaive et d'espee. (f. 367v)

Lamorat's passion, like Tristan's, is requited, but thwarted by social opposition. While he may suffer from love, and reproach Amours for his cruelty, he need make no complaint to his lady. If his *lai* lacks specific references to his own affair, it contains nothing inappropriate to the master musician to whom he sends it. Lamorat, who observes the similarities between his position and Tristan's, becomes here a double of the hero. The story of Lamorat and the Lady of Orcanie, with its parallels to the central story of Tristan and Iseut, constitutes a commentary on that story. In both cases the lovers are doomed, but the suffering caused by separation is such as to make their lives a living death. In his apparent solitude by the fountain, Lamorat sings as Tristan's deputy as well as for himself.

Lamorat's *lai*, along with its gloss, brings together two narrative strands of the romance, for Lamorat's audience is Mark, the enemy of Tristan's love. Mark overhears a knight for whom he feels no anger, and feels the cut of his complaints about Gaheriet: 'Quant le roy March entent cest plait il n'est mie bien asseur. Or vouldroit il voulentiers estre en autre lieu' (f. 368r). Because of his reluctance to reveal himself, Mark is obliged to confront severe criticism of his conduct. Lamorat reminds both audiences – King Mark as well as the reading and listening public – of the passion that is at the root of all the action. And the king is obliged against his will to confront a sympathetic image of the man he is determined to murder.

If the *lai* of Lamorat grows out of a narrative line that parallels the story of Tristan and Iseut, the *lai* of Palamedes resembles Kahedin's first *lai*, for it is inspired by Iseut herself. The Saracen knight Palamedes is perhaps Tristan's closest friend, but he is also his most dangerous rival for the love of the queen. Where Palamedes falls deeply and sincerely in love with Iseut, Tristan's love is portrayed initially as shallow, and inspired by envy of the other's passion: 'Ensi entra en orguel et en bobant Tristanz por les amors ma dame Yselt' (Curtis, I, § 329). Once Tristan and Iseut drink the potion, their passion, of course, is all-consuming, and Palamedes is necessarily excluded. Much later in the romance, after Tristan has been accepted into the Arthurian company and is obliged to leave Iseut, the Saracen re-emerges. His literary role is to act as a foil to Tristan – in effect as a point of comparison for the audience.

In the section leading up to Palamedes' *lai*, the comparison between him and Tristan is intensified by the similarity of their adventures. Both have participated in the tournament of Louvezerp (where Palamedes was discouraged by the brilliance of Tristan's success), and both have been imprisoned by enemies and liberated by Arthurian knights. When Palamedes has been freed by Lancelot, Tristan brings both knights to the Joyeuse Garde, where he has taken refuge with Iseut after escaping one of Mark's traps.

Tortured by his hopeless love for Iseut, Palamedes soon withdraws in solitude to a clearing by a spring, and seeks consolation in song: 'Puis dist chanssonnetes et lais et tout est de madame Yseut. Or chante bas, or chante hault, tout ainssi conme le chant le fait monter et tant chante celui jour en tel maniere que moult s'en vait reconfortant et moult a son cuer enjoie' (B.N., f. fr. 336, f. 88v). He continues to sing, and the text repeatedly stresses that he thinks himself alone, although Tristan has heard his voice and approached to listen. At this point, the text says that Palamedes stops singing and begins a *lai*: 'Quant Palamedes out finé son chant, il se taist un poy; lors reconmence un lay que il avoit fait celle sepmaine meismes tout nouvel' (f. 89r). The opening stanzas sing of the 'dous penser' that absorbs him night and day. Palamedes describes forcefully how love holds him in bondage, but he can only express the possibility of succour in the subjunctive: 'Or m'en doinst Diex eür et joie' (Ménard, VI, § 24, 16). He is the servant of love, a theme stressed by the rhymes of stanza VIII:

Amours, car je vous ain et serf
De cuer plus que nul autre serf,
Ne onques jour ne vous messerf,
Donnés moi plus que ne deserf. (29–32)

For most of the piece, Palamedes speaks to Amour; only in stanza XIII does he change this address to 'dame', named in the next stanza as 'douce Yseut'.

The reference of this *lai* to the central love affair is unmistakable: not only is the song inspired by and addressed to Yseut, but it is overheard by Tristan. Despite the obvious differences in their circumstances, much of Palamedes' song could have been sung by Tristan himself. Palamedes appears here, not as a deputy for the hero like Lamorat, but like Kahedin, as an interloper between the lovers, the usurper of a song more suitable to Tristan himself. This is certainly Tristan's interpretation of the song, and when he recognizes Iseut as its inspiration, he is moved to a jealous rage. Despite his anger, however, Tristan appreciates the quality of a composition unknown to him, and waits quietly until it has ended. The narrative text alludes to Tristan's professional interest as a collector of *lais*: 'l'en ne faisoit nul chant ou royaume de Logres que l'en ne lui aportast; puis que il vint premierement a la Joieuse Garde, chascun chevalier qui trovoit lay ou chant ou rotrouenge l'envoioit a Tristan qui trop merveilleusement s'i delictoit.' (f. 89r). This observation has the effect of insisting upon Tristan's role as connoisseur and collector of *lais*. Others may raise their voices in song, but he is the ultimate authority and arbiter of quality.

During the feast that marks the beginning of the Grail quest, an unnamed knight enters Arthur's court with a verse letter ('brief en forme de lai') for the king. The tenor of this *lai* is to announce the turning of Fortune's wheel and the end of the glory of the Arthurian court. Immediately thereafter, he begins to play, and announces his own *lai*: 'Or escoutés un mien lay que je ay fait nouvellement. J'ay fait mon chant de ma mort si ay fait aussi conme le cine que encontre sa mort va chantant, aussi chante je encontre la moie' (B.N., f. fr. 336, f. 98v). It is in fact his 'swan song' – a *lai mortel* – that he sings, although this title is not used. The generalization of the opening line 'Riens n'est qui ne viengne a sa fin' (Ménard, VI, § 99) is quickly personalized as his own death for love:

Ichi chant, si dirai mon chant;
A estouvoir encore chant,
Car pour s'amour vieng or morant.
Amours, Amours, en mortel voie
M'avés mis . . . (10–14)

The meditation on ending and death in the first half of the song leads to a description of his sufferings for love in the remainder. The final stanza reasserts the immanence of his death ('Amours de chi vois a ma mort' VIII), which occurs in a most dramatic and public fashion. As the *lai* ends, a heavily armed knight stalks in and challenges the singer, who kills himself rather than grant this honour to his enemy.

This shocking event is not explained by the narrative, nor are we given any details about the love affair that inspired the song. In contrast to Kahedin's last *lai*, this song addresses only Love, never the lady. Where Kahedin taught his *lai* to a minstrel who would perform it for Iseut even as its composer expired, this nameless knight seeks no audience beyond the Arthurian court. Where Kahedin died of despair, this singer commits suicide to avoid dishonour. This desperate action recalls Tristan's attempt at suicide after his *lai mortel*, while the challenge of the enemy knight adds the dimension of external violence inherent in Tristan's love story. The musical skill of this knight, who accompanies his song on the harp, stresses the resemblance to Tristan. This is the only occasion where a *lai* by a secondary character is described as having instrumental accompaniment. This musical skill, otherwise reserved for the hero and his beloved, distinguishes this knight, who lacks any distinctive persona of his own, as a stand-in for Tristan himself.

The *lai*, with its sense of impending doom, continues on the personal level the theme of the letter delivered to Arthur. The two lyric pieces form a pair, the first of general, the second of private resonance, but both announce the end of honour and happiness. The lack of individualizing detail or narrative explanation increases the suggestive power of the songs. Just as the letter prophecies the general disaster that will in fact result from the Grail quest, so the second song anticipates the death that will be the result of Tristan's love for Iseut.

At the end of the first year of the quest that follows immediately upon these events, Tristan approaches a spring where he sees a knight turn away two others on the grounds that they do not love, and are therefore unworthy. This knight soon proves to be Helys des Sassogne, the son of the invader of Cornwall killed much earlier by Tristan, whom he is pursuing in search of vengeance. Alone again, Helys falls into a reflective state and then sings a *lai*. The similarities between this scene and the setting of Palamedes' *lai* are evident, and are made stronger still in the narrative passage following the insertion. It is here that we discover that the lady for whom Helys feels such overpowering love is Iseut herself.

The subject of Helys' *lai* is the transforming power of love. The singer describes himself as 'Dolans, chaitif, de povre afaire' (Ménard, VI, § 136).

His lady, the source of goodness and honour, is responsible for all he has accomplished:

> Puis que vous vous entremeïstes
> De moi, a hounour me meïstes,
> De vergoigne ou ja me veïstes
> Au siege de pris m'asseïstes. (21–24)[18]

The author of the romance comments on the quality of the performance: 'Et sachiez de voir que le chevalier chantoit trop bien d'une fort voix bien acordant et le dit des vers que il chantoit estoit aucques bien dictes et aucques bien plaisant de grant maniere,' (B.N., f. fr. 336, f. 114v). Tristan's reaction to the song he overhears confirms this estimate of its merit: 'Quant il a tous les vers finés en chantant si doulcement et si acordablement que Tristan qui l'escoute trop volentiers et trop prise son chant dit a soy meismes que trop merveilleusement a bien dict et chanté' (f. 115r). Although there is no reference to Tristan's collection of *lais* here, we nonetheless see his professional interest and discriminating judgement. Unfortunately, Helys has overestimated the extent of his transformation by love. When he and Tristan reveal their identities in conversation, they discover their grievances, and quickly resort to combat. Eventually Helys is defeated and obliged to renounce his love for Iseut. This incident is clearly a variant of the episode of Palamedes' *lai*. Once again the singer is inspired by Iseut, and has a long-standing rivalry with Tristan; as before, the *lai* provides a moment of lyric reflection in the midst of chivalric adventures, and is itself the provocation of another combat. Helys, however, is not in Palamedes' class, either as a knight or a lover. As that of a new-comer on the scene, his challenge to the hero is quickly dispatched.

The last of this group of *lais*, the 'Lai of the knight with the Red Shield', is yet another variant on the *lai* of reflection.[19] Tristan once again overhears the song of a knight resting by a spring. On this occasion, however, the insertion is set into a description of the hero's pensive state:

> Monsire Tristan chevauchoit pensis moult du[r]ement com cil qi la dame ne pooit oblier [. . .]. Jamés n'avra joie ne bien dusques a tant q'il soit venuz la. La ou il chevauchoient si pensis com je vous cont

[18] Fotitch and Steiner, No. 12, stanza VI, interpret this line: 'Au siege de pris me meïstes'.

[19] This incident, absent from the Ménard edition, occurs in abbreviated form without the insertion in Ms. B.N., f. fr. 336. Löseth in his index, p. 501, under Brunor (3) le noir, suggests that the singer of this *lai* is in fact Brunor.

> tot le grant chemin de la forest qi estoit si belle et si delitable com dit vous ai, il escoute et oït sor senestre une voiz et c'estoit la voiz d'un chevalier. Monsire Tristan areste maintenant q'il entent la voiz et ot que c'estoit un hom qi trop bien chante et trop cointement.
> (Paris, B.N., f. fr. 757, f. 209v)

There is a pause in the singing, and the knight laments in prose:

> Ha! las, [. . .] Je ne la vi onques por mon bien, mes por ma mort, viznément et non por ma vie bien le sai. E[n] sa beauté qi est plus clere qe n'est la biauté dou souleil me mirai come non sachent et de cel mireor m'ocis . . . (f. 210v)

The singer addresses himself to a series of different parties – those who do not love, lovers, Love, and finally his lady. He begins by distancing himself from those who are not in love:

> Vos qui n'amez traiez vous sus
> De moi, por Dieu alez en sus [. . .]
> Pres de moi onc ne vous meez:
> Mors sui, si chanter me veez. (f. 210v)

His song, as he explains to his fellow sufferers, springs from his knowledge of love, which is 'de cest monde enluminement'. The second half of the *lai* addresses his lady, who has rewarded his loyalty with nothing but cruelty, but who is nevertheless the source of his valour:

> Ma dame se j'ai puissance,
> En vous en ai pris vaillance.
> Por ce amerai sanz nussance
> Tant come en vie avrai usance. (f. 210v)

The singer's complaints about his lady's firm resistance distinguish him markedly from Tristan, but much of his song – the sense of isolation from non-lovers, the suffering, and also the great joy of love – could well have been sung by the eavesdropper. As with several of the *lais*, this insertion is performed by a minor character, but is associated with Tristan who shares the singer's mood of pensive reflection. This singer – whose identity and particular circumstances are not explained by the narrative text – acts as Tristan's deputy, composing and performing a song that expresses the substance of the hero's meditation as well as of his own.

The *lais* sung by the secondary characters in the *Roman de Tristan* all show marked similarities to those composed by the hero. All are said to have been composed 'nouvellement', and are presented as the spontaneous lyric expression of intense emotion. Like those of the protagonists, these songs, too, are sung in the text, and sung well. Indeed, the text places great emphasis upon the quality of the singing, usually through the judgement of Tristan – who is portrayed as a connoisseur and collector – and his evaluation is often reinforced by the description of the performance. There is however, no mention of instrumental accompaniment for most of these *lais*. With the exception of the nameless knight at the Grail feast, only Tristan and Iseut use the harp to accompany their songs.

In their function these *lais* also bear a strong resemblance to those of Tristan and Iseut. Most are songs of reflection, like Tristan's 'Lonc temps', while Kahedin's last *lai* and the song of the anonymous knight are *lais mortels* in the most literal sense, for both singers die upon finishing their songs. By their deaths, they not only authenticate their own sincerity, but anticipate the violent fate of the protagonists, who will be killed by Mark as Tristan plays his harp for Iseut. In addition, all of these insertions, whatever their function in the narrative, are at least partially modelled on Tristan's first *lai*, particularly in the description of the setting and the catalogue of symptoms of amorous meditation. The setting for most of the *lais* is a clearing in the forest with a spring, a natural place of repose for a knight errant, but also a narrative equivalent of the 'nature introduction' of so many courtly lyrics. The description of the *locus amoenus* provides a transition from the furious action of chivalric combat to the emotional expression of the lyrics. Prose soliloquies addressed to Love are additional transitional devices that facilitate the shift into and out of the lyric mode. Such passages, as we have seen with the 'Lai of Lamorat', also supply the specific narrative references lacking in the songs themselves.

Also worthy of notice are the circumstances of performance of the *lais*. The anonymous knight at the Grail feast chooses a public occasion for his performance, and for his death. His choice is quite exceptional in the romance, and emphasizes the prophetic quality of both his songs and his fate. All the other singers we have discussed – and in most cases the protagonists themselves – choose to sing in solitude. Like Tristan in his despair, Kahedin, Lamorat, Palamedes, and the Knight of the Red Shield, all seek the isolation of the forest, and the lovely setting of a woodland spring, for private song. Yet none of these performances is in fact private. In every instance the song is heard by an eavesdropper. This consistency in the narrative presentation of the *lais* implies an acknowledgment of the public nature of song. The *lais* are composed not only to be sung, but also to be heard. The inspiration of the songs may be intensely personal and necessarily secret, but the songs themselves have a public dimension.

If they are not intended for a particular audience, as are Kahedin's *lais*, they seem to become public property, even against the intention of the singer. Lamorat, in sending his *lai* to Tristan, acknowledges more directly the loss of privacy inherent in song.

Considered as a group, then, the *lais* in the prose *Tristan* reveal a double nature. If they grow out of the most specific narrative situations, they cannot be confined to that narrative moment. As texts, they exist on another level, and it is not unfair to interpret them in terms of their audience. Lamorat's *lai*, for example, is inspired by his love for the Lady of Orcanie. The fact that Mark is the unintended audience of his song invests it with a meaning for the absent hero. Lamorat, indeed, makes the reference explicit by comparing himself to Tristan, and by sending the *lai* to him. Just as Tristan's first *lai* establishes a pattern for the performance of the later love songs, these references to the hero, both implicit and explicit, establish precedents for interpreting them. In the case of the knight who kills himself at the Grail feast, the only reference to Tristan is implicit – his performance on the harp. This appropriation of a talent otherwise reserved to the protagonists implies that the song created from his own misery also expresses theirs.

The series of *lais* that punctuate the long chivalric elaboration of the legendary love story thus balance the recital of the traditional elements of that story in the first section of the romance. After Tristan leaves Cornwall and pursues his career in other kingdoms, the love affair is commemorated by this series of *lais* composed and sung by various singers, but all referring at least indirectly to Tristan's love. In this way, the singers of *lais* serve as doublings of the hero, and the songs themselves contribute to the thematic unity of a complex work.

Transformations of a Theme: Marriage and Sanctity in the Old French St Alexis Poems

JANICE M. PINDER

THE MAIN THEME of the legend of St Alexis is renunciation, for he gives up wealth, position, family, marriage and even personal identity. However, at the heart of this story lies the special problem posed by marriage for those intent on attaining Christian perfection: the conflict between total devotion to God on the one hand, and the sexual temptations and social obligations inherent in marriage on the other. This is particularly true of the legend as it was elaborated in the Latin West. Already in eleventh-century France Alexis seems to have become a symbol of resistance not only to the attractions of the world in general, but to marriage in particular.[1] Yet, as J. Leclercq has demonstrated, the view of marriage as an obstacle to salvation had never been the sole strand of Church thinking on the subject, even though it was often the dominant one.[2] It was precisely during this period, when the story of Alexis was being

1 In the *Vita* of St Simon of Crépy (d.1082), after telling how Simon admonished his young bride to remain chaste and obtained her consent to a separation, the author exclaims: 'Cui melius similem quam sancto Alexio dixerim?' *Acta Sanctorum*, September, VIII, pp. 745–46, quoted in Baudouin de Gaiffier, ' "Intactam sponsam relinquens": à propos de la *Vie de Saint Alexis*', *Analecta Bollandiana*, 65 (1947), 157–95 (p. 178). The importance of the marriage as an element of the story is reflected by the illuminations in the MSS of the French texts. See Alison Goddard Elliott, *The Vie de Saint Alexis in the Twelfth and Thirteenth Centuries: An Edition and Commentary* (Chapel Hill: University of North Carolina Press, 1983), p. 38, n. 67.

2 The positive strand in Church thinking on marriage, which came to fruition in the twelfth century, is set out by Jean Leclercq in *Monks on Marriage: A Twelfth-Century View* (New York: Seabury Press, 1981), published in French as *Le Mariage vu par les moines au xiie siècle* (Paris: Editions du Cerf, 1983). My references are to the French edition.

retold in the vernacular languages of Europe, that the more tolerant view of marriage was coming to the fore. Although celibacy remained an ideal, it was no longer seen as the appropriate state for all. The radical condemnation of marriage by the heretical movements of the eleventh century had led the Church to sanction and even prescribe it for the laity. Although still an occasion of sin, this sin could be cancelled out if the Church's restrictions on conjugal practice were observed. This qualified approval prepared the way for a view of marriage as a state with its own moral obligations which, if these were fulfilled, could help layfolk not only to avoid sin but to win salvation, a development which culminated in its acceptance as a sacrament.[3]

The vernacular hagiographers who took up the story of Alexis were thus faced with a problem: they had to interpret for a lay audience a legend whose values were rooted in the past, and which sat uneasily with the new marital order the Church was trying to promote. There has been much discussion among modern scholars of the apparent contradiction between the narrative framework, which was designed to express ideals of celibate asceticism, and other Christian ideals such as charity and the duty of husbands to their wives, especially in regard to Alexis's treatment of his bride and his parents.[4] Defenders of the saint's behaviour have pointed rightly to the need to distinguish between holding up a model for direct imitation, and the more general hagiographic function of inspiring the faithful to lead lives of greater holiness.[5] This discussion, however, has been centered on the earliest Old French version of the legend (eleventh century, see below, note 6), and I believe that if we look at the way the story is retold in the later poems, it becomes apparent that reconciling these two sets of Christian ideals was also a concern during

3 This shift is described by G. Le Bras, 'Le Mariage dans la théologie et le droit de l'Église du xie au xiie siècle', *Cahiers de Civilisation Médiévale*, 11 (1968), 191–202, and G. Duby, *Le Chevalier, la femme et le prêtre* (Paris: Hachette, 1981), pp. 56–197.

4 The truly Christian nature of Alexis' asceticism is questioned by Emile Winkler, 'Von der Kunst des Alexiusdichters', *Zeitschrift für romanische Philologie*, 47 (1927), 588–97, Melitta Hürsch, 'Alexiuslied und christliche Askese', *Zeitschrift für französische Sprache und Literatur*, 58 (1934), 414–18, Gerhard Eis, 'Alexiuslied und christliche Askese', *Zeitschrift für französische Sprache und Literatur*, 59 (1935), 232–36, and E. R. Curtius, 'Zur Interpretation des Alexiusliedes', *Zeitschrift für romanische Philologie*, 56 (1936), 113–37. Alexis's conduct is defended by Elise Richter, 'Alexius 95e "Pur felunie nient ne pur lastet" ', *Zeitschrift für französische Sprache und Literatur*, 56 (1932), 65–67, and Leo Spitzer, 'Die Erhellung des "Polyeucte" durch das Alexiuslied', *Archivum Romanicum*, 16 (1932), 480–81. The controversy is summarized in de Gaiffier, pp. 157–61.

5 Matthias Waltz, *Rolandslied, Wilhelmslied, Alexiuslied: Zur Struktur und geschichtlichen Bedeutung*, Studia Romanica, 9 (Heidelberg: Carl Winter, 1965), p. 178, and Spitzer, p. 480, footnote.

the twelfth, thirteenth and fourteenth centuries. These texts represent individual attempts to come to grips with the problem outlined above, as well as to respond to changing literary taste. The development of the legend of St Alexis in Old French, as well as presenting us with contemporary readings of the legend, illustrates in its treatment of the marriage theme the complex interplay of literary and social factors which governed the process of adaptation or *remaniement*, a process which is central to medieval literary production. At the same time, it provides us with a series of windows onto the development of the Church's teaching on marriage as it was presented to lay people in a particular geographic and cultural area.

The textual tradition of the Old French lives of St Alexis is complex. The earliest version (LAPV) was probably composed in the middle of the eleventh century, and was based on a Latin version similar to that printed by the Bollandists.[6] A much-expanded and altered re-telling of this version was recorded in the twelfth century (S), and this was in turn re-worked from assonance into rhyme in the thirteenth century (M) and into alexandrine quatrains in the fourteenth (Q).[7] In addition two independent translations (also based on the *Acta Sanctorum* text or one close to it) were made in the thirteenth century: one in rhyming alexandrine *laisses* (Hz), and the other in octosyllabic rhyming couplets (R). Finally, there is a version in the fourteenth-century poem, the *Tombel de Chartrose* (T), which will remain peripheral to our discussion since it was

6 *Acta Sanctorum*, July IV, pp. 251–53. Reprinted (with revisions) in W. Foerster and E. Koschwitz, *Altfranzösisches Übungsbuch*, 6th edn (Leipzig: Reisland, 1921), pp. 300–08: and in J.-M. Meunier, *La Vie de Saint Alexis* (Paris: Droz, 1933), pp. 11–17. Carl J. Odenkirchen, *The Life of St Alexius in the Old French Version of the Hildesheim Manuscript* (Brookline, Massachusetts and Leyden: Classical Folia Editions, 1978), pp. 34–51, reproduces the Foerster and Koschwitz edition with an English translation. The mid-eleventh-century date, first proposed by Gaston Paris on linguistic grounds, is still the consensus view. For other opinions, see Elliott, p. 15, n. 12.

7 LAPV refers to the text found in five MSS, L, A, P[1], P[2] and V. It was edited by Gaston Paris in G. Paris and L. Pannier, *La Vie de St Alexis, poème du xie siècle et renouvellements des xiie, xiiie, et xive siècles*, Bibliothèque de L'Ecole des Hautes Etudes, 7 (Paris, 1872). This and the many subsequent editions of this text are listed in C. Storey, *An Annotated Bibliography and Guide to Alexis Studies ('La Vie de Saint Alexis')* (Geneva: Droz, 1987), which provides an excellent guide to the editions of all the poems, as well as to St Alexis studies in general. For textual citations from LAPV, I have used Christopher Storey's edition of L: *La Vie de saint Alexis: texte du manuscrit de Hildesheim (L)* (Geneva: Droz, 1968). The other sigla refer to versions, not to individual MSS (although some versions exist in only one MS). S, M, and Q were published by Gaston Paris and Léopold Pannier in the edition cited above, which I shall quote from for those versions. S and M were more recently edited by Alison Godard Elliott (she has published the shorter redaction of M contained in the Carlisle Cathedral MS), see note 1 above.

written for Carthusian monks and shows little interest in the question of Alexis's marriage.[8]

As Baudouin de Gaiffier has pointed out (pp. 164–82), the Western form of the story of Alexis fuses two narrative motifs, which elsewhere exist as alternatives: the flight of the saint before his wedding, and the agreement reached by the couple after marriage to live in chastity, either together or in separate religious communities. In the earliest Eastern versions of the legend only the first motif is present: the flight takes place before the marriage.[9] The superimposition of the second motif in the later Greek versions, to create a story of flight after marriage (though with no mention of agreement by both parties) apparently posed no ethical problem at the time. However, for the public of the twelfth and thirteenth centuries it created difficulties in two areas which were coming to be of increasing concern. These areas both involved the notion of consent, which by the thirteenth century was recognized as an essential condition for a valid marriage.[10] What was Alexis's intention in making the vow of espousal, when he clearly did not want to marry? And if his vow was sincere and the marriage therefore valid, did he leave his bride with her consent, since it was essential for both partners to agree before one could leave to embrace the religious life?[11] Much of the amplification and alteration which distinguishes the later Old French versions from each other as well as from both LAPV and their Latin source can be seen as an attempt to deal with these questions.

The Old French *Alexis* poems are not all independent of one another. As originally pointed out by Gaston Paris in his edition, S, M and Q are all re-workings of LAPV, with M and Q showing some dependence on S. LAPV, S, M and Q belong to what is sometimes referred to as the *Alsis* family of manuscripts because they use the name *Alsis* for the city in which Alexis spent seventeen years. While S, M and Q are clearly related to LAPV in that they take it, rather than a Latin version, as their

8 R was edited by Gaston Paris, 'La Vie de saint Alexis en vers octosyllabiques', *Romania*, 8 (1879), 163–80. Hz and T were edited by Charles E. Stebbins, *A Critical Edition of the 13th and 14th Centuries Old French Poem Versions of the 'Vie de saint Alexis'*, Beihefte zur Zeitschrift für romanische Philologie, 145 (Tübingen: Niemeyer, 1974).

9 The Syriac and Greek legends are summarised in Meunier, pp. 3–6. The simple linear transmission of the legend through Syriac and Greek to Latin was challenged by M. Rösler in *Die Fassungen der Alexiuslegende*, Wiener Beiträge zur englischen Philologie (Vienna; Leipzig, 1905, repr. New York, 1964). Her arguments are summarized in Odenkirchen, pp. 12–31.

10 The consent of both parties came to weigh as heavily as consummation in determining the validity of a marriage, and under Innocent III it became the sole condition (see Le Bras, p. 198).

11 See Le Bras, p. 195 and Duby, p. 179.

starting point (whether by oral or textual transmission), they clearly form a separate group from LAPV and the independent versions Hz, R and T, in the greatly expanded role they accord to the bride.[12] In view of the interrelatedness of S, M and Q, and the fact that S represents the earliest attempt to come to grips with the problem of Alexis's marriage as it is posed in LAPV, I will deal with the modifications particular to this group of texts first.

Gaston Paris saw S as an adaptation of the story made by a *jongleur* for a secular audience, and it certainly has stylistic and thematic affinities with the secular genres of epic and romance. Alison Goddard Elliott, in her detailed analysis of the style of S, argued that its use of formulaic language is evidence of oral composition, and noted resemblances with the epic. On the other hand, H. Schneegans described S as a 'romanticization', and it is true that its concern with psychological motivation, the use of direct speech expressing the inner feelings of characters, and especially the importance accorded to the relationship between a man and a woman, are features associated with secular romance.[13] It is these features which concern us here. In this version, the scene in the bridal chamber is amplified so that it becomes a dialogue, and the bride is able to plead her case. She is the last person to speak to Alexis, and it is she who receives the parchment on which his life-story is written. Furthermore, in one episode it becomes clear that Alexis is not indifferent to her memory after his flight, and that indeed he feels some compunction for the pain he has caused her (S, 493–95). It could be argued that the centrality of the couple to romance narrative, along with the popularity of this new kind of literature in the twelfth century, was the primary motivation for enhancing the role of the bride in this version.[14] But the attempt to transform this story of individual heroism into that of a couple also brings their marriage into the foreground, and invites a more rounded treatment than it was accorded in LAPV.

[12] H. Massmann, *Sanct Alexius Leben in acht gereimten mittelhochdeutschen Behandlungen*, Bibliothek der gesammten deutschen Nationalliteratur, 9 (Quedlinburg and Leipzig, 1843), p. 26, pointed out the existence in the Western *Alexis* tradition of two narrative streams, which he called the *brautlich* and *päpstlich* redactions because in one the document containing the saint's life-story was given to the bride, and in the other to the pope. The French *brautlich* versions seem to be independent of both German and Latin texts in this tradition: see H. Schneegans, 'Die romanhafte Richtung der Alexiuslegende in altfranzösischen und mittelhochdeutschen Gedichten', *Modern Language Notes*, 3 (1888), 247–56 and 307–27 (pp. 307–10).

[13] See G. Paris, p. 200; Elliott, pp. 19–27, 50–76; Schneegans, p. 315.

[14] J. Leclercq (p. 72) writes 'il est intéressant de constater qu'en France, au temps des origines du roman courtois, l'on écrivait aussi, pour les mêmes publics, des récits religieux d'aventures amoureuses, avec ou sans consommation du mariage'. He appears to be referring to LAPV, but what he says is more appropriate to S.

The character of S as a counter-argument to LAPV was demonstrated recently by Alison Goddard Elliott (pp. 31 and 34–39), who pointed out its softening of Alexis's stern asceticism and the emphasis it places on winning the bride's consent to a separation. The overall emphasis of the scene in the bridal chamber, with Alexis explaining his reasons for leaving and his bride trying to make him stay, is on the sentimental, rather than the moral implications of Alexis's departure. It takes on something of the character of a farewell between lovers, with grief on both sides:

> Estes les vous belement departis,
> Plorent des oels, ne se porent tenir, (S, 288–89)

Even Alexis's quest for salvation is to be undertaken on his bride's behalf as well as his own, as a knight might go forth to win glory for his lady:

> 'Certes', dist il, 'Damediu irai querre,
> Qu'il nous reçoive a son regne celestre.' (S, 239–40)

This is made even more explicit in the two later versions (M, 279–86, Q, str. 34), and the motif perhaps owes its endurance not only to its undoubted chivalric overtones, but also to the sense it gives of Alexis performing some sort of service to his bride beyond their separation, and of her continuing to have a part in his ascetic enterprise.

Within this emotional farewell scene, however, there is at least one utterance of the bride which calls attention to what might be described as an aspect of marital ethics. In attempting to persuade Alexis to stay, she evokes the lot of a woman abandoned by her husband:

> Dist la pucele: 'Or sui molt esgarée;
> Mainne me la dunt tu m'as amenée.
> Por coi me lais? Ja m'as tu espousée.
> Que querras ore en estrange contrée?
> Que porai dire ton pere ne ta mere?
> Sempres m'aront de lor terre jetée.
> Puis m'en irai com autre asoignentée.
> Tel honte arai jamais n'iere houneurée.' (S, 166–73)

But the most explicit comment on marriage comes at the end of the scene following Alexis's death, when the *cartre* (letter) bearing the account of Alexis's life, released by the dead man's fingers to the hand of the Pope, flies immediately to the bride:

> Oiés, signour, con grande loiauté
> Tout home doivent a lor moiller porter.

Car tel moustrance fist le jour Damedés,
Que a sa mere ne vaut la cartre aler
Ne a son pere qui l'avoit engenré;
Mais a l'espouse ki bien avoit gardé
Le compaignie de son ami carnel,
La va la cartre par le plaisir Dé; (S, 1106–13)

For the first time, Alexis is held up as an example to married men, and the message here is not one of renunciation of the married state but a commendation of the bond between man and wife (see Elliott, p. 42). The fate of this passage in the later versions illustrates the strengthening of this notion in succeeding centuries. In M the comment is reproduced with elaborations which make it into an even clearer statement of the mutual obligations of married couples:

Chi puet on bien aprendre et escouter
Ke esposailles font forment a amer:[15]
Ke a sa mere ne vout li cartre aler
Ne sor sen pere caoir ne ariester,
Mais sor l'espose le fist Dius ariester,
Ke cascuns hon doit se femme honorer,
Aussi les dames lor signor bien warder;
Et ki ne l' fait tres bien se puet fier
Dedens infier l'en estovra aler
Od les diables tot de fi convierser. (M, 1112–21)

By the fourteenth century, respect for marriage has become a divine teaching and the punishment for disregarding it is presented very explicitly:

Mez le dous Jhesu Crist le fist pour ensegnier
C'ordre de mariage fait forment a prizier,
Quant desus l'espousée fist la lestre lancier,
Sus pere ne sus mere ne la vout envoier.

Personne est bien chetive qui ront son mariage:
Dez lors renie Dieu et se met en l'ommage
Dez anemis d'enfer qui tant sont plains de rage.
(Q, str. 167, 168)

The treatment of the marriage theme in the independent thirteenth-century versions, Hz and R, is more didactic. Returning to the narrative

[15] The Carlisle manuscript has 'Ke mariaiges fait forment a garder'. See Elliott's edition of M^2, l. 939.

outline of the Latin text, they do not give nearly as much weight as S does to the bride's role or explore to the same extent the sentimental aspect of her relationship with Alexis, but they do, along with M and Q, interest themselves in its moral aspect. Like LAPV and S, they describe the whole process of Alexis's marriage in much more detail than the Latin life. This can partly be attributed, of course, to a desire to make the story more accessible and attractive to a lay audience and to indulge a taste for descriptive set-pieces. But I think there is more to it than that. It is instructive to look at these descriptions and to see just what sort of picture they present of this marriage.

The *Vita S. Alexi Confessoris* printed by the Bollandists in the *Acta Sanctorum* gives a very brief account:

> Cum autem ad tempus adolescentiae accessisset, et eum nuptialibus infulis aptum judicasset, elegerunt ei puellam ex genere imperiali, et ornaverunt thalamum, et impositae sunt eis singulae coronae in templo S. Bonifacii martyris per manus honoratissimorum sacerdotum, et sic cum gaudio, et laetitia laetum duxerunt diem. Vespere autem facto dixit Euphemianus filio suo: "Intra, fili, in cubiculum, et visita sponsam tuam."

From the earliest French version onwards, this account is fleshed out in terms comprehensible to an audience familiar with dynastic concerns. The father's reason for wanting to see his son married is made explicit in L:

> Quant veit li pedre que mais n'avrat amfant
> Mais que cel sul que il par amat tant,
> Dunc se purpenset del seclë en avant.
> Or volt que prenget moyler a sun vivant;
> Dunc li acatet filie d'un noble Franc. (L, 36–40)

The negotiations between the two fathers are mentioned (L, str. 9–10). This information is elaborated in virtually all the later versions. M adds a dowry of 1000 *livres* and a castle (M, 74–75), which in Q becomes four castles and land (Q, str. 11). The theme is also present in M and Q in the words of Alexis's father when he instructs his son to join his bride in the bedchamber, as he adds a prayer that God will grant it to Alexis to engender heirs (M, 93–94; Q, str. 15). In Hz, a version independent of this tradition, the father's desire to see his line continued is also stated explicitly:

> Li peres se recorde, mort sont si ancissor,
> De cui il a sa terre, sa ricoise francor;

Ne il n'a que cel fil, si pense et nuit et jor
Que mollier li donra que pora belisor
Et de plus haut linage et de plus douce amor,
Dont Diex li doinst tel fruit qui maintigne s'onor.
(Hz, 126–31)

There could hardly be a better expression of *pensée lignagère* than this, with its evocation of generations past and to come. That Alexis, in his family's eyes, had a duty to care for his inheritance and pass it on to the next generation, is also implicit in the parents' laments in all versions.

The wedding itself, even in the Latin version, follows the widespread medieval pattern of exchange of vows (the point at which the couple was blessed, if the Church was involved at all), and leading of the bride to the house of her husband's family, with music and dancing, for the ceremonial consummation of the marriage. The celebrations, along with the scene in the bridal chamber as the couple are conducted to bed, are of course standard *loci* for rhetorical amplification, but these amplifications are also made to serve a didactic purpose by the poets who use them. Hz and R describe the feasting and dancing at great length, the former contrasting the joy of the celebrations with the sadness to come (Hz, 149–62) and the latter expressing disapproval of worldly enjoyment (R, 124–40). T also describes the celebrations in great detail, contrasting them with Alexis's consciousness of the transitoriness of worldly enjoyment (T, 211–75). R gives a full account of the ceremony in the bedchamber, making it clear that Alexis went through all the public actions of the wedding before he was left alone with his bride (R, 141–58). Descriptions of the bride and bedchamber are found in S, 119–26, M, 94–104, Q, str. 16, 17, and Hz, 177–88. It is clear that the function of these descriptions is not simply to entertain, but to highlight Alexis's strength of purpose. We shall return to these passages when we come to discuss the motivation of Alexis's departure.

The picture of marriage presented in these descriptions is of an arrangement between two families, involving transfer of property and intended chiefly for the begetting of heirs, an intention which is reflected in the concentration of the festivities on the physical consummation of the union. The public acts of the wedding ceremony symbolize and celebrate the propagation of the groom's family rather than the union of two individuals. The resemblance between this picture and the secular 'feudal model' of marriage of northern France in the Middle Ages described by Georges Duby (pp. 42–49) is immediately apparent.

In LAPV this model of marriage is used to represent attachment to the world, and Alexis's reaction to it is to flee. This simple opposition disappears in later versions. We have seen how in S, M, and Q a continuing relationship between Alexis and his bride is described, and her importance and that of the marriage bond is stressed at the end of the story when she receives the *cartre*. These versions make the bride an example of marital fidelity: Alexis is saved through his devotion to God (although in S there is room within this devotion for continuing care for his bride), but she is saved through her devotion to Alexis. In S, she presents her own behaviour in terms of obedience to her husband's instructions:

> Dist la pucele: 'Sire, vostre merci.
> Il m'espousa al los de mes amis.
> Or sui malvaise, si me doit Diex hair,
> Si moi ne membre de çou que il me dist
> A icele eure que de moi departi.
> Quant tu pour lui me vauras retenir,
> Tres or tenrai Damediu a mari:
> Ne me faura se jou le voel servir.' (S, 440–47)

In the two thirteenth-century independent versions, it is in the greatly expanded dialogue in the bridal chamber that we find comments on marriage which do not automatically dismiss it as a form of attachment to the world. In Hz Alexis says to his bride as he gives her half the ring he has just split in two:

> 'Belle suer, membrés vos de vostre espousement,
> Por Dieu vos pri, le voir, a vivre castement
> Et que il vos sovegne de vo enloiement
> Comment somes ensamble par le saint sacrement;
> Or nos [j]oignons a Dieu par bon entendement,
> De bien faire pensomes, de vivre justement.' (Hz, 224–29)

This speech places Alexis in the line of saints who agree to a chaste marriage.[16] But there are some interesting details in the terms in which he speaks of the union. It is indissoluble, regardless of whether or not it has been consummated; it is spoken of as a sacrament, and is presented as a framework within which the couple may serve God chastely.[17] There is clearly a spiritual dimension to the union, although it is not spoken of in those terms. The division of marriage into spiritual and carnal elements

16 Examples are listed by de Gaiffier, pp. 164–82.

17 Marriage was first listed among the sacraments by Hildebert of Lavardin (Duby, p. 192); the sacramental character of marriage was affirmed by the Council of Verona in 1184 (Le Bras, p. 193, n. 19).

had been put forward in the twelfth century by Hugh of Saint Victor and Peter Lombard, and although they saw physical union as an integral part of marriage, it was subordinate to the spiritual union.[18]

This hierarchy of the spiritual and carnal elements of love is expressed far more explicitly in R. It is here that the dialogue in the bedchamber reaches its height as a reasoned exposition of two alternative views of marriage. Alexis begins by outlining the mutual obligations of a couple whose union has been sealed by God:

> 'Dame,' fet il, 'ore est issi:
> Dex qui tot a fet et crié
> Nos a ensemble marié.
> Por ce si est dreit, ce me semble,
> Ke nos aiun amor ensemble,
> Et porton leauté et fei
> Et je a vos, et vos a mei;
> Et nostre amor seit si planiere
> Qu'el seit et veraie et entiere.' (R, 162–70)

His bride, quite reasonably, sees this in terms of sexual fidelity, and assures him that no man will ever share her body or heart with her husband (R, 171–89). However, Alexis is quick to point out her mistake, and to elaborate a doctrine of carnal and spiritual love in which the superiority of spiritual love is ensured by the superiority of the soul over the body (R, 190–213). It is obvious that the author of this poem feared that the unlearned among his audience would take such a theory too literally, for he makes the bride exclaim:

> 'Est donkes pechié mariage?' (R, 215)

This allows Alexis to explain the superiority of virginity, and to point out the dangers that the married state, while not sinful in itself, entails (R, 216–28).

In these two poems, then, while the physical union and social obligations of marriage are set aside as being less pleasing to God and being dangerous to salvation, the spiritual union brought about by the

[18] Duby, pp. 195–96. For spiritual marriage as a category of the wider concept of mystic marriage, see R. Grégoire, 'Il matrimonio mistico', in *Il matrimonio nella società altomedievale* (Spoleto: Il Centro italiano di studi sull'alto medioevo, 1977), II, 701–94 (pp. 758–78). M uses the body/soul distinction in a different way, putting in Alexis' mouth a long quotation from the debate between the Body and Soul which evokes graphically the unhappy fate of the person who has no care for her soul (see Elliott, pp. 44 and 49).

exchange of vows is seen as lasting and divinely ordained, and carrying its own obligations. This distinction can of course be read into the earliest version too, but there it is a matter of interpretation, and here it is put unambiguously into words.

A shift has taken place in the treatment of Alexis's marriage from S onwards. It is presented unequivocally as a valid, lasting union, even though it has not been consummated. In Hz and R an alternative form of marriage, already hinted at in S, M and Q, is articulated, whose spiritual values are superior to those of mere social, physical marriage: rather than opposing marriage and celibacy, as LAPV does, they propose a higher form of union. Several consequences flow from this shift. The model of marriage being used clearly depends on consent rather than consummation for its validity. Therefore it is necessary to show that Alexis made his marriage vow sincerely, of his own free will, and to make absolutely clear his reasons for going away afterwards rather than before. Presenting their union as a spiritual marriage also means that it must be made clear that he has his bride's consent to go. Technically, it was only after consummation that the consent of both parties was required if one or both wanted to join a religious order, but here again it is clear that their union, though unconsummated, was being treated as valid and binding (see Le Bras, p. 195). Here, I believe, we have the motivation for a number of small amplifications in the later versions.

Many of these deal with the reason for Alexis's departure. In the Latin version, we are not told when or why he made the decision to leave. In LAPV the way is prepared a little, since we hear briefly of his unwillingness to marry and his devotion to God at the moment of the wedding. R and Hz, in what had become a standard part of the description of the youth of the saint in vernacular hagiography, describe at length the devotion of the young Alexis to God (R, 81–114, Hz, 93–110). In Hz this devotion to God and fear of the world is crystallized into a kind of promise:

> A orison se couche et a larme et a plor,
> Dieu proie de bon cuer par sa vraie douchor
> Qu'il de mort le defende, qu'il ne caie en error,
> Que de çou c'a promis ne boist son creator. (Hz, 122–25)

Why, then, go through with the wedding, if he was determined to leave afterwards? The French poems present two possible solutions, sometimes concurrently. The first builds on two clues given in LAPV. One comes at the end of the wedding scene, when Alexis's father tells him to join his bride in the bedchamber: Alexis obeys, we are told, because

> Ne volt li emfes sum pedre corocier (L, 54)[19]

S, M, and Q retain the expression of Alexis's reluctance at the marriage negotiations and S, M, and Hz retain the motive of filial obedience when Alexis goes into the bedchamber (S, 100–02, 115; M, 80–83, 94–95; Q, str. 11–12; Hz, 169–70).[20] Q and R transfer this motive to the marriage itself:

> Mez sez amis n'osa couroucier nullement:
> La pucele espousa mout debonnairement. (Q, str. 12)

> N'i osa metre nul contenz
> Por son pere et por ses parenz;
> Mes en son cuer out grand tempeste. (R, 121–23)

In these versions Alexis marries against his better judgement, to carry out his family's wishes. Note, however, that there is no question of his voicing his reluctance or of being forced by his family.

The second element in LAPV which later versions use as a clue to understanding Alexis's behaviour is the description of his first view of his bride in the bedchamber and the prayer he utters:

> Cum veit le lit, esguardat la pulcela;
> Dunc li remembret de sun seinor celeste,
> Que plus ad cher que tut aveir terrestre.
> 'E! Deus!' dist il, 'cum fort pecét m'appresset!
> S'or ne m'en fui, mult criem que ne t'em perde.' (L, 56–60)

It could be argued from this that Alexis had intended until this moment to live chastely with his wife, but on seeing her beauty realized that he would not be able to resist temptation and must flee. That is certainly how the author of Q interprets it:

> Puis dist: 'Dous Jhesu Crist, bien sai, se me couchoie
> Avec ceste pucele, que m'i deliteroie,
> Et vostre dous servise de tous poins delairoie.
> Je seroie trop fol se pour lie vous lesoie.' (Q, str. 20)

S and M, without stating the matter so clearly, convey the impact of the sight of the bride on Alexis by expanding the description of her and of

[19] E. Winkler (p. 588) suggested that Alexis only agreed to marry out of fear of his father, and that he pronounced the vow with certain mental restrictions.

[20] Hz is most explicit about Alexis' reluctance and his fear of angering his father (Hz, 169–73).

the bedchamber (S, 124–28; M, 101–10). These two versions also expand his prayer for help (S, 129–38; M, 111–20). Hz, although it does not belong to the narrative tradition of LAPV, S, M and Q, describes the scene in a similar way. Here the bedchamber is first described, then the bride and her effect on Alexis (Hz, 177–88). Alexis then prays for help against 'si fort destorbier, Del siecle', and strengthened by the injunctions of the Gospel to love God more than family, lands or honour (Matth. 19: 29), decides to leave (Hz, 191–214).

This realisation of human weakness provoked by the sight of the bride is a morally satisfactory solution, accounting as it does for the decision to flee after the wedding. Less satisfactory from this point of view is the motive of a vow of chastity that had already been taken, hinted at by both M and Hz. In M, instead of thinking simply of God, when he sees his bride, Alexis thinks of the Church, which is referred to as his *drue*, as though he had already promised himself to it in some way (M, 105–06). It is as though he had forgotten this promise until he walked into the bedchamber. In Hz, Alexis's knowledge of the danger of marriage is attributed to his education, but his attachment to chastity is cast in the form of a vow taken long ago:

> Bien set en son corage qu'il en sera dampnés
> Se de sa cast[e]é est or si deflorés
> Qu'il promist a garder, ja ert lons tens passés. (Hz, 263–65)
> (cf. Hz, 122–25)

In R, Alexis's mind seems to have been made up from the beginning. There is no description of the bride and no prayer. He launches immediately into his exposition of the superiority of the spiritual aspect of marriage, and justifies his departure by pointing out the dangerous temptations inherent in the (carnally) married state. It is simply not worth the price:

> Si fet que saige li poisson
> Qui fuit le verm por l'ameçon
> Ker trop i a chiere golee,
> Povre e petite, et tost alee. (R, 229–32)

One is left with the impression that this author felt that there was no danger of his audience misinterpreting Alexis's actions as long as the doctrine was set out clearly.

The question of the bride's consent is more straightforward. It is not stated explicitly in LAPV that she has consented at all to Alexis's departure, and in all the versions which reproduce her laments, her grief and incomprehension at his going are made plain. However, from S onwards (except in R) the French authors take care to show that her consent is given, even if she does not understand why.[21] In M, Alexis begins many *laisses* with a request for permission to go away:

> 'Me biele drue, or me done congiet,' (M, 171)
> 'France puchiele, or me laissiés fuir;' (M, 279)
> 'Gentius puchiele, car me laissiés aler:' (M, 289)

Her consent is given, but reluctantly:

> 'Or t'en va, sire, kant ne te puis tenir.' (M, 310)

It is couched in similar terms in S, 208–09, 242 and Q, str. 30. In Hz, the bride agrees readily to exchange a vow of chastity with Alexis:

> Cele dist: 'Volentiers, si com vos commandés,
> Mais que vos ensement autretel me tenés.' (Hz, 275–76)

However, although her consent is given to a chaste marriage, she is not happy about his departure. His request, 'Vo congiet me donés!' (Hz, 281) only produces an enquiry about where he is going, and when he actually goes she weeps and swoons (Hz, 301–09).

In these poems, then, the picture of marriage and its possibilities undergoes a transformation, and most of the plot-changes, added authorial comments, and amplifications of description and dialogue flow from this transformation. However, this does not result in a seamless new work. The constraints of the existing narrative framework do not permit a re-working of the story into a spiritual marriage lived in perfect understanding between Alexis and his bride. It is interesting to speculate on the reasons for the strength of this narrative framework. The authority of the Latin text must of course play a part, especially for R and Hz, for which it is the primary source. But more importantly, the narrative core of this story is the flight from the father's house, and the unrecognized return and life under the stairs for which it is the necessary preparation. Without these events the story ceases to be that of St Alexis. Even for S, M, and Q, which shift the emphasis of the narrative most boldly from the individual to the couple, the flight could not be tampered with, only attenuated. In this group of texts, too, there is an unresolved tension between their attempt to make the bride Alexis's partner and their

[21] Even the author of T, who takes little interest in the bride, and in the marriage question in general, makes her consent clear (T, 349–55).

seizing upon the pathos of her situation. They belong to the narrative tradition which, following LAPV, makes the most of the bride's laments, and it is clear from them that her loyalty is uncomprehendingly fixed on Alexis, without her having understood his purpose. In S, she says to Alexis's parents:

> 'S'il ne revient, ne a toi ne repaire,
> Jou me tenrai vers le roi celestre.' (S, 431–32)

That she does not substitute another husband for Alexis is exemplary; on the other hand, it seems that her devotion to God is only a compensation for the absence of Alexis. Her laments at his death make it clear that she had lived her life in the expectation of seeing him again, as in this example from Q:

> 'Chier amis Alexis, com dure desevree!
> Mout vous ay atendu et en bonne pensee,
> Or m'avez vous lessie de tous biens esgaree.' (Q, str. 184)

This is made even clearer in her lament in R, in which she speaks of wasting her youth in waiting (874–78). Her regret is given an added piquancy by an evocation of the disadvantages of widowhood, which shows her locked still in a vision of marriage which privileges its carnal and social elements:

> 'Ainceis que mi sires morust,
> Aveie je, quel part qu'il fust,
> Grant hennor del non de mari,
> Qu'em m'apelot femme Alexi;
> Mès or sui veuve sanz seignor,
> Sanz cest non et sanz cest ennor;
> Or n'ai je mès point de garant,
> Fors Deu a qui je me commant.
> Certes je suis mout corociée
> Qu'il m'a issi de tot lessiée,
> Quer il out m'amor primereine,
> Si avra il la desreeine.
> Je ne sai nul autre confort
> Que je puisse aveir de sa mort
> Fors que jamès autre n'avrai:
> Virge sui et virge morrai.' (R, 881–96)

In all of these versions her fidelity is exemplary, and it is through her loyalty to Alexis that she is saved, but it is in his wake, rather than beside him: in spite of all the efforts of the vernacular hagiographers to bring her into the foreground, she is not an equal partner in his enterprise.

Our survey of the marriage theme in the Old French *St Alexis* poems reveals two ways of looking at marriage. In LAPV there is a simple opposition between marriage (which is presented in this text largely as a purely social phenomenon), and ascetic service of God. An examination of S suggests that already in the twelfth century there was a desire to tell the story of St Alexis in a more humanly satisfying way, but also a fear that its attitude to marriage might be open to misinterpretation.[22] This and the subsequent versions, with the exception of T, all make some attempt to redeem marriage. In S an appeal to current literary taste is combined with the presentation of a model of obedient wifely fidelity that is divinely sanctioned and rewarded, which counteracts any possible interpretation of the original story as devaluing marriage. The thirteenth-century versions return to a more didactic mode of exposition, although M retains the plot-changes which give the bride greater prominence and R uses courtly language and imagery. Where S and M have used the story as a whole to incorporate a positive view of marriage, Hz and R concentrate all of their efforts on the scene in the bridal chamber. No doubt the expansion of the bride's role in this scene was also responding to a public taste for dialogue and for seeing the couple interact, but it also served a didactic purpose. In R, in particular, the bride's part is constructed in such a way that she represents the audience, asking the questions on which they need to be instructed. While these versions still depict the entanglements of family responsibility and the occasions for lust provided by marriage as something to be avoided, they also acknowledge the existence of a regulated and divinely sanctioned Christian form of marriage. Within the constraints of their narrative framework they manage to slip in a number of clarifications on the most important points of the Church's doctrine of marriage: the solemn, indeed sacramental nature of the bond, the need for the consent of both partners for both marriage and separation, and the superiority of the spiritual over the carnal aspect of marriage. In doing this they are acknowledging that most of the audience of their poems are married lay-people, who must work

[22] The late twelfth-century French life of St Evroul also shows signs of concern about the Alexis story: passages added by the vernacular hagiographer make implicit parallels between Alexis and Evroul, but Evroul is given an interior monologue in which the virtues of marriage, the obligations of partners to each other, and the need to obtain the consent of the other partner before departing are treated at length. See J. Pinder, 'The Intertextuality of Old French Saints' Lives: St Giles, St Evroul and the Marriage of St Alexis', *Parergon*, New Series, 6a (1988), 11–21.

out their salvation within that context and not be encouraged to abandon it.

In the development of the legend, Alexis's marriage is to begin with just the background to his heroic renunciation. The attention given to it in the French texts brings it further into the foreground and makes it exist alongside renunciation as another way of salvation; it becomes clearer (especially in S, M, and Q) that it is the salvation of the bride. As she is given greater prominence and made to voice the possible doubts and questions of the audience, she becomes their representative. The lay men and women who read or listened to the story in its later versions may perhaps have felt called to take inspiration from Alexis's heroism, but they were also being encouraged to work out their own salvation, like the bride, within the more prosaic confines of the married state.

Outdoing Chaucer: Lydgate's *Troy Book* and Henryson's *Testament of Cresseid* as Competitive Imitations of *Troilus and Criseyde*[1]

NICHOLAS WATSON

> Taccia Lucano omai là dov' e' tocca
> del misero Sabello e di Nasidio,
> e attenda a udir quel ch' or si scocca.
> Taccia di Cadmo e d' Aretusa Ovidio,
> chè se quello in serpente e quella in fonte
> converte poetando, io non lo 'nvidio:
> Chè due nature mai a fronte a fronte
> non transmutò si ch' amendue le forme
> a cambiar lor matera fosser pronte. (*Inferno*, XXV, 94–102)[2]

GRINDING HIS EPIC GEARS in the *bolgia* of the thieves – a place of endless metamorphosis in the seventh circle of hell, where two monstrous forms are about to turn into one another – Dante audaciously presents his 'transmutation' of his predecessors' poetic 'matter' as the theft it is, but steals the laurel from them anyway. This paradoxical fusion of homage and displacement – here embodied in an example of what E. R. Curtius

1 A draft of this paper was given at the Kalamazoo Convention on Medieval Studies in May, 1992. I wish to thank C. David Benson for reading the draft and for his helpful comments.

2 'Let Lucan now be silent, where he tells of the wretched Sabellus and of Nasidius, and let him wait to hear what now comes forth. Concerning Cadmus and Arethusa let Ovid be silent, for if he, poetizing, converts the one into a serpent and the other into a fountain, I envy him not; for two natures front to front he never so transmuted that both forms were prompt to exchange their substance.' *The Divine Comedy*, ed. by Charles S. Singleton, 6 vols, Bollinger Series, 80 (Princeton: Princeton University Press, 1977).

calls the 'outdoing' topos[3] – has been an integral feature of Western literary tradition from at least the Golden Age of Ovid, Virgil and Horace on. As Rita Copeland has shown,[4] both individual writers and entire literary cultures have invented themselves through this process of *translatio*, imitating the *auctores* of the past while at the same time seeking to contain and if possible outdo them. When, at the end of *Troilus and Criseyde*, Chaucer instructs his poem to 'kis the steppes where as thow seest space/ Uirgile, Ouide, Omer, Lucan and Stace' (V, ll. 1791–92), he is only using modesty topoi to achieve an end similar to Dante's, proclaiming his poem and his voice as additions to the literary canon, and elevating the English vernacular as worthy (like French and Italian) to stand comparison with Latin.[5] It is this last achievement that justifies Deschamps' praise of Chaucer as 'grant translateur', and lies behind his depiction by Hoccleve, Lydgate and others as founder or (more rarely) 'father' of English poetry.[6] In recent years, Chaucer's self-canonization as poet has received the attention of a growing number of scholars.[7] This paper aims to build on their work by investigating a related matter: that of how Chaucer's poetic descendents made his legacy their own. Many of the fifteenth-century 'Chaucerian' poets are still patronized even by those seeking to rehabilitate them; their rhetorical expressions of gratitude to Chaucer are read at face value (as signs of awareness of inferiority), while the ambition and confidence of many of them are not.[8] Yet our inability to take a century of poetry seriously deprives us of

3 Ernst Robert Curtius, *European Literature in the Latin Middle Ages*, trans. by Willard R. Trask (London: Routledge, 1953), pp. 162–65, quoting (*inter alia*) the same passage of Dante.

4 Rita Copeland, *Rhetoric, Hermeneutics, and Translation in the Middle Ages: Academic Traditions and Vernacular Texts* (Cambridge: Cambridge University Press, 1991).

5 *Troilus and Criseyde*, ed. by B. A. Windeatt (London: Longman, 1984); all further references are to this edition. To compare Dante's 'outdoing' with Chaucer's modesty topoi is not to deny the difference in tone between them, nor the gap between Italian and English humanism which it signifies (see Lee Patterson, *Chaucer and the Subject of History* (Madison: University of Wisconsin Press, 1991), pp. 18–22).

6 For Deschamps, see James I. Wimsatt, *Chaucer and His French Contemporaries: Natural Music in the Fourteenth Century* (Toronto: University of Toronto Press, 1991), pp. 253–54. For fifteenth-century English praise of Chaucer, see Caroline Spurgeon, *Five Hundred Years of Chaucer Criticism and Allusion, 1357–1900* (Cambridge: Cambridge University Press, 1925); for analysis, see A. C. Spearing, *Medieval to Renaissance in English Poetry* (Cambridge: Cambridge University Press, 1985), especially pp. 59–65.

7 See Patterson, *Chaucer and the Subject of History*; Copeland, *Rhetoric, Hermeneutics, and Translation*; Spearing, *Medieval to Renaissance*; and, for discussion of the concept of *auctor*, A. J. Minnis, *Medieval Theory of Authorship: Scholastic Literary Attitudes in the Later Middle Ages* (London: Scolar Press, 1984). For the argument that Chaucer is not the only late medieval English writer to engage in 'self-canonization', see my *Richard Rolle and the Invention of Authority* (Cambridge: Cambridge University Press, 1991).

8 See Derek Pearsall, *John Lydgate* (Charlottesville: University of Virginia Press, 1970), in

the opportunities to study not just what it was that Chaucer founded but the complexities of his act of literary fathering itself. It limits our grasp of his place in literary history as much as our understanding of Dante's importance would be hampered if we ignored Boccaccio and Petrarch. What I hope to show here is that at least two poets, Lydgate and Henryson, had an awareness of Chaucer's significance that went beyond mere imitation to express itself in an ambitious competitiveness worthy of Chaucer himself. Like Dante with Ovid and Lucan, or Boccaccio with Dante, Lydgate and Henryson treat Chaucer not only as source but as challenge, a powerful and even threatening figure, some of whose authority they must annex as a vital part of their self-invention as poets. I will argue that the renarrations of Chaucer's *Troilus and Criseyde* in Lydgate's *Troy Book* and Henryson's *Testament of Cresseid* should be read as complex acts of literary theft which, in at once canonizing Chaucer as an *auctor* and subverting his authority by criticizing or outdoing him, ensured the continuance of the tradition he began. The process of supplementing England's nearest thing to a classical epic was – for these writers and their contemporaries – a kind of *translatio auctoritatis*: a necessary displacement of a literary father in the very texts which defined him as such for centuries.[9]

Lydgate's *Troy Book* is a much-amplified translation of a minor source of *Troilus and Criseyde*, Guido delle Colonne's *Historia Destructionis*

which 'it [is] not denied that Lydgate is prolific, prolix and dull' (p. 14); or C. David Benson, *The History of Troy in Middle English Literature* (Cambridge: Brewer, 1980), which states that 'Lydgate was forced by circumstances to exercise this knowledge [of history] in poetry, a form in which his talents, as he continually reminds us, were modest' (pp. 112–13). For an account of humility topoi and the scholarly tendency to take them at face value, see David Lawton, 'Dullness and the Fifteenth Century', *English Literary History*, 54 (1987), 761–99.

9 The term *translatio auctoritatis* is Minnis', and is modelled on the medieval terms *translatio studii* and *translatio imperii*, for which see Copeland, *Rhetoric, Hermeneutics, and Translation*, pp. 103–35. My thinking on the relationship of male authors to their female characters is indebted especially to Carolyn Dinshaw, *Chaucer's Sexual Politics* (Madison: University of Wisconsin Press, 1989), while all study of the competitive element in the relationships of such authors to their major predecessors is informed by Harold Bloom, *The Anxiety of Influence* (New York: Oxford University Press, 1973), who has been especially influential in A. C. Spearing's writings on fifteenth-century poetry: see *Medieval to Renaissance*, and 'Lydgate's Canterbury Tale: *The Siege of Thebes* and Fifteenth-Century Chaucerianism', in *Fifteenth-Century Studies: Recent Essays*, ed. by Robert F. Yeager (Hamden, CT: Archon, 1984), pp. 333–64. For a study of the fifteenth-century poet John Walton's relationship with Chaucer, which in some ways parallels the present paper, see Ian Johnson's, '*This Brigous Questioun*: Translating Free Will and Predestination in Walton's *Boethius* and Chaucer's *Troilus and Criseyde*', to be published in *Carmina Philosophiae* in 1994.

Troiae.[10] According to its prologue and epilogue, *Troy Book* was commissioned in 1412 by the future Henry V (prologue, ll. 94–147), and finished in 1420 (V, ll. 3368–72), two years before Henry's death – making it the earliest of Lydgate's historical poems and among his first really extended works (it is 30,000 lines long). Written through the course of Henry's brilliant revival of the Hundred Years' War, and fittingly opening with an invocation to Mars, its function as an aid to patriotism and the elevation of the English language is explicit:

> [Prince Henry] wolde that to hyghe and lowe
> The noble story openly wer knowe
> In oure tonge, aboute in euery age,
> And y-writen as wel in oure langage
> As in latyn and in frensche it is;
> That of the story the trouthe we nat mys
> No more than doth eche other nacioun:
> This was the fyn of his entencioun. (prologue, 111–18)[11]

Lydgate offers readers history, not fiction, aligning himself with the 'auctours vs-beforn' (Dares, Dictys, Guido himself) who have winnowed the 'trewe corn' of history from the chaff of legend, and disparaging poets like Homer and Ovid who:

> han contreved by false transumpcioun
> To hyde trouthe falsely vnder cloude
> And the sothe, of malys, for to schroude.
> (prologue, 148–49, 264–66).

By taking over and amplifying Guido's own opening discussion of truth and falsehood, I shall argue that Lydgate also sets the stage for an ex-

10 For editions, see *Lydgate's Troy Book*, ed. by Henry Bergen, Early English Text Society (EETS), extra series (es) 97, 103, 106, 126 (Oxford, 1906–1935), and Guido delle Colonne, *Historia Destructionis Troiae*, ed. by Nathaniel Edward Griffin, Mediaeval Academy Publications, 26 (Cambridge, 1936), trans. by Mary Elizabeth Meek (Bloomington: Indiana University Press, 1974). For accounts of *Troy Book* and its relation to its source, see Anna Torti, 'From "History" to "Tragedy": The Story of Troilus and Criseyde in Lydgate's *Troy Book* and Henryson's *Testament of Cresseid*', in *The European Tragedy of Troilus*, ed. by Piero Boitani (Oxford: Clarendon Press, 1989), pp. 171–98; Lois A. Ebin, *John Lydgate*, Twayne's English Authors Series (Boston, 1985), pp. 39–52; Benson, *History of Troy*, pp. 97–129. For Chaucer's use of Guido, see C. David Benson, ' "O Nyce World": What Chaucer Really Found in Guido delle Colonne's History of Troy', *Chaucer Review*, 13 (1978–79), 308–15.

11 In quoting Lydgate, I normalize *thorn* as *th*, *yogh* as *gh* or *y*, and *&* as *and*, and omit the square brackets in Bergen's edition; I also on occasion modify Bergen's punctuation.

tended critique of a particular poem, *Troilus and Criseyde*, and through it of Chaucer.[12]

In opening with an account of its commissioning by a young future ruler, *Troy Book* announces itself as a work in the 'mirror for princes' tradition, like Hoccleve's *Regement of Princes* – also written for Henry – or the much-translated *Secreta Secretorum*, putatively written by Aristotle for Alexander the Great.[13] Guido's *Historia* is moralistic, but emphasizes the meaninglessness of the events it describes. Lydgate's transformation of his source involves placing yet more emphasis on the didactic passages and restructuring the narrative to make it exemplify specific moral points. *Troy Book* keeps to Guido's order, but reshapes the *Historia*'s thirty-three books into a five-book structure which is presumably meant to recall *Troilus and Criseyde*.[14] This structure recasts the

12 I shall not here consider the other act of displacement in *Troy Book*, that of Guido's *Historia* itself. The ground for this is prepared in the prologue, in a passage expanded from Guido on why he has rewritten existing versions of Dares and Dictys:

> For he [Guido] enlvmyneth by crafte and cadence
> This noble story with many fresche colour
> Of rethorik, and many riche flour
> Of eloquence to make it sownde bet
> He in the story hath ymped in and set [. . .]
> Whom I schal folwe as nyghe as euer I may . . .
> (*Troy Book*, prologue, 362–66, 375)

To 'folwe [Guido] as nyghe as euer I may' proves to involve not literal translation but translation that repeats Guido's practice of 'ymping' (grafting) many 'riche flour[s] of eloquence' onto his source (Guido is covertly referring to his massive unacknowledged use of Benoît de Sainte-Maure's *Roman de Troie*). This amplificatory practice is explained as a continuation of the attempts by earlier *auctores* to 'ympe [. . .] in oure thought' (l. 164) a true memory of the past – 'true' meaning not so much 'historically factual' as 'vivid and heroic' ('more bryght and clere than in any glas', l. 170). Lydgate displaces Guido (doubling the length of his book) exactly as Guido has done his sources, and for the same end: to make the past live as magnificently and instructively as possible.

13 See *Hoccleve's Works: The Regement of Princes and Fourteen Minor Poems*, ed. by F. J. Furnivall, EETS, es 72 (Oxford, 1897); and *Secreta Secretorum*, ed. by M. A. Manzalaoui, EETS, ordinary series (os) 276 (Oxford, 1977). For discussion, see A. H. Gilbert, 'Notes on the Influence of the *Secreta Secretorum*', *Speculum*, 3 (1928), 84–98, and L. K. Born, 'The Perfect Prince: A Study in Thirteenth and Fourteenth Century Ideals', ibid., pp. 470–504. For Middle English advice literature, see *Henry V: The Practice of Kingship*, ed. by G. L. Harriss (Oxford: Oxford University Press, 1985), introduction (by Harriss), and Richard Firth Green, *Poets and Princepleasers: Literature and the English Court in the Late Middle Ages* (Toronto: University of Toronto Press, 1980), chapter 5.

14 For the five-book structure of *Troilus and Criseyde*, see John Norton-Smith, *Geoffrey Chaucer* (London: Routledge, 1974), chapter 6. Norton-Smith argues that Chaucer imitates the five-act structure of Senecan tragedy (pp. 160–69). An alternative influence might be Boethius' *Consolation of Philosophy*, but the five-fold structural division of Chaucer's work is a rarity in late medieval literature. Lydgate's adoption of it is unlikely to be coincidental; as Lesley Lawton points out (in 'The Illustration of Late Medieval Secular Texts, with Special Reference to Lydgate's *Troy Book*', in *Manuscripts and*

narrative as a formal tragedy, the pivot of which is the death of Hector – virtually the poem's protagonist – at the climactic end of book III: an event caused not by the fortunes of war, as in the *Historia*, but by a lapse from noble prudence on the part of the Trojan prince himself (Hector exposes his breast to Achilles while greedily stripping a dead Greek of his armour):

> But out, allas! on fals couetyse!
> Whos gredy fret, the whiche is gret pite, [gnawing]
> In hertis may nat lightly staunchid be;
> The etyk gnaweth be so gret distresse, [hectic]
> That it diffaceth the highe worthines,
> Ful ofte sythe, of thies conquerours,
> And of her fame rent aweie the flours
> . . .
> Allas, why was he tho so rekeles,
> This flour of knyghthood, of manhod pereles,
> Whan that his fo, al that ilke day,
> For hym allone in a-wayte lay! [ambush]
> (III. 5354–60, 5383–86)

The significance of this moment is clear both from its placing and from the fact that (as David Benson has shown) Lydgate here shifts his source, translating not from Guido but from Christine de Pizan's *Epistre d'Othea*, another 'mirror for princes' which expounds a letter by the goddess of prudence, 'Othea', instructing Hector in just the virtue he here abandons.[15] After Hector's death, moreover, the ambivalence about war latent in many passages in the early books – one characteristic of the 'mirror for princes' tradition, and expected of a monk such as Lydgate – is pushed to the surface.[16] From here on, the poem is emphatic in its insistence on the brutality of war, and draws to a close with a lengthy prayer for peace (although this is now the peace of the early 1420s by which England's 'Hector' was hoping to consolidate the gains made at Agincourt). Thus if we view the poem as a refashioning of the *Historia* into a work of advice for its young royal reader, it emerges as a serious and crafted exposition of

Readers in Fifteenth-Century England, ed. by Derek Pearsall (Cambridge: Brewer, 1983), pp. 54–59, n. 57), the illustrated MSS of the work consistently emphasize these structural divisions, which are not paralleled in any extant copies of the *Historia*. The most obvious explanation for Lydgate's choice of structure is that it was intended to forge a link between *Troy Book* and *Troilus and Criseyde*.

15 Benson, *The History of Troy in Middle English Literature*, pp. 124–29.

16 For the implied 'pacifism' of much Middle English advice literature, see Harriss, introduction to *Henry V*, pp. 1–10; Lawton, 'Dullness and the Fifteenth Century', pp. 775–87.

princely virtue, and the dangers that threaten it. The apparent randomness of the reflections which Lydgate offers on the poem's events is not mere thoughtlessness, but an expression of the difficulties any of the maxims of advice literature encounter when faced with real situations. In effect, Lydgate dramatizes the *Secreta Secretorum* tradition in order to point up the dangerous gap between theory and practice. *Troy Book* is a far more complex and interesting poem than scholars generally suppose.

What, then, of its relation to *Troilus and Criseyde* and its attitude to Chaucer? On the face of it, Lydgate is here the confessedly derivative poet, tamely structuring his poem in the same five-book form as Chaucer, taking over the decasyllabic couplets of most of the *Canterbury Tales* and recycling much of Chaucer's imagery, syntax and vocabulary, and so on. Nor is his indebtedness surreptitious: among the most famous passages of *Troy Book* are those praising Chaucer as Lydgate's 'maistre', and swearing allegiance to his memory:

> For he owre englishe gilte with his sawes,
> Rude and boistous firste be olde dawes,
> That was ful fer from al perfeccioun
> And but of litel reputacioun
> Til that he cam, and thorugh his poetrie
> Gan oure tonge firste to magnifie
> And adourne it with his elloquence:
> To whom honour, laude and reuerence
> Thorugh-oute this londe youe be and songe,
> So that the laurer of oure englishe tonge
> Be to hym youe for his excellence
> . . .
> My maister Galfride, as for chefe poete
> That euere was yit in oure langage
> . . .
> And for my part I wil neuer fyne,
> So as I can, hym to magnifie
> In my writynge, pleinly, til I dye.
> (III. 4237–47, 4256–57, 4260–63)

This attitude of deference – expressed though it is in terms that leave Lydgate room for a high view of his own status[17] – has strategic import for

[17] Chaucer is praised as chief poet 'that euer was *yit*', while his achievement – that of *beginning* 'oure tonge firste to magnifie' – is implicitly taken over by Lydgate's own intention 'hym to magnifie in my writynge'. The double use of 'magnifie' brings out its ambiguity (it means both 'praise' and 'enlarge' or 'develop'; see also 'pleinly', which means both 'simply' and 'fully'), its alternative connotations expressing different relationships between the poets.

the poem's patriotic purpose of making the 'noble story' available in 'oure tonge'; the work's *auctor* may be Italian, but its true lodestar is a great English poet. Yet behind this deference, and partly undercutting it, lies a set of manoeuvres which position Chaucer and his Troy book differently. Not surprisingly, the point of attack is Lydgate's retelling of Guido's version of the story of Criseyde.

Like his own major source, Benoît's *Roman de Troie*, Guido regards the story of Criseyde (or 'Briseyde', as she is called by Benoît and Guido, though not Lydgate) as a minor repetition of the Troy narrative's main action, which is initiated by Paris' abduction of Helen, and has Medea's elopement with Jason (a vital episode of Lydgate's book I) as part of its past. Lydgate follows the *Historia* in regarding women as suspect by definition, and strengthens the metaphorical links Guido makes between their supposed falsity and several other phenomena: the sea-storms that punctuate the narrative; the figure of Fortune, which these storms also symbolize; death, decay, and the passage of time, which Lydgate refers to as 'the serpent of age' (prologue, l. 156); and the lying poets, who side with time in perverting memory of the past, prevented only by the vigilance of historians: 'For ner her writyng nowe memorial,/ Dethe with his swerde schulde haue slayen al' (prologue, ll. 171–72).[18] *Troy Book* thus views its memorializing of past heroism as being, *inter alia*, a counterattack against the baleful influence of women, fictions, and poets, and it is this structure of oppositions, as much as Lydgate's dependence on the misogynist Guido, that determines his treatment of the Criseyde narrative. Yet this sort of structure places Lydgate in an awkward relationship to his 'maister' Chaucer – for *Troilus and Criseyde*, whatever its final attitude to its heroine may be, is loud in expressions of sympathy for her. Moreover, Lydgate shares with Chaucer a powerful motive for appearing to be sympathetic towards women, the fact that he is writing a vernacular work that is immediately accessible to them in a

[18] Lydgate links these themes and phenomena mainly through the use of 'image sets'. Much of *Troy Book* is structured around oppositions between these forces of disharmony – to which can be added darkness, tarnishing (e.g., prologue, ll. 165, 173, 175), treachery, dishonour, infection (e.g., IV. ll. 2780–857) – and forces of harmony: heroism, nobility and prudence, brightness, calm and peace, health, mirrors, pageantry, the rhetorical high style, the process of poetic memorializing. A major purpose of many of Lydgate's expansions of Guido is the elaboration of these oppositional structures: see his account of Hector's embalming (with the aid of gold pipes) and enshrinement in a 'riche crafty tabernacle' (III. ll. 5579–764), which many fifteenth-century poets would condemn as a 'paynems corsed olde rite' (*Troilus and Criseyde*, V, l. 1849), but which here becomes a virtuoso figure, inscribed at the notional centre of *Troy Book*, of its own 'riche crafty' enshrinement of the Trojan past.

way that Guido's Latin is not.[19] Lydgate's handling of the Criseyde story is thus a test of his ability to mediate between a Latin source, a 'maister' whom it is in his interests to canonize, and a vernacular readership. His confidence in emphasizing rather than evading his difficulties, and ingenuity in playing off these competing interests against one another, go far towards explaining his success in establishing his credentials as the inheritor of Chaucer's mantle, a serious *auctor* in his own right.

Lydgate's retelling of the story of Criseyde follows the order of the *Historia*, being broken up into several episodes: book II contains a description of Criseyde; book III gives an account of her leaving Troy and Troilus, followed by a retrospective narration of the story of their love and a preview of her betrayal; and book IV describes her visits to Diomede's tent and abandonment of Troilus. But rather than translating Guido's Latin for these episodes, Lydgate ostentatiously turns to his 'maister', basing most of the first of Criseyde's appearances on parts of *Troilus and Criseyde*, and pretending to diffidence in describing her when Chaucer (whose death is lamented at length) has incomparably done so first (II, ll. 4677–735). The portrait of Criseyde which nonetheless follows is amplified from Chaucer (*Troilus and Criseyde*, V, ll. 806–26), but spiked with a few of Guido's less complimentary details (II, ll. 4760–62). For all the barrage of deference to Chaucer, the effect of introducing him as Lydgate's 'maister' at the moment Criseyde enters the poem is to initiate what remains a close association between him and one of *Troy Book*'s emblems of female falsity. Lydgate's awe of his 'maister' is tempered from the start by his contempt for Chaucer's 'mistress'.

The association between Chaucer and Criseyde is reinforced by the next mention of both figures, in book III. Here, Lydgate's account of Criseyde's departure from and love affair with Troilus is structured on Guido's, but mostly consists of an admiring thumbnail sketch of parts of *Troilus and Criseyde* (III, ll. 4186–263). Again, Lydgate ostensibly sides with his 'maister' against his *auctor* Guido, who at this point in the *Historia* launches into an anti-feminist tirade. Yet at the same time as *Troy Book* chastizes Guido for his views on women and purports to defend them against his calumnies, it first dutifully translates and even expands them. Moreover, Lydgate's defence, when it comes, proves to be a transparently parodic gesture of obedience to Chaucer's 'routhe':

[19] For discussions of the misogynistic digressions in *Troy Book*, and their humorous intent, see Torti, 'From "History" to "Tragedy" ', pp. 176–79 and Pearsall, *John Lydgate*, pp. 134–36.

> And though Guydo writ, thei [women] han of kynde
> To be double, men shulde it goodly take,
> And ther ageyn no maner grucching make:
> Nature in werkynge hath ful gret power,
> And it wer harde for any that is here
> The cours of hir to holden or restreyne
> . . .
> Therfore, eche man with al his fulle myght
> Shulde thanke God, and take paciently:
> For yif wommen be double naturelly,
> Why shulde men leyn on hem the blame?
> (III. 4398–403, 4406–09)

So, according to Lydgate, Guido blames women for falsity because he pays no attention to its basis in nature – he is *insufficiently essentialist*: when he 'mysseith' Criseyde, 'late him be with sorwe!' (III, l. 4416).

That *Troy Book* stands with Guido against Chaucer and his pity for Criseyde becomes finally clear in book IV's account of her acceptance of Diomede, where Lydgate no longer keeps up any pretence of sympathy, condemning her in a powerful passage of original verse:

> Loo! what pite is in wommanhede,
> What mercy eke and benygne routhe –
> That newly can al her olde trouthe,
> Of nature, late slyppe a-syde
> Rather thanne thei shulde se abide
> Any man in meschef for hir sake!
> . . .
> Daunger is noon but counterfet disdeyn;
> The se is calme and fro rokkis pleyn:
> For mercyles neuer man ne deide
> That soughte grace! – recorde of Cryseyde . . .
> (IV. 2148–53, 2161–64)

Chaucer is not mentioned during this episode, but Lydgate's aggression is all but overtly turned against him too: it is the narrator in *Troilus and Criseyde*, who has excused Criseyde by using the language of 'pite' and 'routhe', that is here so firmly exposed as merely a set of synonyms for 'female lechery'.

Lydgate does purport to refashion a positive image of women, mainly by praising virginity and claiming Criseyde, Medea, Helen are untypical – few in number set beside, for example, the eleven thousand virgins of Cologne (III, ll. 4370–97). But by letting his indignation at Criseyde emerge through an elaborately respectful retelling of Chaucer, Lydgate manages to imply two different things: that, thanks to Chaucer, *Troy Book* can be part of a real literary tradition; and that, as a result of Chaucer's doubtful moral allegiances, his own poem improves on *Troilus and Criseyde*. Chaucer, who is scarcely mentioned in *Troy Book* except in association with Criseyde,[20] is inexorably linked with the group of themes connected with that of 'false women'. He is shown to be aligned not with the true 'auctours vs-beforn' whom Lydgate is following, but with the lying poets, Ovid and Homer, who share Criseyde's susceptibility to falsity, frivolity and change. In pitying Criseyde, *Troy Book* strongly implies, Chaucer has fallen prey to a weakness dangerously analogous to the one embodied by Criseyde: he has been seduced by a beautifully adorned lie.

The weight of this charge becomes clear when we look at how the Criseyde story is positioned within the five-book structure which Lydgate perhaps borrowed from Chaucer. Its two main episodes in books III and IV are divided by long scenes of fighting and political debate, and by the poem's most important incident, the death of Hector. This is lamented at length, in a passage which rewrites part of Chaucer's opening invocation to the furies (*Troilus and Criseyde*, I, ll. 1–14) in a context clearly meant to lend it a new moral seriousness:

> To hem [the muses], allas! I clepe dar nor crye,
> My troubled penne of grace for to guye –
> Nouther to Clyo nor Callyope,
> But to Allecto and Thesyphone,
> And Megera that euere doth compleine,
> As thei that lyve euere in wo and peyne
> Eternally, and in turment dwelle
> With Cerberus depe doun in helle,
> Whom I mote praie to be gracious
> To my mater, whiche is so furious.
> For to a whight that is compleynynge,
> A drery fere is right wel sittynge;
> And to a mater meynt with hevynes
> Acordeth wel a chere of drerynes . . . (III. 5443–56)[21]

[20] The exception is V. ll. 3521–30, where Chaucer's kindness about the work of other poets is used to plead for a tolerant reception for *Troy Book*. The humble conclusion here, that nobody is alive worthy 'his ynkhorn for to holde', characteristically doubles as a threat: there is also unlikely to be anyone alive (in spite of V. ll. 3531–39) worthy to criticize Lydgate.

[21] See Chaucer's Thesiphone 'sorwynge euere in peyne', and 'ffor wel sit it, the sothe for to seyne,/ A woful wight to han a drery feere,/ And to a sorwful tale a sory cheere' (ll. 9–14).

Here, Lydgate implies, in the wasted death of a heroic prince, not in the erotic fiction of *Troilus and Criseyde*, lies true tragedy (see III, l. 5440). *Troilus and Criseyde* excludes the larger action of the siege of Troy from consideration, addressing itself to an audience of noble lovers who are sent elsewhere for information about what comes to seem the unimportant military action surrounding Criseyde and Troilus' love (*Troilus and Criseyde*, I, ll. 141–47). *Troy Book* asserts the opposite priorities. The climax of its five-book structure is occupied not by a scene of love-making but a moral and military disaster, while the love story is an unimportant digression from the action which Lydgate dismisses with a shrug: 'her-of no more' (IV, ll. 2178). Even Troilus seems little affected by his loss of Criseyde, fighting not to avenge it but to defend his homeland; his anger at Diomede is momentary.[22] In short, *Troy Book* imitates the structure and tragic tone of *Troilus and Criseyde*, but displaces it as a major historical poem by pushing its narrative to the periphery of its own sphere of interest, and by exposing its concerns as finally unworthy of the reader's attention.

Modern readers of Chaucer and Lydgate, used to treating one with reverence, the other almost with scorn, may find the intertextual relation I have sketched and the ambition that underlies it to be merely amusing, more evidence of the later poet's inability fully to plumb even his own inadequacy. Yet as a version of the 'outdoing' topos which I began by exemplifying from Dante, Lydgate's aggression towards Chaucer can be justified as the inevitable response of an aspiring poet to any revered *auctor*, particularly the founding father of an entire vernacular tradition: a response which English poets indeed had to learn to make if they were to benefit from Chaucer's example. Moreover, the displacement of *Troilus and Criseyde* can also be taken as a necessary gesture within *Troy Book*'s role as mirror for princes. From the viewpoint of the early fifteenth century, the courtly productions of the Ricardian era must have seemed dangerously aestheticized, lacking in the rigour that Henry V strove to embody; *Troilus and Criseyde*, with its brilliant and diverse sympathies, was a clear case in point.[23] Lydgate's task in *Troy Book*, one

[22] In IV, ll. 2051–73, before Criseyde's last appearance, Troilus' attack on Diomede is out of envy (ll. 2064–66), but this is the only time love forces its way onto the field. By IV, ll. 2254–344 Troilus and Diomede are fighting like anyone else – for all that this scene ends (l. 2344) by repeating Pandarus' praise of Troilus as 'Ector the secounde' (*Troilus and Criseyde*, II, l. 158).

[23] For Henry V's 'moral rigour', see Harriss, *Henry V*, pp. 201–10 (Harriss' conclusion), and (for its religious manifestations) chapter 5, 'Religious Change under Henry V', by Jeremy Catto; an early account of his life which emphasizes this same rigour is *The First Life of King Henry the Fifth*, ed. by C. L. Kingsford (Oxford: Clarendon Press, 1911). For discussions of Ricardian court culture which stress its coterie nature, see *English Court*

proper to a monk, seems to have been to reinstate the matter of Troy as something from which moral truths could again be learned: to point the way back from a mere 'enditinge of worldly vanitee' – as Chaucer himself calls *Troilus and Criseyde* in his 'Retractions' – which seemingly incites young male readers to imitate Troilus' earthly passions, and direct their minds instead towards the serious affairs of knighthood and government. The stories of Prince Hal's conversion from unruly youth to responsible ruler which Shakespeare adapted for his two *Henry IV* plays may be legendary, but express something of contemporary perceptions of his personality (few monarchs but the most earnest are accorded their own conversion story).[24] *Troy Book*, I suggest, effects a comparable transformation to the matter of Troy and the manner of English poetry. It aims to institutionalize the moralizing temper of Henry's sensibility, and of contemporary poets such as Gower, within the cosmopolitan, elaborate and aristocratic *stil nuovo* that Lydgate and his contemporaries considered was Chaucer's major legacy to them.[25] Given the exegencies of this moral agenda, 'my maister Chaucer', that kindly genius who stares out at us so inoffensively from *Troy Book*'s epilogue (V, ll. 3521–30) or the pages of Hoccleve's *Regement of Princes*,[26] must from the beginning be a carefully contained figure.

Lydgate straitjackets Chaucer by praising him in a public voice, while in private allowing the implication to grow that he should be numbered among the lying poets whose retellings of the matter of Troy pervert the truth. My other example of the 'outdoing' of *Troilus and Criseyde*, Henryson's *Testament of Cresseid* – which tells how, after being abandoned by Diomede, Cresseid curses the gods and is smitten with leprosy in punishment, then meets Troilus by chance and dies repenting her wickedness when he fails to recognize her – adopts the opposite strategy. The *Testament* is a critique of Chaucer – of his failure to treat his heroine with rigorous justice – whose author legitimizes his own poetic voice by exploiting the very features of *Troilus and Criseyde* he seems to criticize.

Culture in the Later Middle Ages, ed. by V. J. Scattergood and J. W. Sherborne (London: Duckworth, 1983).

24 Both contemporary and later commentators frequently interpret the snow-storm which accompanied Henry's coronation on April 9, 1413 as a sign that he had put aside the winter of an apparently riotous youth. For references, see Charles Lethbridge Kingsford, *English Historical Literature* (New York: Franklin, 1962; orig. pub., 1913), pp. 65–66.

25 See Pearsall, *John Lydgate*, chapter 2, 'Chaucer and the Literary Background', and the tributes to Chaucer as rhetorician in Spurgeon, *Five Hundred Years of Chaucer Criticism*.

26 See *Hoccleve's Regement of Princes*, p. 180, st. 714, where Hoccleve inserts a portrait of Chaucer into his poem; for analysis, see Jeanne E. Krochalis, 'Hoccleve's Chaucer Portrait', *Chaucer Review*, 21 (1985), 120–32.

On one level, the poem insists on the moralistic attitude towards Criseyde which Chaucer's narrator suspends and which *Troy Book* adopts for its own ends; that Cresseid pronounces her own condemnation (having achieved, in the eyes of some scholars, a belated tragic dignity)[27] only twists the knife in the wound. But on another level, the *Testament* is as ambiguous in its attitudes as anything Chaucer ever wrote: the status of narrator, narrative and *moralitas* are all left open, in an act of poetic virtuosity that is a challenge both to Chaucer and, perhaps, to the historiographic tradition of *Troy Book*.[28] There is real logic behind the poem's fate in Thynne's 1532 edition of Chaucer's works where, half a century after its composition, it made the first of its many appearances as Chaucer's own epilogue to *Troilus and Criseyde*.[29]

The *Testament* has been more satisfactorily analysed than has *Troy Book*,[30] and my discussion can thus be focused on the specific issues raised by the transition to the poem's main narrative from its frame. After an opening imitation of the first lines of *Troilus and Criseyde*,[31] the frame sets a puzzle by first calling the poem a 'tragedie' (l. 3), a historical genre in the Middle Ages, then proceeding both to use and to differ from many of the topoi associated with the fictional genre of secular dream poetry.[32] There is a narrator praying to Venus, but here an old man (like Amans in Gower's *Confessio Amantis*), who (unlike Amans) is not in love but wants to be; there is a spring setting, which takes place at night during a hailstorm; and there is a symbolic set of planetary conjunctions, which

27 See, e.g. Spearing, *Medieval to Renaissance*, pp. 165–87. There is a high level of critical disagreement about most aspects of the *Testament*, including this one: for this disagreement, and an attempt to explain it, see Malcolm Pittock, 'The Complexity of Henryson's *The Testament of Cresseid*', *Essays in Criticism*, 40 (1990), 198–221.

28 It has not been established that Henryson knew *Troy Book*, but there can be no doubt that he was familiar either with it or with another form of Guido's *Historia*. See Gretchen Mieszkowsi, 'The Reputation of Criseyde, 1155–1500', *Transactions of the Connecticut Academy of Arts and Sciences*, 43 (1971), 71–153.

29 The *Testament* circulated as part of Chaucer's poem for three hundred years, in spite of periodic claims that it was not his. See *The Poems of Robert Henryson*, ed. by Denton Fox (Oxford: Clarendon Press, 1981), pp. xciv–xcv, cii–civ (all quotations from the *Testament* are taken from this edition; *yogh* is normalized as y, punctuation slightly modified).

30 For bibliography to 1980, see Fox's edition; more than twenty studies have been published since then.

31 'Ane doolie sessoun to ane cairfull dyte/ Suld correspond and be equiualent' (ll. 1–2). See note 21 for the source passage, and above for Lydgate's version of it.

32 For the topoi of dream poetry, see A. C. Spearing, *Medieval Dream Poetry* (Cambridge: Cambridge University Press, 1976). For tragedy as a historical genre, see Paul Strohm, '*Story*, *Spelle*, *Geste*, *Romaunce*, *Tragedie*: Generic Distinctions in Middle English Troy Narratives', *Speculum*, 46 (1971), 348–59.

can never occur.[33] When the narrator leaves his oratory to sit by a fire, pour himself a drink, and read in a 'quair' containing *Troilus and Criseyde* – 'Writtin be worthie Chaucer glorious' (l. 41) – he does so 'to cut the winter nicht and mak it schort' (l. 39), like the dreamer in *The Book of the Duchess* with his book. But after putting this book down, the narrator does not fall asleep as he would in a dream poem, but rather, 'to *brek* my sleip', takes up a mysterious 'uther quair' (l. 61), in which he discovers what is recounted in the rest of the poem, about 'the fatall destenie/ Of fair Cresseid, that endit wretchitlie' (ll. 62–63). These mixed generic signals – a dream poem that is not a dream poem, a tragedy that is not a history – are all-important to the pivotal stanza that follows:

> Quha wait gif all that Chauceir wrait was trew?
> Nor I wait nocht gif this narratioun
> Be authoreist, or fenyeit of the new
> Be sum poeit, throw his inuentioun
> Maid to report the lamentatioun
> And wofull end of this lustie Creisseid,
> And quhat distres scho thoillit, and quhat deid. [suffered]
> (64–70)

What this stanza does on a simple level is to assure us that, in spite of the use of the word 'tragedie', we are not too far from the world of the dream poem, for the narrative we are to enter is not an 'authoreist' history but a fiction: 'I wait nocht' is transparent, and intended to be so. In a nice inversion of the usual relationship between poet and narrator, the latter introduces us to 'sum poeit' who has contrived an original ending to Cresseid's story: the stanza is an indirect poetic vaunt. Yet this claim to novelty is more daring than it appears, for by making it of a 'tragic' narrative whose context is historical, Henryson defines himself exactly as one of the 'lying poets' castigated by Guido and Lydgate; he is boasting of his intention to taint history with fiction. Thus the challenge issued in the first line of the stanza, 'Quha wait gif all that Chauceir wrait was trew?' is radically ambiguous. On the one hand, it insinuates Lydgate's point, that Chaucer's relations with the 'false' Cresseid renders his poem suspect, and leaves room for 'new' treatments; Henryson shoulders aside the care with which Chaucer leaves her fate suspended, and imposes on her a poetic closure in which she is confronted at last with her own 'truth'. Yet, on the other hand, Henryson is 'authorizing' his own fictional 'tragedie' by sheltering behind a reading of *Troilus and Criseyde* as

[33] See Fox, *Poems of Henryson*, p. 341, note to *Testament*, ll. 11–14; see pp. xcii–xciii for the more general confusion of the seasons in the poem.

fiction: if Chaucer invents parts of his 'litel [. . .] tragedye' (*Troilus and Criseyde*, V, l. 1786) – with its appeals to the pseudo-authority Lollius and access to the private spaces of its characters' lives – then surely 'sum poeit' can follow.[34] In short, at the moment its authority is being challenged, *Troilus and Criseyde* is also being invoked to legitimize the writing of fictions that are set in the waking world of history and 'unauthorized' except as products of the 'feigning' poetic imagination. The stanza is a declaration of poetic independence of a peculiarly dependent kind.[35]

Henryson's sense of Chaucer as his literary 'master' is thus at once more complicated and less fraught than Lydgate's, his dependence seen less as burden, more as opportunity; in spite of a challenge to the older writer, 'Chauceir' and 'sum poeit' indeed emerge from this stanza as colleagues, not as senior and junior ('poeit' is a term of dignity). One reason for this contrast with Lydgate is no doubt Henryson's distance in time and space from Chaucer, but more important is the radical divide between the two later writers' attitudes towards poetry itself, viewed by Lydgate as a tool of institutional morality and by Henryson as a way of scrutinizing such morality. Where Lydgate makes room for his own poetic voice by exposing the moral ambiguity of *Troilus and Criseyde*, Henryson therefore takes the opposite approach of widening the ambiguity as much as possible (and it is here Lydgate himself may be numbered among the *Testament*'s targets). This approach becomes clear in the stanzas following that just quoted, which repay detailed analysis:

> Quhen Diomeid had all his appetyte,
> And mair, fulfillit of this fair ladie,
> Vpon ane vther he set his haill delyte,
> And send to hir ane lybell of repudie [declaration]
> And hir excludit fra his companie.
> Than desolait scho walkit vp and doun,
> And, sum men sayis, into the court, commoun.
>
> O fair Creisseid, the flour and A per se
> Of Troy and Grece, how was thow fortunait
> To change in filth all thy feminitie,

[34] It may be that this point should be made differently, by stressing that 'Quha wait gif all that Chauceir wrait was trew?' implies that some of *Troilus and Criseyde* is historical, while (as the rest of the stanza makes clear) all of the *Testament* is 'feigning'. If we read the stanza like this, Henryson's 'sheltering' of his poem behind Chaucer conceals another boast, that by writing pure fiction he is showing more imaginative independence than Chaucer.

[35] For helpful treatments of this stanza, see Pittock, 'The Complexity of Henryson's *Testament of Cresseid*', pp. 206–09, and Alicia K. Nitecki, ' "Fenyeit of the New": Authority in *The Testament of Cresseid*', *Journal of Narrative Technique*, 15 (1985), 120–32.

And be with fleschelie lust sa maculait
And go amang the Greikis air and lait, [early]
Sa giglotlike takand thy foull plesance! [wantonly]
I haue pietie thow suld fall sic mischance!

Yit neuertheles, quhat euer men deme or say
In scornefull langage of thy brukkilnes, [weakness]
I sall excuse, als far furth as I may,
Thy womanheid, thy wisdome and fairnes,
The quhilk fortoun hes put to sic distres
As hir pleisit, and nathing throw the gilt
Of the – throw wickit langage to be spilt! (71–91)

In one sense, this is a Lydgatian passage, which parodies the compassion of Chaucer's narrator in the manner of *Troy Book*'s comic attacks on Guido's misogyny; the pity Henryson's narrator expresses for Cresseid is doomed in advance by the way the story has been stacked against her. But where the humour of *Troy Book* is a veneer over misogynistic didacticism, this passage actively scrutinizes the relationship between moralizing commentator and moralized woman, in a manner antipathetic to Lydgate's view of his authority as poet and more challenging of Chaucer than any of Lydgate's criticisms. For Henryson's complicated framing of Cresseid's story holds a mirror up to the process by which her character has been formed by a succession of men: a process in which Lydgate, Chaucer and he himself are implicated. The 'unauthorized' second 'quair' tells of how Diomede repudiates 'this lustie Cresseid' by letter (as though to temper its 'unauthorized' status, the *Testament* is full of statements written down by its characters)[36] when he finds his desire for her sated, leaving her to 'walk up and down', a victim of ever more overt sexual innuendos. The truth of what 'sum men sayis' about Cresseid's promiscuity – whether their comments even appear in the 'quair', which later contradicts what is here asserted, and which can anyhow make no legitimate claims for its veracity – remains very dubious.[37] Not so, however, to

[36] See also Cresseid's 'testament' (ll. 577–91), and the epitaph for Cresseid (ll. 607–09), which 'sum said' Troilus wrote for her (l. 603).

[37] There is evidence within the poem that the narrative in the 'vther quair' does not sustain the rumours of Cresseid's promiscuity. After the apostrophe, the narrative continues with Cresseid's departure for Calkas' mansion, as though Diomede's rejection has just occurred: 'This fair lady, in this wyse destitute/ Of all comfort and consolatioun/ Richt priuelie, but fellowschip or refute,/ Disagysit passit far out of the toun' (ll. 92–95). Later, when she declines to visit Venus's temple, she does so to avoid 'hir expuls fra Diomeid the king' being known 'of the pepill' (ll. 118–19), one of her many inexorably exposed attempts to avoid public exposure. It is hard to see either how she had time for promiscuity or prostitution, or how she could practise either while still retaining the public dignity she here clings to.

the narrator, who in the next stanzas (which I assume contain his reflections on the 'quair', not part of it) fastens fervidly on their euphemistic gossip, and transforms it into a scenario in which Cresseid features not as victim but as sexual predator, 'takand [her] foull plesance'. 'Thocht lufe be hait, yit in ane man of age/ It kendillis nocht sa sone as in youtheid' (ll. 29–30), the narrator has confessed, before turning to the two 'quairs' which he hopes will help his sluggish amatory juices to flow; but already the only difference between himself and Diomede is that his invention of Cresseid as erotic object has not yet spent itself. His apostrophe is a fine display of the variety of male sexual 'plesance' to be gained from reading or writing about Cresseid: from that of erotic language ('fleschelie lust sa maculait') to that of moralistic fervour ('to change in filth all thy feminitie'), or from that of imagining her sins (she goes among the Greeks 'air and lait') to that of excusing them, 'quhat euer men deme or say'. By combining in one series of perverse excitements the attitudes to Cresseid of a Diomede, a sentimental Chaucerian narrator and a Lydgate, these stanzas reveal all of them – lust, pity, and moralizing judgement – as equally the products of the fantasizing male imagination.

What gives this passage a biting relevance from our present perspective is its juxtaposition with the stanza about the *Testament*'s fictionality, for it is this juxtaposition which enables Henryson to complete the chain of male commentators who have combined to make and unmake Cresseid, by including Chaucer, perhaps Lydgate, and himself among them. If 'sum men', including the narrator, have shared in the pleasure of inventing stories about Cresseid which attribute to her their own desires, no one has done this with so much at stake as her poets. After all, Henryson's fiction owes its existence to his willingness to tell falsities about the false Cresseid of 'history', and thus to take part in the process of fantasizing he so subtly exposes. Unlike the narrator, he is not using Cresseid for sexual ends, but he is certainly using her, both as the basis of his self-invention as a writer of fictions, and as the conduit for a transfer of authority between his poetic source Chaucer and himself. His poetic lies, like those of Chaucer (for which both hope to gain the fame that is the reward of poets), rest on the lying scandals other men have spread about her putative lies, for which she has gained only infamy. In a passage Henryson partly dramatizes here, Chaucer has her lamenting her lost 'name of trouthe' and fearfully anticipating how 'thise bokes wol me shende', before himself grieving that 'Hir name, allas, is punysshed so wide' (*Troilus and Criseyde*, V, ll. 1055, 1060, 1095) and insisting on his eagerness to forgive her (ll. 1097–99). At the root of the *Testament*'s 'outdoing' of its source is the perception that Chaucer's attempt to make his book supportive of its heroine, rather than adding to her 'punishment', is partly disingenuous, since as a fiction-maker he has as much at stake in her falsity as any moralizing writer such as Lydgate could possibly have. Lydgate, and the historiographic tradition that he represents, conceals the dependence of his own ethical structure – one which conceives of truth as ordered, noble, strong, and male – on the very principles of disorder, weakness, femininity he castigates; there is no room in *Troy Book*'s discourse for the recognitions that would be involved in acknowledging such dependence. Henryson's point – one similar in some respects to recent feminist analyses of *Troilus and Criseyde*, which have taught us much about the masculism of the poem's viewpoint[38] – is that Chaucer is not as different here from Lydgate as we would expect, for he glosses over both the extent of his own connivance at the picture of Cresseid that he inherited and the fact that neither he nor anyone who tells her story can avoid exploiting her, so wholly is she now a product of what 'sum men sayis'. To pretend otherwise, for these complicated stanzas, is to fall into the diffuse sentimentality of the *Testament*'s narrator: a trap Henryson himself, with his systematic exposure of the interests, strategies and lies which are at the heart of his own and his predecessors' poetic projects, avoids. The *Testament* is not a feminist poem in its depiction of male-female power relations, any more than it is a socialist one in its depiction of an underclass of lepers; neither phenomenon is viewed as capable of change, and Henryson's own interests are with the *status quo*. But as the weather at the poem's outset signals, it is a poem which promotes an icily clear vision of both poetry and reality: 'The northin wind had purifyit the air/ And sched the mistie cloudis fra the sky' (ll. 15–16). As the 'northin wind' blows the warmer spring clouds from the sky, so Henryson displaces Chaucer's compassion with a cold, clear dispassion.

Scholarly discussion of the 'Chaucerian' poets of the fifteenth century often treats them as a source of near-contemporary 'views' of Chaucer, interpreting the poetry as, in effect, a body of secondary literature with no independent interest. Even exceptional works like the *Testament* are praised as outstanding exercises in *reading*, while notionally bad ones, like *Troy Book*, serve to cast our own subtler understanding of the master poet in a reassuringly bright light. My argument here can be reduced to this: that fifteenth-century poets did not merely try and fail to imitate what they thought Chaucer had done, they tried to show and do what he had not done, and thus to make room for their own ambitions. Competition is the sincerest form of literary flattery, and also the most revealing:

38 See Dinshaw, *Chaucer's Sexual Poetics*, chapter 1 and Elaine Tuttle Hansen, *Chaucer and the Fictions of Gender* (Berkeley: University of California Press, 1992), chapter 6.

witness the struggles of poets from Pope to Keats to assimilate the inspiring but debilitating influence of *Paradise Lost*. In the fifteenth century, competition with 'master' Chaucer was as established a mode as imitation, if the two can truly be distinguished. Indeed, there are signs that taking issue with *Troilus and Criseyde* was something of a topos. Besides the poems examined here, there is the case of John Walton's poetic Boethius, whose 'outdoing' of Chaucer has recently been analysed by Ian Johnson.[39] There is also that of John Metham's *Amoryus and Cleopes*, a version of the Pyramus and Thisbe story with many allusions to *Troilus and Criseyde* – apparently serving the purpose of justifying its intense interest in astrology and the 'heathen' past – which piously ends by having the entire cast (the two principals having first been resurrected) convert to Christianity, as though in condemnation of Chaucer's sympathetic depiction of 'payens corsed olde rites' (*Troilus and Criseyde*, V, l. 1849).[40] To understand more fully this body of poetry and its relationship with Chaucer's, we need to look at how and why it differs from him, to understand its reading of his work as in the root sense *interested* reading, and take its high hopes for itself seriously. My own high hope is that this paper has shown something of what might be gained by adopting such an approach.[41]

[39] See John Walton, *Boethius: De Consolatione Philosophiae* (1410), ed. by Mark Science, EETS, os 170 (Oxford, 1927), and Ian Johnson, *'This Brigous Questioun'*.

[40] *The Works of John Metham*, ed. by Hardin Craig, EETS, os 132 (Oxford, 1916). *Amoryus and Cleopes* is written in rime royal in four books, three with prologues in the style of *Troilus and Criseyde* (e.g. ll. 1024–30), the first being a direct (and metrically disastrous) imitation of Chaucer's opening (ll. 1–7). The poem includes a scene in which Amoryus sees Cleopes in a temple, as Troilus does Criseyde, and ends by listing Criseyde (most unusually) among the virtuous classical women (l. 2172), and praising both Chaucer and Lydgate. Its imitation and implied criticism of *Troilus and Criseyde* has apparently not been previously noted.

[41] Since this article was finished in June, 1992, three studies of immediate relevance to it have been published: Barbara Nolan, *Chaucer and the Tradition of the 'Roman Antique'* (Cambridge: Cambridge University Press, 1992), which provides much useful commentary on the background from which both Chaucer's and Lydgate's texts emerged; Paul Strohm, *Hochon's Arrow: The Social Imagination of Fourteenth-Century Texts* (Princeton: Princeton University Press, 1992), which has a fine account of the cultural transition between Ricardian and Lancastrian England; and Seth Lerer, *Chaucer and His Readers: Imagining the Author in Late-Medieval England* (Princeton: Princeton University Press, 1993). I should also have noted an earlier article by Strohm, his 'Chaucer's Fifteenth-Century Audience and the Narrowing of the "Chaucer Tradition",' *Studies in the Age of Chaucer* 4 (1982), 3–32.

Transpositions of Dreams to Reality in Middle High German Narratives[1]

ALBRECHT CLASSEN

IN RECENT YEARS literary scholarship has rediscovered the particular value of dreams within medieval culture. In the Middle Ages dreams were generally viewed as reflections of a higher reality, and their study and interpretation were considered to be a crucial means by which to reach a heightened understanding of one's existence.[2] The dream was not only (as we tend to think today, influenced as we are by Freudian and Jungian traditions) a reflection of the unconscious or of archetypes, but it served primarily as a vehicle to communicate with God, Fate, Fortune, and other extra-human forces. Within the dream the individual could encounter both his/her self and his/her destiny. The literature of the Middle Ages reflects this fascination with the dream, but we have only just begun to understand the importance of dreams for medieval man.[3] One way of defining the difference between the modern and medieval periods is to emphasise the contrasting approaches to dreams in each age. It is safe to say that dreams were considered to be real phenomena in the

[1] Dear Elspeth, with this paper I should like to express my thanks for your exceptional and inspiring teaching methods in the study of medieval literature and for showing me how to appreciate fully its beauty. If I ever had a teacher who taught me to understand the true value of comparative and interdisciplinary studies, it was you. Your absolutely unique seminars at St Hilda's made my two-year graduate studies in Oxford from 1982 to 1984 worthwhile. Thank you.

[2] There are a number of ways to interpret the function of dreams in medieval literature. In a related article I have outlined, on the basis of similar or related material, a different reading; see 'Die narrative Funktion des Traumes in mittelhochdeutscher Literatur', forthcoming in *Mediaevistik*, 5.

[3] See *I sogni nel medioevo. Seminario internazionale, Roma, 2–4 ottobre 1983*, ed. by Tullio Gregory, Lessico Intellettuale Europeo, 35 (Rome: Edizioni dell'Ateneo, 1985).

Middle Ages, whereas we are more likely to see in them a document of our unconscious.[4]

My concern in this paper is with concrete and visually realistic dreams, that is non-religious dreams or visions, dreams which the protagonists experience in their physical existence.[5] The narrative meanings of the protagonists' dreams will be investigated, along with their function in terms of their structural and thematic impact. What happens to the dreamer during and after the dream? Why is he/she dreaming? What is the purpose of the dream within its literary context?[6]

It is a remarkable fact that a high proportion of medieval texts contain dream-motifs.[7] Also, in many cases when the main characters fall asleep the narrative is interrupted by a form of authorial commentary, although the narrator might not step in to interpret the dream or the events leading up to the dream as such. The content of the dream provides the necessary information for the reader/listener to comprehend the message. Often, however, we can observe that the protagonists are the worst interpreters of their own dreams, sometimes because they refuse to understand the meaning, sometimes because they are not in a position to decode the signs contained in the dream.[8]

4 See *The Oxford Book of Dreams*, ed. by Stephen Brook (Oxford: Oxford University Press, 1987) and Peter Burke, 'L'histoire sociale des rêves', *Annales. Economies – Sociétés – Civilisations*, 28 (1973), 329–42.

5 Regarding mystical visions in the Middle Ages see *Visionary Literature*, ed. by Elizabeth Alvilda Petroff (Oxford: Oxford University Press, 1986), pp. 5ff.; *Mittelalterliche Visionsliteratur. Eine Anthologie* ed. and trans. by Peter Dinzelbacher (Darmstadt: Wissenschaftliche Buchgesellschaft, 1989); E. Benz, *Die Vision. Erfahrungsformen und Bilderwelt* (Stuttgart: Klett, 1969), and P. Dinzelbacher, 'Körperliche und seelische Vorbedingungen religiöser Träume und Visionen', in *I sogni nel medioevo*, pp. 57–86.

6 I shall not be including in my discussion allegorical dreams such as Dante's *Divina Commedia*, Guillaume de Lorris' and Jean de Meun's *Roman de la Rose*, Chaucer's *House of Fame* and Boccaccio's *Amorosa Visione*, among many others. They belong to a different genre and have received sufficient scholarly attention in the last few years; see A. C. Spearing, *Medieval Dream-Poetry* (Cambridge: Cambridge University Press, 1976); J. Stephen Russell, *The English Dream Vision. Anatomy of a Form* (Columbus: Ohio State University Press, 1988). Similarly I am not here concerned with the tradition of dream books and the equation between individual dreams and their literary models; see Steven R. Fischer, *The Complete Medieval Dreambook. A Multilingual, Alphabetical 'Somnia Danielis' Collation* (Bern-Frankfurt a. M.: Lang, 1982).

7 See Steven R. Fischer, *The Dream in the Middle High German Epic. Introduction to the Study of the Dream as a Literary Device to the Younger Contemporaries of Gottfried and Wolfram*, Australian and New Zealand Studies in German Language and Literature, 10 (Bern-Frankfurt a. M.: Lang, 1978), and Alice Cornelia Loftin, 'Vision', *Dictionary of the Middle Ages*, ed. by Joseph R. Strayer, vol. 12 (New York: Scribner, 1989), 475–78.

8 See, for a modern perspective on this problem, Zygmunt A. Piotrowski, *Dreams, a Key to Self-Knowledge* (Hillsdale, NJ: L. Erlbaum, 1986); Ernest Lawrence Rossi, *Dreams and the Growth of Personality. Expanding Awareness in Psychotherapy*, 2nd edn, Pergamon General Psychology Series, 26 (New York: Brunner/Mazel, 1985).

It does not really matter which literary genre we consult regarding the functions of dreams and their interpretation, since lyric poetry, the heroic epic, and the courtly romance freely play with this motif. The *Nibelungenlied*, for instance, presents several important dreams, which highlight both the future development of the plot and the position which the protagonists are going to assume in future events. Kriemhild experiences a frightening dream, a nightmare, long before she has, it seems, reached puberty.[9] Her night vision is closely linked with her public honour: 'in disen hôhen êren tróumte Kriemhildè' (13, 1,)[10] and associated with the prime symbol of courtly love, the falcon: 'wie si zügc cinen valken' (13, 2).[11] As expected, this bird excels both through its beauty and wildness: 'stárc scóen' und wildè' (13, 2) which are characteristic aspects of courtly culture. Beauty stands for the highest ideals of *minne* and the devotion of a chivalric knight to his beloved mistress, whereas 'wildness' represents a utopian concept both within and outside courtly society, and the danger inherent in courtly love. Only lovers accept the idea of 'wildness' and live, metaphorically speaking, in a forest far away from the court. Examples of this are Tristan and Isolde in Gottfried von Straßburg's *Tristan* (love cave), Sigûne and Schionatulander in Wolfram von Eschenbach's *Titurel*, and we can even refer to the allegorical lover Amans in Guillaume de Lorris' *Roman de la Rose*, who encounters the 'wild' within the cultivated garden as a barrier between himself and the Rose, the object of his love.[12] In other words, by dreaming and envisioning the wild as a threatening force, Kriemhild participates, quite unconsciously and also unwillingly, in the sophisticated courtly culture of her time. The poet positions her by means of her dream within the context of *Minnesang* and thus indicates, in clear contrast to the expectations raised by the heroic genre, that courtly ideals of suffering and joy, of beauty and courtly education will have their impact on the female

[9] For nightmares in the Middle Ages, see Claude Lecouteux, 'Mara – Ephialtes – Incubus. Le cauchemar chez les peuples germaniques', *Etudes Germaniques*, 42 (1987), 1–24.

[10] Quoted from *Das Nibelungenlied*, ed. by Helmut de Boor, based on the edn by Karl Bartsch, 13th rev. edn, Deutsche Klassiker des Mittelalters (Wiesbaden: Brockhaus, 1956).

[11] See Helmut Birkhan, 'Wie kam die Falknerei nach Europa?', *Zeitschrift für Jagdwissenschaft*, 18 (1972), 152–66; for an updated bibliography on this topic, see Otfrid Ehrismann, *Nibelungenlied. Epoche – Werk – Wirkung*, Arbeitsbücher zur Literaturgeschichte (Munich: Beck, 1987), pp. 93ff.

[12] See Guillaume de Lorris and Jean de Meun, *The Romance of the Rose* trans. by Harry W. Robbings, ed., and with an introduction by Charles W. Dunn (New York: Dutton, 1962), p. 37, ll. 1767ff. and Christian Schmidt-Cadalbert, 'Der wilde Wald. Zur Darstellung und Funktion eines Raumes in der mhdt. Literatur', in *Gotes und der werlde hulde. Literatur in Mittelalter und Neuzeit. Festschrift für Heinz Rupp zum 70. Geburtstag*, ed. by Rüdiger Schnell (Bern-Stuttgart: Francke, 1989), pp. 24–47.

protagonist in the *Nibelungenlied*. Whatever the meaning of Kriemhild's dream, it clearly summarizes and epitomizes many of the later tragic events in her life; the dream is a reflection of herself and also a distorted mirror image.[13] Kriemhild's insecurity and helplessness in the face of her dream are of similar significance. She turns to her mother Uote for advice, yet she is not able to penetrate the deeper meaning of the dream either: 'sine kúndes niht besceiden baz der gúotèn' (14, 2) and informs her only that the falcon symbolizes her future lover. This falcon might escape her, however, if she does not take good care of him: 'du muost in sciere vloren hân' (14, 4,). The author seems to have been aware of the falcon image employed by Der von Kürenberg in his love poetry,[14] and may have alluded to his contemporary's work in order to encourage his audience to investigate the deeper, tragic meaning of the dream.

Examining the attitude of the heroine and her mother, we notice, above all, that neither is able to interpret the dream or even to fathom the dream's content. The mother connects the falcon with the loving knight who will later appear in Kriemhild's life, yet she does not heed the warning signals that this falcon will be torn to pieces. Just as Der von Kürenberg has the lady lament the loss of her falcon, who is flying far away from her, Uote interprets the dream bird as Kriemhild's wooer who might be snatched away by other women. From this point of view, it makes sense to admonish her daughter to strive to keep the falcon. Not surprisingly, Kriemhild reacts only to her mother's analysis of the dream and rejects any possible insinuations that she herself might be the object of amorous wooing, vowing to avoid both 'liebé mit leide' (17, 3, 'love with sorrow') and thus to remain aloof from worldly cares. The dream, nevertheless, contains rather unusual features, which are to become crucial in the life both of Kriemhild and Siegfried. The poet has her elaborate the dream and the falcon image: 'den ir zwêne arn erkrummen' (13, 3, 'which two eagles will attack'). The meaning though is not that Kriemhild will suffer from the usual love pains, but that her lover will be killed. The image is strange, a falcon attacked and killed by two eagles. Eagles represent royal birds, and thus could point only to Hagen and Gunther, although the former lacks this rank, and the latter is shamefully flawed in his performance as king. In more general terms, however, Hagen is the

13 Jean-Claude Schmitt, 'Rêver au XIIe siècle', *I sogni nel medioevo*, pp. 291–316 (p. 297): 'Le rêve est une expérience totale, qui concerne en même temps le corps et l'âme du rêveur. Le sommeil nocturne est le moyen privilégié de cette expérience tout à la fois physique et spirituelle.'

14 *Des Minnesangs Frühling*, ed. by Karl Lachmann, Moriz Haupt, Friedrich Vogt and Carl von Kraus, 38th edn rev. by Hugo Moser and Helmut Tervooren, 2 vols (Stuttgart: Hirzel, 1988), I. *Texte*, pp. 25ff.

actual leader of the court, in effect the king of his world, whereas Gunther appears as weak only because of the contrast with the Other World and Siegfried's and Brünhild's challenge. His performance later at Etzel's court and in the battle against Kriemhild's men shows him in a positive light which allows us to equate him and Hagen with eagles. In other words, the dream anticipates future events in an exemplary way and also indicates the very sorrow which Kriemhild will have to suffer.

When the narrator steps in at the end of the first *âventiure* he provides us with the correct interpretation of the dream and thus indicates how little the two women have understood its true meaning. On one point Uote had not been wrong, however. Siegfried is about to enter Kriemhild's life, and it is appropriate to have Kriemhild dream of his arrival just before it actually occurs. But the mother disregards, just as much as her daughter, the second part of the dream containing the message of the falcon's death: 'durch sîn eines sterben' (19, 4, 'because of his dying alone') and is therefore unaware of the consequences of Siegfried's murder, which the narrator has to supply: 'starp vil maneger muoter kint.' (19, 4, 'many mothers' children died'). According to Jerold C. Frakes, 'in the *Nibelungenlied* the convention of the prophetic dream is subsumed under the more general category of epic prediction'.[15] But he concludes that this and the following dream reveal a discordance between Kriemhild and Burgundian society, since on each occasion the aggressor is turned into the victim and his image as aggressor becomes increasingly obscured (p. 187). In contrast I should like to suggest that the misunderstandings, illusions, and self-deceptions are forces at work in the whole of Burgundian society. Neither Gunther nor Uote, neither Dankwart nor Giselher nor any other protagonist comprehends the function of the forces from the Other World and their undermining and destabilizing effects. This is not to say that the outsiders Brünhild or Siegfried fully grasp what is going on either, since they are victimized as well. In fact, the whole world seems to be on the brink of collapse, and the dream serves to express the imminent danger.

Why does their world collapse? The dream, and through it the poet, provides the answer that because the harmony of society is jeopardized and the problems of the ensuing conflicts are not understood by the heroes, the survival of human society is at stake. Not surprisingly, the following dream images reflect a topsy-turvy world in which the hunter has become the hunted, and where man is being threatened by nature.[16]

15 'Kriemhild's Three Dreams', *Zeitschrift für deutsches Altertum und deutsche Literatur*, 113 (1984), 173–87 (p. 175).

16 See Volker Honemann, 'Unibos und Amis', in *Kleinere Erzählformen im Mittelalter*.

Kriemhild's second dream presents a boar hunting and killing Siegfried (921),[17] the third one relates that the earth collapses under him, representing the revolt of nature against man (924). Again we observe that neither the dreamer nor the addressee of the dream, Siegfried, is capable of comprehending the meaning of the enigmatic images. Yet, this is the very point of the dreams. If their message is lost on them, the protagonists face their destiny without being prepared for it. And those who listen to them are equally unable to comprehend the semiotics of their dreams.[18] Siegfried is a good example of this, since Kriemhild warns him twice through dream images of his forthcoming death. He proves to be so much caught in his illusions that even the most frightful signals about his life do not reach him: 'Er sprach: 'mîn triutinne, ich kum in kurzen tagen./Ine wéiz hie niht der liute, die mir iht hazzes tragen' (923, 1ff., 'He said, "my dear beloved, in a few days I will be back. I do not know anybody here who would hate me" '). And Uote has utterly failed to comprehend what Kriemhild's dream signifies. Even worse, she does not listen to her daughter's words carefully enough to hear the end of the story and thus fails in her interpretation.

Dreams are thus revealed to be a powerful strategy employed by the poet. The very meaning he tries to convey through his literary work is misunderstood or not even perceived by his protagonists. The less they are able to interpret the dream, however, the more the poet seems to invite his audience to reach a higher degree of comprehension. In other words, the use of dreams, at least in the *Nibelungenlied*, represents a crucial step in the narrative development and defines either the actual turning point or the future catastrophe, conditioned by present failings.

Wolfram von Eschenbach's *Parzival* contains several powerful examples of how dreams are integrated into the narrative sequence in order to create an intermediate climax at which the protagonists either win or lose. Both Herzeloyde and Parzival experience terribly frightening dreams, but neither succeeds in interpreting their messages. This very failure in fact proves to be disastrous for both of them, and both realize afterwards that their concept of reality has been undermined. It is

Paderborner Colloquium 1987, ed. by K. Grubmüller, L.P. Johnson and H.-H. Steinhoff, Schriften der Universitäts-Gesamthochschule-Paderborn. Reihe Sprach- und Literaturwissenschaft, 10 (Paderborn: Schöningh, 1988), pp. 67–82 (p. 80).

17 Regarding the symbolic function of the boar in Germanic and medieval superstition, see Ludwig Herold, 'Eber', *Handbuch des deutschen Aberglaubens*, ed. by E. Hoffmann-Krayer and H. Bächthold-Stäubli, II: *Handwörterbuch zur deutschen Volkskunde*, Section 1: 'Aberglauben' (Berlin-Leipzig: de Gruyter, 1929/30), cols 517–23.

18 See Umberto Eco, 'Denotation', in *On the Medieval Theory of Signs*, ed. by Umberto Eco and Costantino Marmo, Foundations of Semiotics, 21 (Amsterdam-Philadelphia: John Benjamins, 1989), pp. 43–77.

significant that for both characters the dreams function as important interludes which require close attention, and neither of them is willing to fulfil the requirement. Moreover, Wolfram connects Parzival's dreams to the one his mother has: 'sô daz der junge wol gevar/sîner muoter troum gar widerwac' (245, 6ff., 'so that the young man dreamt the other part of his mother's dream') and thus establishes a narrative continuum of deficiencies in dream analysis, which have consequences for the hero's waking life.[19]

Even Gawain is portrayed as a dreamer (628, 12ff.), yet he continues with his battle against his beloved only while he is asleep and thus is immediately in a position to learn from his dreams or, as one might also say, to connect the worlds of sleep and reality. In his case, dreaming represents a successful combination of the real and the prophesied, of the present and the future, and thus the happy outcome of the fight is only a matter of time. The problems of Herzeloyde and Parzival, on the other hand, lie in their lack of intellectual acuity and in their unwillingness to transgress the strict barriers between reality and non-reality. This is not surprising; after all, they are the main representatives of their society. Yet this society is deeply divided, without leadership and devoid of generally accepted ideals. While Parzival is dreaming, Herzeloyde is dead and Anfortas is suffering.[20] In other words, because the dream is not functionally integrated into Parzival's society, the courtly world is disjointed and agonizes over its future.

In Gottfried von Straßburg's *Tristan*, however, the dream operates on a different level because the dreamer is not the main protagonist and yet becomes, via the dream, the main agent for Tristan and Isolde to experience their love for each other in the sharpest and deadliest form. The seneschal envisions a boar entering the king's chamber and soiling his bed (ll. 13513ff.).[21] The whole court stands by helplessly and incompetently defends Marke's honour. The fact that it is a boar, however, which runs through Marjodô's dream is revealing in itself because it can symbolize Christ, the lover, the wild, and Otherness, amongst other

19 Wolfram von Eschenbach, *Parzival*, ed. by Karl Lachmann, 7th edn by Eduard Hartl (Berlin: de Gruyter, 1952).

20 Helmut Brackert, ' "Der lac an riterschefte tôt". Parzival und das Leiden der Frauen', in *'Ist zwîvel herzen nâchgebûr'. Günther Schweikle zum 60. Geburtstag*, ed. by R. Krüger, J. Kühnel, and J. Kuolt, Helfant Studien, S 5 (Stuttgart: Helfant, 1989), pp. 143–63; Will Hasty, *Adventure as Social Performance. A Study of the German Court Epic*, Untersuchungen zur deutschen Literaturgeschichte, 52 (Tübingen: Niemeyer, 1990), pp. 38 ff.; Fischer, *The Dream*, pp. 126ff.

21 Quoted from *Das Tristan-Epos Gottfrieds von Straßburg. Mit der Fortsetzung des Ulrich von Türheim nach der Heidelberger Handschrift Cod. Pal. Germ. 360*, ed. by Wolfgang Spiewok, Deutsche Texte des Mittelalters, 75 (Berlin: Akademie-Verlag, 1989).

characteristics.[22] Tristan embodies all of these elements; he is in fact the boar and even carries its picture on his shield (ll. 4942, 6614).[23]

Something significant happens through the dream, which heightens the tension and drama of the romance. The envious seneschal informs the king, and only now is jealousy, the major counterforce of love, allowed to enter Marke's heart. Because of the dream the actual drama begins, and we would be hard pressed to say who is living in reality and who in a dream. Marke constantly changes his beliefs regarding the lovers and the accusations of their adultery. When he accuses them of wrongdoing, he is close to the truth; when he accepts them back to his court, he submits voluntarily to the illusion. We might argue that the love cave represents a sophisticated form of architectural dream out of which Tristan and Isolde are allowed to return to reality/society once Marke has entered his own dream.

As in the case of Herzeloyde and Parzival, the dream functions as a narrative medium to indicate the possible, perhaps even necessary, transgressions by the protagonists when reality is deceiving them to such an extent that it becomes illusory. For instance, when the Irish seneschal claims the hand of Isolde the Fair, which in itself represents another type of social transgression, her mother searches in her dreams to find out the truth and learns from her nocturnal visions that a foreigner has slain the dragon and that Isolde will not marry the seneschal: 'daz si in ir troume gesach,/daz es niht also geschach,/als der lantschal sagete' (ll. 9303–05, 'she saw in her dream that it did not happen in the way the seneschal claimed').

In the verse novella *Morîz von Craûn*, the dreamer offers, through his falling asleep, the necessary forum for his lady and her chambermaid to discuss the fundamental issues underlying the love relationship with him in particular and love in general.[24] His dream is a nightmare, although we

22 See note 17 and compare, for instance, the boar which Bertilak de Hautdesert hunts down and kills in *Sir Gawain and the Green Knight*. When a boar attacks Count Emrich in the late medieval German prose romance *Melusine* by Thüring von Ringoltingen (1456), it is indirectly responsible for his death. The count defends himself quite successfully, but when his cousin Reymund intervenes, he accidentally kills him in the confusing struggle against the ferocious animal.

23 See *Gottfried von Straßburg: Tristan*, ed. and trans. by Rüdiger Krohn, 3 vols, Universal-Bibliothek, 4471–73 (Stuttgart: Reclam, 1980), III: *Kommentar, Nachwort und Register*, p. 136. More traditional in his interpretation is Lambertus Okken, *Kommentar zum Tristan-Roman Gottfrieds von Straßburg*, Amsterdamer Publikationen zur Sprache und Literatur, 81 (Amsterdam: Rodopi, 1988), III, 90ff.

24 *Moriz von Craûn*, ed. by Ulrich Pretzel, 4th edn, Altdeutsche Textbibliothek, 45 (Tübingen: Niemeyer, 1973). I have discussed all relevant research literature on this text in my translation and commentary, *Moriz von Craûn*, Universal-Bibliothek, 8796

do not hear in detail what the dream contains. Morîz confesses, however, that it could not have been worse: ' "ich slief sô unsanfte nie./ich wânde, mîn vrouwe waere hie/unt wolde niht mîn grüezen." ' (ll. 1397–99, ' "I have never slept so badly, I thought my lady was here and would not greet me" '). His labours in his dreams seem almost like birth pains, and in fact, the metaphysical child which he has produced (like the one which Emperor Nero was said to have borne and which was a toad, l. 162) is a horrible one, signifying the end of love. His lady does not only intend, as he learns from the chambermaid, to abandon him as her lover, she has also decided to give up loving altogether. Morîz is not willing to accept such sweeping condemnation, enters the bedroom forcibly and claims his 'reward' from his beloved. Thereafter, Morîz declares the end of his attempts at wooing and leaves the sorrowful woman alone. It seems that this nightmare is the ultimate transformation of the actual nightmare situation in which Morîz and his lady are caught, since both have committed a number of sins against love. She postpones his reward for too long, and he displays an unprecedented arrogance in tournament preparations and forgets the ideal of *mâze* (moderation). Eventually the lady rejects her lover altogether, and he secures his prize by committing rape (Fischer, p. 98). Reality itself proves to be the real nightmare, and Morîz' dream represents the stage at which the painful truth seems to have dawned upon him. In his dream he sees the lady with him (l. 1398), whereas in reality she has left him. But this very reality appears distorted and dream-like, as the chambermaid stresses in her description of her lady's appearance: ' "dô quam sî rehte alse ein alp/ûf mich her geslichen" ' (ll. 1418ff., ' "she crept up on me just like an elf" '). I would argue that the *Morîz*-poet projects two levels of existence, one of a dream world, the other of courtly reality. The fact that both protagonists are unable to distinguish between them indicates the direction of their fate: total frustration, dissatisfaction with themselves, sorrow and unfulfilled desires, lamenting and loneliness (this, at least, in the case of the lady).

A similar phenomenon can be observed in the case of Hartmann's *Iwein*, where the hero's utter failure to keep his promise given to Laudine to return to her after one year on the 'tournament circuit' leads him to fall into a state of madness – he becomes a wild man.[25] This state can be

(Stuttgart: Reclam, 1992). There has been, however, no significant examination of Moriz' dream yet.

[25] See David Arthur Wells, 'Die Ikonographie von Daniel IV. und der Wahnsinn des Löwenritters', in *Interpretation und Edition deutscher Texte des Mittelalters: Festschrift für John Asher zum 60. Geburtstag*, ed. by Kathryn Smits, Werner Besch, and Victor Lange (Berlin: E. Schmidt, 1981), pp. 39–57); David Wells, *The Wild Man from the 'Epic of Gilgamesh' to Hartmann von Aue's 'Iwein': Reflections on the Development of a Theme in*

compared to dreaming, since Iwein is totally distracted and will not recall later what has happened to him. His repentance and feeling of shame drive him crazy and force him into a dream-like or nightmarish state (ll. 3231ff.), as his own words reveal when his sanity is returning:

> wider sich selben er dô sprach
> 'bistûz Iwein, ode wer?
> hân ich geslâfen unze her? (3508–10)[26]
>
> (he said to himself, 'Are you Iwein or who are you? Have I been sleeping until now?')

It is not unusual for medieval poets to contrast reality with the spiritual world either through the imagery of dreams or madness,[27] and Hartmann's *Iwein* is no exception. The question remains, however, whether Iwein falls into a dream or whether his state is in fact being contrasted with reality through his dreamlike loss of civilization. More to the point, what is Iwein's reality? His previous chivalric existence has proved to be tainted with murder (Ascâlon), deceit, emotional blackmail, arrogance, jealousy, envy, ignorance and neglect. Only after his return from the dream does he embark on a path towards total recovery in both physical and spiritual terms. Thus the interaction between dream and 'reality' provides the necessary medium for the protagonist to begin to grasp his role in life, his future course of action, and the meaning of life itself. As Kurt Ruh observed, 'der "Iwein" [ist] die Dichtung, in der die Gespanntheit der Artusideologie zum erstenmal deutlich wird.'[28] From this perspective the dreams in *Morîz* and in *Parzival* work in the opposite direction, but start from the same position. In *Tristan* neither

World Literature (Belfast: Queen's University of Belfast, 1975); P. B. R. Doob, *Nebuchadnezzar's Children: Conventions of Madness in Middle English Literature* (New Haven–London: Yale University Press, 1974). Compare especially the *lai Bisclavret* by Marie de France. Susan L. Clark's study *Hartmann von Aue: Landscapes of the Mind* (Houston, Texas: Rice University Press, 1989) pp. 187ff., does not provide any particular insight into the use of the dream as a narrative strategy.

26 See *Iwein*, ed. by G. F. Benecke and K. Lachmann, 7th edn, rev. by Ludwig Wolff, 2 vols (Berlin: de Gruyter, 1968).

27 See R. Bernheimer, *Wild Men in the Middle Ages: A Study in Art, Sentiment and Demonology* (Cambridge, Mass.: Harvard University Press, 1952); František Graus, 'Goldenes Zeitalter, Zeitschelte und Lob der alten Zeit', in *Idee-Gestalt-Geschichte: Festschrift Klaus von See. Studien zur europäischen Kulturtradition*, ed. by Gerd Wolfgang Weber (Odense: Odense University Press, 1988), pp. 187–222 (pp. 213ff.).

28 Kurt Ruh, 'Zur Interpretation von Hartmanns 'Iwein,' first publ. in *Philologie deutsch: Festschrift zum 70. Geburtstag von Walter Henzen*, ed. by W. Kohlschmidt and P. Zinsli (Bern: Francke, 1965), here quoted from *Hartmann von Aue*, ed. by Hugo Kuhn and Christoph Cormeau, Wege der Forschung, 359 (Darmstadt: Wissenschaftliche Buchgesellschaft, 1973), pp. 408–25 (p. 425); see also Fischer, *The Dream*, pp. 103ff.

dream nor reality is negatively qualified; instead they interact with each other and facilitate the protagonists' establishment of a basis for their love relationship. We might even wish the characters to experience dreams, because without them their lives would not take the decisive turn towards the spiritual and concrete love cave.

Dreams operate on a level where they enable the narrative to express its fundamental message in a poetic image, and the proper interpretation of dreams determines the course of future events. In Wernher the Gartenaere's *Helmbrecht*, old Meier Helmbrecht relates several dreams to his son, all of which will come true.[29] In these dreams he foresees the tragic destiny of his son, who is caught first by the sheriffs, and one year later by the peasants whom he has maltreated earlier. The poet's aim is didactic, warning both the protagonist and his audience to heed dreams since they tell the truth. Yet, the way in which the prophecies are revealed to the young Helmbrecht contains significant elements. The father keeps them to himself until he has no ammunition left to deter his son from becoming a robber knight. He himself has, however, aided and abetted him by providing Helmbrecht with the necessary equipment – in his case an expensive steed. Why did he not relate the dreams earlier? Does he make them up when he is searching desperately for convincing reasons? No, the dreams were real, since they are later fulfilled and thus prove their anticipatory power.[30] He had dreamt them earlier, but he had postponed revealing them to his son because he had become an accomplice in preparing his son for his future career. The father's dream analysis represents his own reawakening from illusory dreams about his son's rise to nobility, and an attempt to rescue him from an early and miserable death.[31] The dreams are the hinges upon which the narrative turns. They are, however, introduced too late to affect the turn of events and serve only as the moral teaching of the narrative.

In *Helmbrecht*, as in the previous works discussed above, the status of dreams approximates to that of reality, for reality is neither better nor closer to the truth than dreams are. The dream was an important narrative strategy employed by the authors of classical MHG verse narratives to focus on the one experience in man's life which placed him in a state

29 See Wernher der Gartenaere, *Helmbrecht*, ed. by Friedrich Panzer, 8th edn rev. by Kurt Ruh, ATB, 11 (Tübingen: Niemeyer, 1968).

30 See Ulrich Seelbach, *Kommentar zum 'Helmbrecht' von Wernher dem Gartenaere*, GAG, 469 (Göppingen: Kümmerle, 1987), pp. 99ff.

31 See Anton Schwob, 'Das mittelhochdeutsche Märe von 'Helmbrecht' vor dem Hintergrund der mittelalterlichen ordo-Lehre', in *Geistliche und weltliche Epik des Mittelalters in Österreich* ed. by D. McLintock, A. Stevens, and Fred Wagner, Publications of the Institute of Germanic Studies, 37, GAG, 446 (Göppingen: Kümmerle, 1987), pp. 1–17.

somewhere between sleep and wakefulness. The ambiguity thus produced served to illuminate the underlying forces and motives of the protagonists. The crucial question for the protagonists is, however, how to interpret the dreams, how to evaluate them and what importance to grant them. We learn from these medieval texts that the proper approach and response to dreams leads the individual to fulfil his destiny, while the wrong approach, or the disregard of dreams, leads to his tragic end. This suggests that dreams were considered essential elements in medieval culture and required close attention. To ignore them could be fatal.

The Story's Voyage through the Text: Transformations of the Narrative in *Beowulf*

ANNE SAVAGE

DIFFERENT IDEAS ABOUT *Beowulf* as narrative have manifested themselves in many kinds of discussion: of the narratives in *Beowulf*, their sources, author(s), interpretations in whole or in part, of how they were composed, and how they ended up in a single poem.[1] The critical picture for over a century has been coloured by readings which see the poem as, for example, a collection of fabulous and historical Germanic narratives;[2] as a 'pagan' tale with 'Christian' elements or vice versa.[3] There have been

[1] All references to *Beowulf* are to the edition by Fr. Klaeber, 3rd edn (Lexington, MA: Heath, 1950).

[2] While there have been many different approaches to the fabulous in *Beowulf*, most students are probably familiar with this idea through Klaeber's edition, and possibly also Garmonsway's *Beowulf and its Analogues* (see below). While Tolkien's famous British Academy lecture, 'The Monsters and the Critics' (*Proceedings of the British Academy*, 22 (1936), 245–95), which remains standard introductory reading, produced a non-anthropological, fairly 'straight' view of the monsters, large numbers of students are already familiar with Tolkien's own dragon, Smaug, and his Orcs (Grendel-like goblins, only smaller), from *The Hobbit* and *The Lord of the Rings*, when they come to read *Beowulf*; their views of the people in *Beowulf* are thus influenced by Tolkien's own stories of the Riders of Rohan (and this certainly seems to do more good than harm). *Beowulf and its Analogues*, trans. by G. N. Garmonsway and Jacqueline Simpson (London: Dent, 1968, rev. 1980) contains along with a translation of the poem the parallel Scandinavian material, both fabulous and mundane. Many of the attempts to give *Beowulf* a date have relied on the historical basis of some of the narratives, e.g. Gruntvig's identification of Gregory of Tours' description of Chlochilaicus' Frisian raid as Hygelac's (N. F. S. Gruntvig, 'Om Bjovulf's Drape', *Dannevirke*, 2 (1817), 207–89).

[3] For example, see F. A. Blackburn, 'The Christian Colouring in the *Beowulf*', *PMLA*, 12 (1897), 205–25; H. Munro Chadwick, *The Heroic Age* (New York: Cambridge University Press, 1912), pp. 47–56. A major early concern of *Beowulf* criticism was origins, and primarily the origins of different stories. Much later, Margaret Goldsmith, *The Mode and*

perceptions of disjunctures in a 'main' storyline for reasons such as allegorical or thematic considerations,[4] multiple authorship of the poem as an oral-formulaic anthology of stories or as a textual creation in a manuscript.[5] Even when paleographical analyses do not discuss the poem's narrative structure, they have long influenced ideas about the poem's composition, just as oral-formulaic approaches have done. But almost always ideas about the poem's composition focus on the nature of the narrative and the way the many pieces are perceived to fit – or not to fit.[6]

This paper will examine the poem as a medium for stories, and the status of those stories in relation to each other – the ways they point to each other, and the ways they change in nature in the course of the

Meaning of Beowulf (London: Athlone Press, 1970), rallied a vast number of learned sources in service of an allegorical reading of the poem; Goldsmith, too, approached the poem in search of sources, and found biblical and patristic references everywhere. Her reading has been extremely influential, and has produced a 'standard' view (next to other, quite opposing, 'standard' views) that the poem is allegorical – that the large-scale narrative and the other narratives contained within it are to be read as a Christian allegory of man's life, not as themselves, but with religious ironization of secular heroic values.

4 For example, see J. Blomfield, 'The Style and Structure of *Beowulf*', *Review of English Studies*, 16 (1938), 396–403; Adrien Bonjour, 'The Digressions in *Beowulf*', Medium Aevum Monographs, 5 (Oxford: Basil Blackwell, 1965). While these approaches and others that have followed emphasize thematic links, the term 'digressions' has stuck; we still think in terms of a 'main' narrative with at least *apparent* changes of subject which we must override to bring the whole together.

5 For example, see Arthur Brodeur, *The Art of Beowulf* (Berkeley and Los Angeles: University of California Press, 1959). While Jeff Opland's *Anglo-Saxon Oral Poetry* (New Haven: Yale University Press, 1980) does not analyze individual poems to any great extent, but focuses on performance, I think his work has been generally influential on the idea of narrative in *Beowulf* as springing from or still being largely within an oral tradition; this view has counterbalanced the heavily literary and learned 'source studies' approaches to narratives in the poem, which tend to exclude a general audience from an authorially *intended* understanding of the poem and its unity, positing instead a learned audience capable of decoding the poem. W. F. Bolton's *Alcuin and Beowulf: An Eighth-Century View* (New Brunswick, New Jersey: Rutgers University Press, 1978) is a good example of this learned approach, but there are many others.

6 For two very different approaches see, Kevin S. Kiernan 'The Eleventh-Century Origin of *Beowulf* and the *Beowulf* Manuscript', in *The Dating of Beowulf* (ed. by Colin Chase (Toronto: University of Toronto Press, 1981) pp. 9–21) and Leonard E. Boyle, O.P., *ibid.* pp. 23–32. Kiernan, here and in his book (*'Beowulf' and the 'Beowulf' Manuscript* (New Brunswick, NJ: Rutgers University Press, 1981), constructs an extremely complicated series of hypotheses based on the idea that the manuscript shows evidence of being the only one there ever was, an original composition by two authors, the first and second scribes. In contrast, Leonard Boyle's lucid, tightly-knit description posits an exemplar, in which case we would be free to choose whatever theory of *composition* we wish. We can thus go to theories of textual composition like Kiernan's, for a heavily literary view of Old English poetry; or, if we believe that the manuscript was simply copied more or less as is from an exemplar, we may theorize anything from the poem's being a copy of a performance to a transitional oral-literary work.

poem. Narratives exist in different currents of time; it is chiefly their *movement* through a temporal continuum, and their placing in the continuum of the poem, that draws our attention to their status. Not only do they exist in a linear relation to each other, but *their nature changes* in the course of the poem: they are transformed by being told to different audiences by different tellers, and by having different time frames.

There are two frames of reference within which the narratives I will be discussing here, and the poem *Beowulf* as a narrative, stand: the audience to whom a given narrative is directed by the teller, and the relationship of an audiencc to the past. To a society whose tradition of storytelling rests on the double foundation of remembered history and an exemplary reading of history, some of the most significant aspects of a narrative like *Beowulf*, and the narratives within *Beowulf*, must have been the awareness of opening and closure, and the privileged hindsight of the audience: the awareness, as a narrative line progresses, that the 'present' of that narrative is in the process of becoming a past for the people in it, and that the listeners to the story are aware of it as something complete and significant in a way hidden to the participants.

There are many illustrations of such an awareness in the fabric of Old English literature; I shall cite one here for its value as a contrast. The cross in *The Dream of the Rood* tells its story as a tree in the forest, a gallows, the cross on which Christ was crucified, and the rediscovered, risen cross, whose image is ordinarily visible as a symbolically adorned altar cross, and whose image *will appear* in the heavens on the day of judgement; the expanse of time encompassed by the vision is eternity, which encloses history. First the cross appears to the dreamer silently in the heavens in its risen state, then its appearance changes, and then it speaks, describing its transformation from a naive participant in the crucifixion to a risen being with an eternal existence and divine power; it has been changed into something that exists outside the temporal framework of history. It tells its own story to a listener (and of course the larger audience, listening to the listener's retelling) *to whom it conveys a meaning the story can only have once complete*. The listener, the dreamer-poet, undergoes a transformation similar to the cross's, from confusion and distress to informed longing; and the audience of the poem too, is clearly meant to be transformed *by the completeness of the narrative*, which moves into eternity at the end of the poem; that is, there is an explicit insistence that the story of the tree is the story of the cross is the story of the dreamer/ audience/ all creation.

Finality or the lack of it in a narrative or collection of them is an important determiner of how it or they are to be understood. *The Dream of the Rood*, a poem focused on the continuity of earthly life into eternal, is emphatic about its completeness, the wholeness of its perspective; in contrast, as the many narratives in *Beowulf* pass by, the audience of the poem and different audiences in the poem are aware of different degrees and kinds of completeness or lack of it.[7] As modern readers we are aware of other kinds which grow out of the poem's place in its present contexts: the classroom, critical analysis, the performances available on tape, and so on.

Some stories in the poem draw unusual attention to themselves by virtue of *not being told*: the story of the extinct, unnamed people who held the gold before its burial in the mound (ll. 2232–70) and the arrival of the dragon (ll. 2270–80), are examples. The poetic lament of the Last Survivor, along with its introduction and conclusion (ll. 2231–70), occupy one of those peculiar Old English poetic spaces which seem simultaneously to be occupied by both words and silence, like, for example, parts of *The Wanderer*:[8]

> Ne maeg werig mod   wyrde wiðstondan,
> ne se hreo hyge   helpe gefremman:
> fordon domgeorne   dreorigne oft
> in hyra breostcofan   bindað faeste,

7 Since we have no contemporary outside references to *Beowulf* and know very little about the performance and/or reading of Old English poetry in Anglo-Saxon culture, we do not know, for example, what audience(s) heard this poem, or under what circumstances, or how often the same or different audiences heard it. Different kinds of awareness in the *Beowulf* audience are visible in the relationships between narratives in the poem; a given listener need not be familiar with the poem in order to register them. The mention of Sigemund, for example, while indicating that there are many stories about him, highlights one of those: his slaying of the dragon (l. 886). While a first-time hearer who did not know the 'plot' of *Beowulf* would not say 'Aha!' at the very mention of the dragon, a parallel would be established when the dragon enters the narrative in line 2211. There are other verbal pointers to assist the listener in perceiving the parallel: Sigemund attacks the dragon *under harne stan* ('under grey stone', l. 887); so does Beowulf (l. 2553); both are alone when they do so (ll. 888; 2532ff.); both are the survivors of many trials (ll. 875–82; 2542–43). Likewise, while someone hearing *Beowulf* for the first time might not know that Grendel's mother is going to appear after Grendel is dead and the Danes are breathing freely for the first time in twelve years, the audience is warned before she arrives in such a way as to draw a great deal of attention to the Danes' mistaken belief that the monster-episode is over: 'Wyrd ne cuþon,/ geosceaft grimme, swa hit agangen wearð/ eorla manegum, siþðan æfen cwom [. . .] Sum sare angeald/ æfenræste [. . .] Þæt gesyne wearþ,/ widcuþ werum, þætte wrecend þa gyt/ lifde æfter laþum [. . .] Grendles modor,/ ides aglæcwif. (ll. 1233–78).

8 I am grateful to James W. Earl for his useful discussion of the role of silence in *Beowulf* and *The Wanderer* in '*Beowulf* and the Origins of Civilization', in *Speaking Two Languages: Traditional Disciplines and Contemporary Theory in Medieval Studies*, ed. by Allen J. Frantzen (New York: SUNY Press, 1991), pp. 65–89.

swa ic modsefan   minne sceolde . . .
. . . feterum saelan   (*The Wanderer*, 15–19)[9]

(The weary heart cannot withstand *wyrd*, the troubled spirit cannot give help: so those eager for reputation often seal sadness fast in their breasts, as I my own thoughts have had to do, bind them with chains. [The speaker has been lamenting his care in a poem which is fictionally private – addressed to no audience; a main theme is reticence about suffering.])

The Last Survivor, like the wanderer, is speaking to no-one but himself. The point of these stories in *Beowulf* is that *no-one was present to witness them so that they could be transformed into poetry*, that is memory; the *Beowulf* audience is privileged, endowed with omniscience of events very nearly out of the time-frame, actions at which no-one was present. The dragon in Beowulf's kingdom is hidden, having fallen asleep on the gold three hundred years before with no witnesses, so that there is no way for the represented participants in the action to avoid its accidental awakening and its meeting with the hero; and there is no-one but the audience of *Beowulf* itself to perceive the symmetry in the destruction of the unknown people several hundred years before and the forthcoming extinction of the Geats.

Beowulf begins with a story which is in the distant past, the story of the good king, Scyld; this leads genealogically and proverbially into the 'now' of the poem, the time of Hrothgar's prime and the building of the great hall, Heorot – and then the monstrous Grendel's arrival and predation on the inhabitants. In terms of a narrative line, this one continues until the end of the poem, yet it is transformed on the way there by many shifts in frame of reference: other stories are constantly flowing into and out of it, so that as a story itself it must always be seen in relationship to, for example, the account of the creation of the world (ll. 90–98), or the history of the Grendel-kind's war with God (ll. 102–14), the story of Hildeburh (ll. 1068–159) or Sigemund (ll. 874–97) or the buried gold (ll. 2221–80). And as a narrative line which creates a fictional continuum, it has the most extreme degrees of concentration and expansion within itself, from the detail-by-detail account of Grendel's approach to Heorot and the fight, to such temporal leaps as

syððan Beowulfe   brade rice
on hand gehwearf;   he geheold tela

[9] *The Wanderer*, ed. by T. P. Dunning and A. J. Bliss (London: Methuen and Co., 1969).

fiftig wintra – wæs ða frod cyning,
eald eþelweard –, oð ðæt an ongan
deorcum nihtum draca rics[i]an (2207–11)

Swa se ðeodsceaða þreo hund wintra
heold on hrusan hordærna sum
eacencræftig, oð ðaet hyne an abealch
mon on mode. (2278–81)

(And then the broad kingdom came into the hand of Beowulf; he held it well *for fifty winters* – he was then a wise king, old guardian of the land – until a dragon began to rule in the dark nights [. . .] So this enemy of the people *for three hundred years* held a treasure house in the earth, until a man enraged him in his spirit.)

Also, much of the main narrative line is told in its own past: that is, the narrative line often turns back on itself, so that events *happen* in the normal, linear order (in the manner in which humans perceive them), but are not recounted until later in the poem, or are recounted differently there. For example, we have Beowulf's fight with Grendel related with great care in natural order (ll. 746–836); but then Beowulf himself relates it, along with other things, in an entirely different mode to Hygelac, when he gets home (ll. 2069–100). There is a brief description of the defeat and death of Hygelac just before the above-mentioned stretch of Beowulf's fifty years of kingship (ll. 2354–66), but the story of Beowulf's relationship with his adopted family, and the events which led to Hygelac becoming his lord are not *told* until Beowulf is sitting alone just before the dragon-fight and his own death (ll. 2425–515), remembering his youth, the kindness of Hygelac's father, Hrethel, and the personal suffering and battles in which the family were involved.

So, there is a single linear narrative which encompasses the time from Scyld's life to the end of Beowulf's; embedded within it are others which are recounted after they have happened. Sometimes they are altogether outside that linear narrative, that is, they have happened long before it started, and sometimes they are within it; there are different audiences for these, sometimes present in the poem and sometimes outside it (that is, the Anglo-Saxon audience(s) of *Beowulf* itself).

Let us look more closely now at audiences, and at their relationships to the many stories of different lengths which exist outside or sometimes on the margins of the main narrative line: the longer of these are often called 'the digressions in *Beowulf*'. They exist within several frames: delivered to a particular audience or audiences; with direct or indirect reference to another story. Some, like the marriage of Hildeburh and

Finn, are told within the main narrative, and are formally opened and closed for a particular audience:

> Þær wæs sang ond sweg samod ætgædere
> fore Healfdenes hildewisan,
> gomenwudu greted, gid oft wrecen,
> ðonne healgamen Hroþgares scop
> æfter medobence mænan scolde,
> [be] Finnes eaferum, ða hie se fær begeat,
> hæleð Healf-Dena, Hnæf Scyldinga
> in Freswæle feallan scolde.
> Ne huru Hildeburh herian þorfte
> Eotena treowe;
> . . .
> . . . Leoð wæs asungen,
> gleomannes gyd. Gamen eft astah,
> beorhtode bencsweg, byrelas sealdon
> win of wunderfatum. (1063–72, 1159–62)
>
> (There were song and convivial sounds mingled together before Halfdane's battle-leader, the gleewood was greeted often, a tale often told; then Hrothgar's scop related the story along the mead-benches about the sons of Finn; when the terror seized them, the hero of the Half-Danes, Hnaef of the Scyldings, had to fall in the Frisian slaughter. Hildeburh indeed had no need to praise the faith of the Jutes [. . .] The tale was told, the scop's story. Speech rose again, the table-talk brightened, cupbearers poured wine from beautiful vessels.)

Some, like the origin of Grendel (ll. 102–14), or the story of the buried gold (ll. 2221–80), are told to the audience of *Beowulf* itself, and are not introduced or closed as separate narratives, but woven seamlessly into the poem, even though the instrumental event for the founding of the Grendel line, the murder of Abel by Cain, is ancient biblical history not far removed from the creation itself, and, in the case of the buried gold and the dragon, the events occurred three hundred years before the hoard was inadvertently opened again and that narrative met the one of Beowulf's life.

The extreme points of the 'audience' frame of reference, then, are manifested by on the one hand stories directed to an audience inscribed within the narrative of *Beowulf*, such as the narrative of Hildeburh and Finn's disastrous marriage, performed by the poet to listeners in Hrothgar's hall; and on the other hand by stories directed to no audience but that of the *poem*, such as the death in war of all the Last Survivor's people, and of himself (ll. 2231–70) – events which were not witnessed and could not be passed on as stories providing reliable historical information. The narrator's account of Beowulf's time at Heorot, told to the audience of *Beowulf* (ll. 224–1904), is at one extreme, directed only to an outer audience; but as an example of narrative directed very specifically to a particular audience within the poem, Beowulf's own account of the events at Heorot, including his battle with Grendel, is told in Hygelac's hall, in reply to his question as to how Beowulf's expedition had gone (ll. 1999–2162). Unlike the performance by the scop in Hrothgar's hall, it is not a *poem*, and is introduced only by Hygelac's question, and closed only as direct speech gives way to an account of gift-giving.

Sometimes a story moves, then, in the course of the poem, from one frame of audience reference to another, or exists in one frame for the people in the poem and another for the audience of *Beowulf*. The episode concerning Hildeburh and Finn, for example, is told in the course of an evening's entertainment in Heorot; for the *Beowulf*-audience, however, it stands in a clear parallel relation to Beowulf's dire forecast in Hygelac's hall about the fate of Freawaru's (Hrothgar's daughter) and Ingeld's marriage – that the fragile peace it creates will be broken by loyalties to the slain which will surface, at first verbally (ll. 2041–58), and then in violent action (ll. 2058–65) and still more killing.[10]

The events concerning the families of Hildeburh and Finn happened

[10] Beowulf himself is speaking these lines to Hygelac: 'Þonne cwið æt beore se ðe beah gesyhð,/ eald æscwiga, se ðe eall gem(an),/ garcwealm gumena – him bið grim sefa –,/ onginneð geomormod geong(um) cempan/ þurh hreðra gehygd higes cunnian/ wigbealu weccean, ond þæt word acwyð:/ "Meaht ðu, min wine, mece gecnawan,/ þone þin fæder to gefeohte bær/ under heregriman hindeman siðe,/ dyre iren, þær hyne Dene slogon,/ weoldon wælstowe, syððan Wiðergyld læg,/ æfter hæleþa hryre, hwate Scyldungas?/ Nu her þara banena byre nathwylces/ frætwum hremig on flet gæð,/ morðres gylpeð, ond þone maðþum byreð,/ þone þe ðu mid rihte rædan sceoldest."/ Manað swa ond myndgað mæla gehwylce/ sarum wordum, oð ðaet sæl cymeð,/ þæt se fæmnan þegn fore fæder dædum/ æfter billes bite blodfag swefeð,/ ealdres scyldig; him se oðer þonan/ losað (li)figende, con him land geare./ þonne bioð (ab)rocene on ba healfe/ aðsweord eorla.' (ll. 2041–64) ('Then he will say over beer, the one who sees a ring, an old spear-warrior who remembers it all – the death of men by spears, there is a grim spirit in him – he will begin mournfully to tempt the spirit of a young fighter through the feelings of the heart, to awaken war, and will say this: "Can't you recognize that sword, my friend, which your father bore to battle, wearing his fierce helmet? That precious iron sword, when the Danes killed him? They ruled the battlefield, the arrogant Scyldings, after Withergyld lay dead, after the fall of heroes. Now here one of the killers goes across the hall-floor rejoicing in his booty, boasts of the murder, and carries the treasure which you should have, if there were justice." And in this way he will urge and remind with painful words, until the time comes when the woman's retainer sleeps bloodstained after the bite of a sword on account of his father's deeds, has forfeited life, while the other loses himself, stays alive – he knows the land well. And then the oaths of men on swords will be broken on both sides.')

long enough ago to be shaped into a poem offered as an evening's entertainment which does not mar the happiness of the occasion; Beowulf's 'spontaneous' exposition-analysis of Freawaru and Ingeld's forthcoming marriage exists within the main narrative as a simple forecast of events – but of course the *Beowulf*-poet has shaped it into poetic form, not simply metrically but thematically. The tragedy of Hildeburh and her family has moved in time from political situation to completed event to poem; that of Freawaru and Ingeld is in the process of becoming a political situation which will undergo the same change as it moves through time. While for the audience to whom Beowulf speaks at Hygelac's court it remains a grim prediction, for the audience of *Beowulf* this change is complete, the events long ago came to pass, were worked into poetry, and there is no *stylistic* difference between the first story and the second for the audience of *Beowulf*. For them – and for us – both have been worked upon by time and memory, have become poetry, and the fact that they are, in the context of *Beowulf*, stories with the same status is significant in itself: the main narrative too has undergone this transformation in time and memory from event to poem; it is what happens to all narratives worth remembering. In this sense, all narratives stand in a *potential* poetic relationship to one another.

The ultimate movable story is that of the hero himself, which is suddenly introduced through a peripheral connection – the poem has been about the Danish line, its glorious peak under Hrothgar, and the latter's affliction when old by Grendel. Beowulf comes into this story from the outside, across the sea, simply because he has heard the stories about Grendel and wishes to help the king. From this point on, the poem is no longer about Hrothgar, but about Beowulf, whose heroic person has justly appropriated the narrative, and to whom the final narrative stands as a memorial.

Beowulf is introduced as follows: the poet has just finished his condemnation of the sin of despair into which the Danes have fallen, and described the terrible stasis in their situation (ll. 189–93) when he introduces 'Higelaces þegn' (l. 194) (not mentioning Beowulf by name, but by which lord he serves), who, in a different country among a different people, hears the stories of Hrothgar's misfortune. His name is not given until he arrives at the door of Heorot (l. 343), but he is described much earlier: 'se wæs moncynnes mægenes strengest/ on þæm ðæge þysses lifes/ æþele ond eacen' (he was the strongest of mankind in those days of this life, noble and mighty, ll. 196–98). The story of Grendel's persecutions of the Danes and his ruin of Hrothgar's kingship *seems* to have come to a point where it is over in the sense that no-one can do anything to change it:

ne mihte snotor hæleð
wean onwendan
. . .
. . . se snotera bad,
hwæþ*er* him Alwalda aefre wille
æfter weaspelle wyrpe gefremman. (190–91, 1313–15)

(The wise hero could not alter his woes [. . .] the wise one waited to see if the All-ruler would ever wish, after a time of woe, to bring a change.)

Beowulf determines to end it properly, and so he does – not once, but twice, having to deal unexpectedly with Grendel's mother after everyone thought the death of Grendel to be the end of their monster trouble. We might even say that he ends the story three times, in that he refuses to take more than a hero's due although it seems that he could do so, since Hrothgar has declared he will hold him as a son. He does not *complicate* the future of the Danish line, and thus closes the Grendel story rather than causing it to turn into a story about something else, such as his own usurpation of the kingship.

In Old English poetry, one way of measuring heroic accomplishment is the degree to which one's actions outlive their present to be retold as exemplary actions of the past:

Forþon þæt bið eorla gehwam æftercweþendra
lof lifigendra lastworda betst,
þæt he gewyrce, ær he on weg scyle,
fremum on foldan wið feonda niþ,
deorum daedum deofle togeanes,
þæt hine ælda bearn æfter hergen,
ond his lof siþþan lifge mid englum
awa to ealdre, ecan lifes blæd,
dream mid duguþum. (*The Seafarer*, 72–80)

(So that is best for everyone – the praise of the living speaking afterwards, the best of final words: so that they perform, before they must go on their way, deeds on the earth against the devil – so that the children of man praise them after, and their praise from then on will live with the angels, forever and ever, eternal life's glory.)[11]

[11] Given the standard *spoken* use of the third-person plural forms as a singular generic pronoun in Modern English, and given the number of Anglo-Saxon female saints who live up to this exemplum, I feel the use of this form of generic pronoun is justified here.

In the world of *Beowulf*, both as a fictional present in which the hero exists, and the 'present' of the poem's telling, exemplary stories focusing on individual achievement – or its failure – are always available in the fabric of human memory as poetry. We see this process in action when, after Beowulf has killed Grendel, we are told that one of Hrothgar's thanes, 'guma gilphlæden, gidda gemyndig' (a man loaded with proud words, mindful of stories, l. 868), is telling tales as the people celebrate their new freedom from fear. He composes a poem about Beowulf's success:

> secg eft ongan
> sið Beowulfes snyttrum styrian,
> ond on sped wrecan spel gerade,
> wordum wrixlan . . . (871–74)
>
> (Further, the man began with skill to tell Beowulf's adventure, wrought the tale rightly, linked word with word.)

He has inserted Beowulf's heroic action into the past by converting something which has only just ceased to be a present event – is still a happy *occasion* – into the same medium which preserves the celebration of Scyld's achievements marking the ancestral origins of the Swedes – the same medium in which *Beowulf* still exists: Old English poetry. On the one hand, the effect is equivalence: both Scyld and Beowulf are great warriors, whose strength in battle provides shelter for others. This is clearly a flattering poem, since Beowulf is a young retainer, not a founding father, and his battle-skills, unlike Scyld's, have only just been tested against one monster, though a terrible one; Scyld is described at the beginning of the poem with respect to the years of keeping his neighbours, near and far, too terrified to attack him – instead they had to pay him tribute so he would not attack them (*Beowulf*, ll. 4–11); 'þæt wæs god cyning! (*that* was a good king! l. 11). So the idea of equivalence is simultaneously undermined by obvious contrast. For the audience within *Beowulf*, some of Hrothgar's thanes, the contrast is straightforwardly between youth and age; the compliment is forward-looking into a bright future for Beowulf, the young man. For the outer audience, the contrast is complicated by the awareness that what for the inscribed audience is a present moment has undergone the change that all such moments do: it has become the past, in this case an illustrious past in a life comparable to Scyld's in heroic scale, preserved in a monumental poem about the young man grown old and then killed in battle. In terms of the moment's relationship to poetry, for the internal audience that relationship is celebratory, fresh, hopeful and again, forward-looking. For the audience of

Beowulf the celebration has acquired the sadness of closure: the poem preserves the past within the context of the hero's *entire* heroic past. It is backward-looking: he is dead, and unlike Scyld he had no worthy successor to keep his people from harm. The Geats are gone, swept away in the aftermath of war and slavery when neighbours learn that Beowulf is dead. (While these events do not occur in *Beowulf*, the poem ends with the dire certainty that they will; the disappearance of the Geats from recorded history around this time seems to indicate that they did, whether or not the hero himself was a fiction). For both audiences, the preservative and celebratory roles of poetry are important, but for the external audience under the pressure of other narratives (one of which includes the end of the hero's life in disaster) these roles are shown always to be open to further consideration.

The *Beowulf*-poet's awareness of the double audience-frame, which has just been highlighted by the insertion of Beowulf the hero into the medium of Old English poetry, is illustrated by the way in which the same thane who makes the poem about Beowulf's killing of Grendel then moves on to other, much older stories:

welhwylc gecwæð,
þæt he fram Sigemunde[s]   secgan hyrde
ellendædum,   uncuþes fela,
Wælsinges gewin,   wide siðas,
þara þe gumena bearn   gearwe ne wiston   (874–78)

(He told just about everything he had heard about Sigemund's courageous acts, the many unknown struggles of the Waelsing, his great adventures, which the children of men do not readily know, the feuds and dire conflicts . . .)

Among these adventures is Sigemund's killing of the dragon and gaining of its hoard without the help of his faithful supporter Fitela (l. 899). The irony of narrative itself here is something the poet and audience of *Beowulf* are clearly aware of: the celebrating of Grendel's death during which Sigemund's tale is told is premature, since Grendel's mother that very night enters Heorot unchallenged and kills Aeschere; Beowulf too will kill a dragon and gain its hoard, but *even though* a single thane, Wiglaf, faithfully supports him, he will die of his wounds, and all the gold will be burnt by his grieving people on his funeral pyre and buried again in his mound.

One of the commonplaces of *Beowulf* criticism, anywhere along the continuum of oral-formulaic to literary-allegorical, is the idea that the stories are exemplary: whether in terms of Germanic-heroic secular values or Christian didacticism, it is important that people know stories about great actions in the past. However, the stories in *Beowulf* constantly draw attention to the fact that an audience's perceptions of openings and closures are naïve. This is surely one of the most subtle lessons of narrative. On the one hand, the audience of *Beowulf* know that they know more than the tellers of stories in the work; and they know that their Christianity gives them some knowledge about the way the 'whole' story, from creation to its end, will go. But they also know that whatever knowledge they have is partial, that a Christian perspective is also limited:

> Is seo forðgesceaft
> digol and dyrne; drihten ana wat,
> nergende faeder. Naeni eft cymeð
> hider under hrofas, þæt her for soð
> mannum secge hwylc sy meotodes gesceaft
>
> (*Maxims II*, 61–65)[12]
>
> (The future is locked and lightless; the Lord alone knows it, saving Father. No-one ever returns here under the hall-roofs who can truly tell people what the Measurer's decree is.)

The speaker recounting true events under the roof of the hall is in Old English poetry an image of the power of human knowledge and interpretation, but also of their limitations, and the power of words to create as well as reveal illusions. Transience is a universal theme in Old English poetry as well as a staple of the Anglo-Saxon homily: *Beowulf* not only amply explores this theme with respect to human life, but also exposes the transience of narrative significance, the inability of a narrative to tell the whole story. Human tellers may open and close as wisely as they can, but they relate their stories, and interpret them, in a limited field of vision, which may prevent them from perceiving the irony of their own position.[13]

[12] Quoted from *The Anglo-Saxon Poetic Records* VI: *The Anglo-Saxon Minor Poems*, ed. by E. V. K. Dobbie (New York: Columbia University Press, 1942).

[13] This is also true of the different stances – confident interpretations of *Beowulf* and Old English poetry as a whole – which Anglo-Saxonists have taken in the past, and are no doubt taking now. Allen J. Frantzen, *Desire For Origins: New Language, Old English, and Teaching the Tradition* (New Brunswick and London: Rutgers University Press, 1990), looks at the way schools of thought *requiring* the view that Anglo-Saxon civilization was superior to Roman, democratic, 'pure', etc. have alternated with those regarding it as crude, rude and embarrassing to the enlightened civilization now considering it ('Origins, Orientalism, and Anglo-Saxonism in the Sixteenth and Nineteenth Centuries', pp. 27–61). Concepts of the sophistication of the narrative have vacillated along these lines.

The poet has, then, very consciously, established two levels of audience relationship to the past. Most of the events in the poem are presented as 'history known by someone in the poem', common knowledge either because someone existing within the fictional framework of the poem was 'there' when something happened, or heard about what happened from an 'eye-witness'. Examples would be the major events of Scyld's life and the genealogical list leading to Hrothgar; the conception and building of Heorot; the divine origins of the world; Hildeburh, Finn and Hengest; the story of the ring of the Brosings; the story of the sword-hilt told by the writing on it; Sigemund; Heremod; and so on, including the story of Hygelac's fall and the unsettled period afterwards. Some events, however, are simply not available as information except to the outer audience, the audience of *Beowulf*: the life of Christ and the dragon's claiming of the hoard for itself three hundred years before its reawakening are in this category.

The existence of 'what happened' in these two categories points to the importance of narrative in another way: the *isolation* of a people from a story can have dire consequences. There is an important past which *belongs* only to the audience, though it is also invisibly *in* the past of the people in the poem: the life of Christ and its consequences, which have not yet reached the Germanic people at the time of the events in the poem. This unshared past history results both in the condemnation of some of the Danes for turning in their despair about Grendel to devil-worship, a heathen practice, and the condemnation of anyone in the *Beowulf* audience who, knowing better as a Christian, does anything similar out of despair (ll. 175–88). The isolation of the story of the Last Survivor, the gold, and the dragon illustrates this in another way: because no-one knew of this, the dragon was accidentally disturbed, Beowulf and the Geats met their ends; the Geats as a people were extinguished like the anonymous people whose gold moves from one grave (theirs) to another (Beowulf's, but symbolically the grave of the Geats as a people). This may well be a Christian poet's way of ending the poem with a sober farewell to a pagan past, but even if so, the poet has taken a great deal of trouble to establish it as a *shared* past. The Christian audience of *Beowulf* is not allowed to isolate itself from that past.

For the *Beowulf* audience, then, these different layers of relationship to the past emphasize both their closeness to and distance from a non-Christian, Germanic antiquity: some stories are part of a shared past, but some are not, and it is awareness of the Christian story which splits the frames of audience reference in the poem. When the Germanic peoples within the poem were telling their stories, Christianity was out of their reach, beyond their narrative compass; they are Germanic, but not

Anglo-Saxons, whose Christianity was brought to them later. *Beowulf* itself is told, however, by an author to an audience with a foot in each narrative circle, the unknowing and the knowing. An important point of contact is the story of creation from Genesis (ll. 90–98) which establishes ancient Germanic history in about as correct a relationship to the *Beowulf* audience as possible: the Genesis story is not known to the Danes and sung in the new hall because they are Christians or even because they possess the Old Testament, but because *it is their past*, and they know it as such because they have preserved it in poetry. Other stories from the Germanic past are thereby validated, *so long as they are recognized as incomplete* by the Anglo-Saxon audience. We need not see Alcuin's famous rhetorical question 'Quid Hinieldus cum Christo?' as condemning all Germanic heroic narrative at all times, but simply insisting that the monastic refectory not model itself on the beer-hall;[14] after all, some monastic authority thought *Beowulf* worth preserving.

One of the side-effects of the way *Beowulf* reveals both the strengths and the limitations of narrative is the way it leaves us as a modern audience stranded in ambivalence towards its hero – I speak in terms of an audience of critics, a body of critical responses often entirely opposed to one another. At the end of the story, are we able to judge its hero? It is a story about an exemplary hero – but, what, exactly, is he exemplary of, and is that the whole story?

Certainly he is exemplary of heroic values; but both the behaviour of the hero and the structuring of the many narratives that comprise the poem indicate a mournful awareness in the poet that heroic values are acted out in many ways, and that actions may be entirely in the spirit of these values while their effects are catastrophic, undoing the society the

[14] 'Verba Dei legantur in sacerdotali convivio. Ibi decet lectorem audiri, non citharistam; sermones patrum, non carmina gentilium. Quid Hinieldus cum Christo? Angusta est domus: utrosque tenere non poterit. Non vult rex celestis cum paganis et perditis nominetenus regibus communionem habere; quia rex ille aeternus regnat in caelis, ille paganus perditus plangit in inferno. Voces legentium audire in domibus tuis, non ridentium turbam in plateis.' Alcuin's Epistle IV. to Hygbald, Bishop of Lindisfarne, in 797 (*Monumenta Germaniae Historica*, p. 183). Alcuin's language is quite severe; it seems that inveighing against drunkenness, fancy dress and secular entertainments in monasteries is thematic in his letters. Opland, *Anglo-Saxon Oral Poetry*, (from which the text of this letter is quoted), comments that Alcuin meant to include only 'wandering popular entertainers' and not 'the eulogising poet' in his condemnation; he notes, 'that such entertainers were welcome visitors in Anglo-Saxon monasteries is suggested by the Council on English affairs in Rome and confirmed by the Council at Clofeshoh in 747, and one need not argue this point further' (p. 147). It is anyway clear that *Beowulf* was not likely to evoke *ridentium turbam in plateis* any more than it does now in the classroom.

values are meant to hold together. Again, this usually happens because the 'end' of a given narrative of which someone is a part is not visible until the story is 'complete' – and then it is too late. Beowulf's attempt to kill the dragon singlehandedly and enrich his people with the hoard is generous and courageous; the poet declares this to be so in his own voice, 'strengo getruwode/ anes mannes; ne bið swylc earges sið!' (he trusted in the strength of one man; such is not the way of a coward! ll. 2540–41) and in the voice of the Geats grieving over the burial mound:

> cwædon þæt he wære wyruldcyning[a]
> manna mildust ond mon(ðw)ærust,
> leodum liðost ond lofgeornost. (3180–82)
>
> (They said that he was of all worldly kings the most gentle of men, and most trustworthy, kindest to his people, and most eager for praise.)

In *Beowulf* the men who forge the alliances and take the oaths are the same people who break them and make war, leaving the women who made equally heroic political marriages grieving over the pyres of the extended families they created as a way of establishing peace. The hero who keeps at bay the destructive forces of war upon his people, as well as personal greed in himself, and who is wise, generous and just, is the same king who dies without a son as heir and leaves his people open to invasion, death and slavery. His insistence on facing the dragon alone is exemplary, both because of and in spite of its being incautious; though in disobedience to Beowulf's express command to stay out of the fight, Wiglaf's behaviour in coming to Beowulf's aid is exemplary, because of his loyalty, but he is clearly not able to fill the void left by a dead Beowulf, either as a leader or an example. The retainers who run away are bad examples, because they run away out of fear rather than obedience to their lord's command to let him fight the dragon alone.

The *exemplum* is not always a *simple* picture of what we should or should not do, and for the Anglo-Saxon audience it may sometimes amount to a verbal emblem of cultivated ambivalence. What an Anglo-Saxon audience is *supposed to* make of Germanic-heroic values is too often assumed to be absolute. Where the verbal *exemplum* is not a static picture, but a narrative or series of them, it captures the most difficult moral lesson: that moral judgements are provisional until a story is truly complete.[15] When we ourselves are part of the story – part of the

[15] While within a different genre altogether, that is exemplary prose with one foot in the

construction placed on a narrative composed of many narratives – our sense of closure is always going to be transient.

'The story' as a concept in its different forms in *Beowulf*, and *Beowulf* itself, are icons of memory and the power and impotence of memory, as stories move through the poem collectively in the form of poems about the past; as events which become poems in the course of the narrative and are narrated as stories; as events which are 'unrecorded,' yet still become part of the *Beowulf* story. For fictive audiences within *Beowulf*, and for the Anglo-Saxon audience, the accessibility *through poetry* of, for example, the creation of the world (ll. 90–98), and the life of Scyld Scefing (ll. 1–52), is witness both to memory as a victory over the limits of human life, and memory as a limited power. For the Anglo-Saxon audience, Beowulf's life takes form mysteriously, from a not very promising start ('Hean wæs lange [. . .] swyðe (wen)don, þæt he sleac wære', He was miserable for a long time [. . .] they firmly believed he was worthless, ll. 2183–87), and grows, in relation to different pasts and presents, into a story which is a monument both to the past and to a present which has much in common with it, not least because the present in which the monument stands will become the past too. For modern readers also the story of Beowulf emerges out of the unknown: the pagan Germanic world the poem is on one level 'about' and the Christian Anglo-Saxon world which the poem is also 'about'. We know very little about either of these worlds, or about *Beowulf*. Against odds heavily stacked in favour of its disappearance, a manuscript of the poem – perhaps the only one that ever existed – survived the passage of time and the burning of libraries, when so many other manuscripts did not. As poetry, *Beowulf* has survived the dissection, the many conflicting analyses and conclusions of critics.[16] As a narrative it tells us about the ways in which stories meet within a culture, flow into significant relationships, and are changed into other stories. Its history as a story continues to illuminate this process as it shifts through editions, translations, rock musicals, films, comic books, animated cartoons, and the dreams of critics which become part of the

historical and the other in the homiletic, the portrait of William the Conqueror in the Laud Chronicle's entry for 1087 is a very concise illustration of the way that juxtaposed anecdotes and opposing judgements produce no *final*, simple moral statement about the king.

16 The survival of the poem in both undergraduate and graduate syllabuses is remarkable also, given the difficulty of reading Old English – especially *so much* Old English – and the varying degrees of opacity, oddity, and strain against slippage which characterize any translation.

textual interlace of critical awareness.[17] It is part of a shared present which is always in the process of becoming the past, and it changes shape as it moves on.[18]

[17] See, for example, James W. Earl, '*Beowulf* and the Origins of Civilization', in which he analyses a dream of his.

[18] I would like to thank Jocelyn Wogan-Browne for her enormous help in rewriting this paper, which was in very rough form when she received it.

How Long is a Trojan War? Aspects of Time in the *Roman de Troie* and its Sources

PENNY ELEY

NO ONE COULD ACCUSE the Old French *Roman de Troie*[1] of being a slavish imitation of either of the two short Latin pseudo-histories of the Trojan War on which it is based.[2] Benoît de Sainte-Maure adapted his sources on a grand scale, replacing a laconic 'fit magna caedes' with battle scenes up to 2,500 lines in length, and interweaving them with sophisticated accounts of love-affairs which receive either the briefest of mentions or no mention at all in the originals. Such major modifications tell us a good deal about the author's perception of audience expectations in the second half of the twelfth century.[3] Equally illuminating, however, are some of the minor alterations which Benoît made, and which cannot be so readily attributed to the need to re-create flat prose narratives for a public whose responses had been conditioned by the *chansons de geste*, the *Roman de Thèbes* and *Pyramus et Thisbé*. The chronology of the Trojan War is a case in point.[4]

1 Benoît de Sainte-Maure, *Le Roman de Troie*, ed. by Léopold Constans, SATF, 6 vols (Paris: Firmin-Didot, 1904–12).

2 Dares Phrygius, *De Excidio Troiae Historia*, ed. by Ferdinand Meister (Leipzig: Teubner, 1873); Dictys Cretensis, *Ephemeris Belli Troiani*, ed. by Werner Eisenhut (Leipzig: Teubner, 1958).

3 See Penny Sullivan, 'Translation and Adaptation in the *Roman de Troie*', in *The Spirit of the Court: Selected Proceedings of the Fourth Congress of the International Courtly Literature Society (Toronto, 1983)*, ed. by Glyn S. Burgess and Robert A. Taylor (Cambridge: Brewer, 1985), pp. 350–59.

4 The basic reference for the treatment of time in medieval French writing remains Richard Glasser, *Time in French Life and Thought*, trans. by C. G. Pearson (Manchester University Press, 1972), esp. Chapters 1–3 (first published as *Studien zur Geschichte des französischen Zeitbegriffs* (Munich: Hueber, 1936)). Other useful contributions include

Throughout its length, the text of Dares' *Historia* is punctuated by references to the duration of the various phases of the conflict. The majority of these references are very precise, giving an exact number of days, months or years, and show remarkably little variation from one MS to another. There are only three relatively minor gaps in the information required to draw up a complete internal chronology for the text (see Table I). The impression of historical accuracy which this creates is further reinforced in the final section of the work, which states that the Trojan War lasted for ten years, six months and twelve days.[5] Such precision commands respect: everyone knows the tradition according to which the Greeks spent ten years at Troy, but surely only one of the participants (which is what Dares purports to be) could have known *exactly* how long the conflict lasted. The only problem is that a closer inspection reveals a significant discrepancy between the authoritative time-frame established in section XLIV and the chronological detail provided by the text. Even if we allow for a rather generous interpretation of the phrase 'aliquot dies' and the periods not specified in the text (and in all these cases the context implies a fairly short duration), the internal chronology suggests a total length for the war of less than eight-and-a half years, some two years short of the final figure. Such a lack of consistency not only highlights the fraudulent nature of the text, but also points to one of the principal elements in its strategy of deception:

Georges Poulet, *Etudes sur le temps humain*, 4 vols (Paris: Plon, 1950–68), I, I–XLVII; Philippe Ménard, 'Le Temps et la durée dans les romans de Chrétien de Troyes', *Le Moyen Age*, 73 (1967), 375–401; *Aspects of Time*, ed. by C. A. Patrides (Manchester University Press; University of Toronto Press, 1976), pp. 1–56; Minette Grunmann-Gaudet, 'The Representation of Time in *La Chanson de Roland*', in *The Nature of Medieval Narrative*, ed. by Minette Grunmann-Gaudet and Robin F. Jones, French Forum Monographs, 22 (Lexington, KY: French Forum, 1980), pp. 77–97; Richard Lock, *Aspects of Time in Medieval Literature*, Garland Publications in Comparative Literature (New York and London: Garland, 1985); Bernard Guidot, *Recherches sur la chanson de geste au XIIIe siècle, d'après certaines oeuvres du cycle de Guillaume d'Orange*, 2 vols (Aix-en-Provence: Université de Provence, 1986), pp. 714–30; *Le Temps et la durée dans la littérature au moyen âge et à la Renaissance*, ed. Yvonne Bellenger (Paris: Nizet, 1986), and Joseph J. Duggan, 'The Experience of Time as a Fundamental Element of the Stock of Knowledge in Medieval Society', in *Grundriss der romanischen Literaturen des Mittelalters Volume XI.1: La Littérature historiographique des origines à 1500*, ed. by Hans Ulrich Gumbrecht, Ursula Link-Heer and Peter-Michael Spangenberg (Heidelberg: Winter, 1987), pp. 127–34.

[5] 'Historians considered precise indications of time as an attribute of serious historical writing.' Glasser, p. 73. There is no mention in Dictys of the overall length of the war, although II,9 does contain a reference to the fact that eight years had passed between the Greeks' first making preparations for war and their sailing from Aulis.

namely, the use of a purely superficial precision to confer a spurious historicity.[6]

The success of this strategy can be judged in part by the extent to which Benoît reproduces the internal chronology of the *Historia* in the first 24,000 lines of his *Roman de Troie* (hereafter *RT*), as can be seen from Table II.

TABLE I: INTERNAL CHRONOLOGY OF DARES' *HISTORIA*

Section	Events	Duration
XV–XVIII	Invasion	
	occupation of Tenedon	?
XIX–XX	1st battle	2 days
	truce	2 years
XX–XXII	2nd battle	80 days
	truce	3 years
XXIII	3rd battle	30 days
	truce	6 months
XXIII	4th battle	12 days
	truce	30 days
XXIV–XXV	5th battle (death of Hector)	1 day
	truce	2 months
XXVI–XXVII	6th battle	aliquot dies
	truce	1 year
XXVII–XXX	7th battle	7 days
	truce	2 months
XXX–XXXI	8th battle	aliquot dies
	truce	6 months
XXXII	9th battle	aliquot dies
	truce	30 days
XXXIII–XXXV	10th battle	6 days*
	truce inc. murder of Achilles	20 days**
	truce	? (short)
XXXV–XLI	Final battle, inc.	aliquot dies x2
	2 sieges	? (short)

* var. 7   ** var. 30

6 Another instance of this can found in the precise numbers of Greek and Trojan casualties (886,000 and 676,000 respectively) also given in section XLIV. For the first of these figures to be possible, each of the Greek ships which set out for Troy would have had to be carrying nearly a thousand men.

TABLE II: INTERNAL CHRONOLOGY OF *RT*

Lines	Events	Duration
5583–7060	Invasion	
	occupation of Tenedon	over 1 year
7061–10560	1st & 2nd battles	1+1 days
	truce	2 months*
10561–13892	3rd–7th battles	1+1+1+1+80 days
	truce	3 months
13893–15186	8th battle	30 days
	truce	6 months
15187–15262	9th battle	12 days
	truce	30 days
15263–17044	10th battle (death of Hector)	1 day
	truce	2 months
17045–18475	11th battle	several days
	truce	? (not in source)[7]
18476–19959	12th & 13th battles	1+7 days
	truce	2 months**
19960–20417	14th & 15th battles	1 day +?
	truce	6 months***
20418–20878	16th & 17th battles	1+8 days#
	truce	?(short)
20879–22598	18th & 19th battles	6+10? days
	truce inc. murder of Achilles	30 days
	truce	1 month
22599–24396	20th battle	1 day
	siege	over 2 months##
	final battle	over 2 months
	final siege	? (9 days)

* var. 1 month ** var. 3 months *** var. 1 year
# var. 10, 20 days ## var. over 3 months

[7] In l. 17348 Benoît states that his source does not indicate how long this truce lasted. Only one of the extant MSS, L, omits the words 'Palamedes indutias fecit in annum' in section XXVI, which might suggest that it, rather than G, was Benoît's original (Meister argues the case for G on pp. XXVI–XXIX). However, G is the only MS to give the length of the truce during which Achilles is murdered as thirty days, which is the figure which appears in *RT*. Taken together, these two facts suggest that Benoît may have been working from a lost MS of the same family, intermediate between G and L.

The overall pattern of twelve main phases separated by truces of varying lengths is identical in the two texts. Benoît has increased the total number of battles from eleven to twenty-one, by dividing the two-day battle in the second phase into two separate battles, and by adding one or more days' fighting to phases three and eight to twelve inclusive; however, the regular alternation of truces and consecutive days or weeks of battles remains the same as in Dares.[8] The only significant alterations are to be found in the durations of the first and second truces and of the final battle. According to Dares, the first truce lasts for two years, and the second for three; in *RT* the numbers remain the same, but the years are transformed into months. The reason for this modification would appear to be a concern for *vraisemblance*, made more acute by Benoît's own re-interpretation of the length of the occupation of Tenedon. Sections XVII–XIX of the *Historia* clearly imply that only a short time elapsed between the sack of Tenedon and the Greeks' attack on Troy itself. In *RT*, this becomes a period of well over a year (see ll. 7005–06), a change apparently motivated by the desire to increase suspense by delaying the fateful first encounter between the two armies. Greeks and Trojans having finally joined battle after this extended phoney war, would it not have been faintly absurd to suggest that they then spent less than three months out of the next five-and-a-quarter years actually fighting one another?

A similar concern with literary values would seem to lie behind Benoît's decision to change the length of the final battle from 'aliquot dies' to over two months (*RT* ll. 23777–80 and 23792–94). For an author and audience conditioned by the mental and emotional structures of the *chansons de geste*, the last battle must be seen to provide a fitting climax to an epic struggle. Since *RT* is written from an unmistakably pro-Trojan point of view, the issue must also appear to remain in doubt, and hopes of cheating fate must remain alive, for as long as possible. Hence both the duration of the fighting in *RT*, and the explicit recognition of how evenly-matched the two sides were until the death of Panthesilée finally tipped the balance in favour of the Greeks:

> Demi jor dura cel estrif,
> Que nus ne s'en pot resortir
> Ne eschaper ne defoïr,

8 Benoît numbers the battles up to and including the nineteenth (l. 21243); this is followed by a truce, a further battle and the first siege; the second, definitive siege is preceded by a long period of uninterrupted fighting which Constans divided somewhat arbitrarily into three battles.

> Ne ne saveient qui veintreit
> Ne as queus d'eus le chans sereit. (24348–52)

There remains the question of the overall length of the war. Benoît maintains the oracle's prediction that Troy would fall in the tenth year of the conflict, and makes two other references to the fact that the war at Troy lasted for ten years (*RT* ll. 254 and 14973). He does not, however, reproduce the precise figure of ten years, six months and twelve days given by Dares, despite having adopted his source's chronology, with very few modifications, for the major events of the conflict. This represents a deliberate omission on Benoît's part. We can be certain that section XLIV was not missing from his copy of Dares, since in line 27440 he refers to the fact that Antenor was accompanied into exile by 2,500 followers, a number taken directly from the final section of the *Historia*. Moreover, there is a very much greater discrepancy between internal chronology and overall time-frame in the case of *RT* than there is in Dares: the total duration of the events listed in Table II is just over five years at best. Taken together, these facts suggest a quite different textual strategy from that of the *Historia*. The loss of precision with regard to time seems to imply that *RT* makes no pretence of historicity, but belongs instead to a category of narrative in which the principal function of time is something other than establishing a relationship between the events narrated and external reality.

In this respect, it is interesting to compare *RT* with the works of Benoît's contemporary Wace. The precise datings in the *Roman de Rou* prompted Richard Glasser to comment on Wace's 'sense of temporal order and of historical reality', a sense which he felt was conspicuously absent in other twelfth-century narratives (p. 15). Similar comments might also be made about the *Brut*, where Wace scrupulously reproduces Geoffrey of Monmouth's synchronisation of the reigns of the early kings of Britain with notable events in biblical and classical history. In one instance he even improves upon his source, by giving the precise date of Caesar's invasion of Gaul, which does not figure in the *Historia Regum Britanniae*.[9] Although Glasser did not address the question of genre directly, his use of the term 'rhymed chronicle' to describe *Rou* implies that the explanation for the difference between Wace and other vernacular authors of the period is to be found in the kind of writing they were engaged in. All the other texts which Glasser cites as examples of

[9] *Le Roman de Brut de Wace*, ed. by Ivor Arnold, SATF, 2 vols (Paris, 1938 and 1940), ll. 3827–30: 'Seissante anz ainz que Jesu Crist/De Seinte Marie nasquist,/Ert Julius Cesar meüz,/De Rome ert en France venuz.'

twelfth-century attitudes towards time (principally *chansons de geste*) are in fact pieces of extended narrative *fiction*, conceived and received as entertainment. The absence of a 'sense of temporal order' in such texts is part of the 'émancipation du récit par rapport à la temporalité diégétique' which Genette sees as one of the hallmarks of fictional narratives.[10] The fact that Wace took pains to maintain and even to increase the temporal precision of his sources suggests that he saw himself as a chronicler, not a *romancier*. Equally, the fact that Benoît does *not* establish explicit links between intra- and extra-diegetic time, and, moreover, actually rejects the precision of his source with regard to the length of the war, signals that *RT* was intended to be read as fiction, not history.[11] This is certainly how it was received by the thirteenth-century compilers of MSS B (BN fr. 375), E (BN fr. 794), H (BN fr. 1450) and the Middleton MS at the University of Nottingham, who chose to present *RT* alongside a wide variety of vernacular romances, *chansons de geste*, and even fabliaux. We can only speculate about the reasons for the shift in perception evidenced by the fourteenth-century Italian MS F (BN fr. 821), in which *RT* appears with Cato, Boethius, a *Passion de Nostre Seigneur* and parts of the *Histoire ancienne jusqu'à César*.

Many of the other conclusions reached by Glasser about medieval vernacular writing remain valid, provided that the implicit assumption that they relate to fictional rather than non-fictional narratives is borne in mind.[12] Of particular relevance here is what he has to say about the predominance of affective time in twelfth-century writing. A distinction needs to be drawn, however, between the concepts of 'affective' and 'subjective' time. Subjective time can be defined as time perceived in relation to the experience of the human subject, rather than to objective historical chronology. The phrase affective time, on the other hand, describes the use of temporal indications to evoke a particular emotional response, which is conditioned by the symbolic associations of certain

10 Gérard Genette, *Figures III*, (Paris: Seuil, 1972), pp. 178–82 and 228–37 (p. 179). For a lucid summary of critical discussions of the relationship between history and fiction, see Paul Ricoeur, 'Pour une théorie du discours narratif' and 'Récit fictif – récit narratif' in *La Narrativité*, ed. by Dorian Tiffeneau, Collection Phénoménologie et Herméneutique (Paris: Editions du CNRS, 1980), pp. 5–68 and 251–71 respectively.

11 Had Benoît's perception of his task been different, the information he needed to link the Trojan War with biblical or pre-classical history was readily available in Book 3 of the *Imago Mundi* attributed to Honorius of Autun (*PL*, 172, cols 168–70).

12 This distinction is also implicit in Philippe Ménard's review of Richard Lock, *Aspects of Time*, *Cahiers de Civilisation Médiévale*, 30 (1987), 283–84, and in Bernard Guidot's article 'Mesure du temps et flou chronologique dans quelques chansons de geste du XIIIe siècle', in *Le Temps et la durée*, pp. 55–70 (also published in *Annales de l'Est*, 38 (1986), 171–86).

seasons, durations, or times of day, rather than to draw attention to the quantifiable passage of time. Examples of the affective use of time in *RT* can be found in the many temporal references which represent additions to Dares and Dictys. Such additions occur throughout the text: allusions to the time of day or night (Jason's Argonauts embark in the evening, l. 1128; the Greek fleet founders after none on the second day of a great storm in the Aegean, ll. 27618–19); to the duration of events such as feasts (that held by Peleus for Jason lasts seven days, l. 814) or journeys (the Paflagonians take ten months and three weeks to reach Troy, ll. 6825–26), and even to the days of the week (Telegonus reaches Ulixès' stronghold on the first day of the week, ll. 30044–45). In almost every case, the addition of a reference to time reflects the author's desire to impress upon his audience the grandeur of an occasion or the difficulties and dangers faced by his characters.

Some events are marked by the presence of clusters of such references, forming detailed 'micro-chronologies' which represent significant expansions of the temporal indications given by the sources. Two examples will illustrate the point. According to Dares, the abduction of Helen from the temple on Cythera was to take place sometime during the night:

> Alexander imperat, ut omnes in navibus sint parati, nocte classem solvant, de fano Helenam eripiant secum eam auferant. (section x)

In *RT*, on the other hand, the timing of the raid is established with great precision. A decision is taken to attack at night, after the moon has set (l. 4459); as evening falls, some of the Trojans take the opportunity to have a meal (ll. 4476–79); the moon shines brightly at nightfall, but sets before 'prinsome' (ll. 4479–81); the raid takes place in darkness, but it is broad daylight before the Trojans manage to set sail with their prisoners (ll. 4585–86). Likewise, Dictys gives few indications of time when describing Antenor's negotiations with the Greeks, leading up to the surrender of the Palladion. Antenor returns to Troy at an unspecified time (IV,22 and V,4), and then attends a banquet; early next morning he goes to a meeting of the council (V,1); at daybreak the following day he and Aeneas go out to the ships (V,4). In Benoît's version, Antenor returns from his first visit to the Greek camp late in the evening (l. 24969), and spends a long time at table with the other leaders (l. 24979). Next morning there is a meeting, and the rest of the day is spent collecting the dead (ll. 25253–57); that night Antenor's son Glaucon is buried and mourned till dawn (ll. 25260–61). The negotiators ride back to the Greek camp at first light (ll. 25308–89), and it is still early when the Greek council meets (ll. 25334–36).

It is noticeable that these micro-chronologies tend to be associated with events of particular significance within the story of the conflict, events which are also likely to be marked by clusters of authorial interventions and other foregrounding devices.[13] In one of these episodes, the murder of Achilles, Benoît not only adds indications of time to his source, but also modifies Dares' timing so as to increase the dramatic intensity of his own narration. Section XXXIV of the *Historia* tells how Hecuba persuades Alexander (Paris) to kill Achilles, and how he then makes his preparations:

> Noctu de exercitu eligunter fortissimi et in fano Apollonis collocantur, signum accipiunt. Hecuba ad Achillem, sicuti condixerat, nuntium mittit. Achilles leatus Polyxena amans postera die ad fanum se venturum constituit. Interea Achilles sequenti die cum Antilocho Nestoris filio ad constitutum veniunt.

In *RT* events are delayed so that the act of treachery is committed under cover of darkness: the rendez-vous is fixed for the following evening, before moonrise (ll. 21983–88). Paris sets his ambush at nightfall (ll. 22097–98), and Achilles and Antilochus set out after dark (ll. 22157–62).[14] The audience is then invited to visualise the two Greeks arriving at their destination both literally and metaphorically in the dark:

> Li lieus fu soutis e segreiz:
> Hisdor lor en prist e esfreiz.
> Descendu sont li dui vassal:
> Chascuns aresne son cheval;
> Li sans lor monte a mont el vis. (22169–73)

A cry is heard, spears are hurled and armed men leap out of the darkness. The dark deed is done and the bodies of Achilles and Antilochus thrown out of the temple before daybreak (ll. 22310–11); Paris then waits until it is light before organising the burial of his own men (ll. 22312–16). In Dares, the transition from night to day is little more than an incidental detail, reminiscent of the rather mechanical, unmotivated use of

[13] See my article 'Author and Audience in the *Roman de Troie*', in *Courtly Literature: Culture and Context*, ed. by Keith Busby and Erik Kooper, Utrecht Publications in General and Comparative Literature, 25 (Amsterdam: John Benjamins, 1990), pp. 179–90 (pp. 185–86).

[14] There is an inconsistency here, in that the moon is shining as they leave (l. 22161). Perhaps Benoît simply forgot what he had written some two hundred lines earlier; perhaps his concern for *vraisemblance* overrode other considerations (how could the two Greeks expect to find their way through the enemy lines in total darkness?).

references to dawn and nightfall in many *chansons de geste*.[15] In *RT*, on the other hand, nightfall, darkness, dawn and daylight are woven into a complex symbolic structure illustrating the moral depths to which war ultimately reduces those who provoke it.

The description of the murder of Achilles, and others like it, indicate that in *RT* references to time are more than simple conventional markers of the forward progress of the narrative. They form part of a careful literary patterning, in which their value is affective and symbolic rather than temporal. Additions are made to the sources not because the length of Peleus' feast or the time at which Glaucon was buried have a bearing on subsequent events, but because they serve to emphasise the extent of the king's duplicity or to foreground the physical and emotional stress suffered by Antenor. Likewise, when Benoît's Achilles says in line 18421, and again in line 19578, that the war has already been going on for at least five years, this is not intended to be a statement of temporal fact (a glance at Table II will show that this cannot be the case). Its function is rather to provide supporting evidence for the hero's supposed war-weariness, and also to signal to the audience, who know that the war is destined to last for ten years, that a great deal more drama and suffering lies ahead before the oracle's prediction can be fulfilled. In the same way, coherent internal chronologies may be created for individual episodes, but their purpose is not to bring the events narrated into relation with extra-diegetic time or with the text's own overall time frame. It is, rather, to heighten the audience's awareness of key events and to maintain the dramatic momentum at high points in the narrative.

These additions to and modifications of source material in *RT* also raise questions about the process of composition of this lengthy and complex work. While there may be some evidence in the text of concern with overall structure, it is clear from our analysis that time does not function as a structuring principle in *RT*, nor is it thematised after the fashion of Chrétien's *Yvain*.[16] The identification of a significant number of carefully structured micro-chronologies (in addition to those noted above, we should include the relationship between Jason and Medea, Antenor's mission to Greece, the first attack on Troy, Achilles' negotiations with Priam and Hecuba, the twentieth battle and the sack of Troy) points to a process in which the primary focus is the episode, conceived as an autonomous temporal unit located within a sequence whose coherence is thematic (the escalation and resolution of the most famous war in literature) rather than chronological.

15 See Guidot, *Recherches*, pp. 727–29.
16 See Lock, pp. 62–79.

This idea is reinforced by the fact that there is almost no chronological cross-referencing between episodes. We learn that the Amazons set out for Troy during the siege which signalled the end of the twentieth battle, but apart from this, explicit statements about certain events taking place before, during or after others are conspicuous by their absence.[17] This is particularly noticeable in the last 3,000 lines of the text, which deal with the homecomings of individual members of the Greek army. It is clear from Dictys, on whom this section is based, that the events narrated here take place simultaneously in various parts of the Aegean: Book VI of the *Ephemeris* is marked by the recurrence of the adverb 'interim' and the phrase 'per idem tempus', which link the various stories into a reasonably coherent whole.[18] *RT* follows Dictys very closely in terms of the number and sequence of episodes, and even in such precise detail as the fact that the goings-on at the wedding of Peleus and Thetis led to the occasion becoming known as 'the banquet of the gods' (Dictys VI,7; *RT* ll. 29165–74). And yet, only two of the dozen or so temporal links between episodes in the *Ephemeris* are preserved by Benoît (*RT* ll. 28549–50 and 29057–59). The others are either ignored, or replaced by the kind of brief résumé and/or direct address to the audience which characterises the start of a new development in Beroul's *Tristran* or some of the earlier *chansons de geste*. So, for example, whereas Dictys explicitly links the arrival of Menelaus and Helen on Crete with Orestes' killing of Clytemnestra and Aegisthus ('per idem tempus Menelaus adpulsus Cretam cuncta super Agamemnone regnoque eius cognoscit', VI,3), Benoît prefers a purely fortuitous connection between the two events:

> Si com le demenot Fortune
> Ert reis Menelaus arivez
> En Crete mout desbaretez. (28412–14)

On the other hand, when the same phrase 'per idem tempus' is used to establish a relationship between the deaths of Neoptolemus and Ulysses (Dictys VI,14), Benoît replaces it with a four-line introduction which both re-affirms his role as story-teller and underlines the importance of this, the final episode in his saga:

> Ore entendez ici après
> Com faitement dans Ulixès

[17] The only other notable exception comes in ll. 29079–86 where, in an addition to Dictys, Benoît announces that he will now relate what happened to Pirrus after he survived the terrible storm described earlier (in ll. 27561–619).

[18] See Dictys, Book VI, sections 2,3,5,6,7,13,14 and 15.

Fu morz e trespassez de vie:
Tel merveille n'iert mais oïe. (29815–18)

In a context where the fortunes of many different individuals are being followed, the omission of temporal links between episodes results in a confusing and fragmented narrative which compares unfavourably with its relatively more structured source. Benoît may have moved away from parataxis at the level of sentence structure, but his rejection of the temporal hypotaxis offered by Dictys indicates to what extent his literary technique remains rooted in the traditions of the *chansons de geste*. Even when presented with a viable solution to the problem of relating simultaneous events in a linear narrative, our author deliberately chooses to isolate individual elements and place them in a simple sequence of juxtaposed episodes. The use of interlace in vernacular fiction is still very much in the future.[19]

How long, then, is a Trojan War? The answer seems to depend on how an author perceives the kind of writing he is engaged in – or, perhaps, how he wants his writing to be received by his audience or readers. Providing a precise (though spurious) answer to the question becomes a major element in Dares' strategy of presenting the *Historia* as history. Rejecting that answer in favour of the emotionally resonant imprecision of tradition and legend is one way in which Benoît de Sainte-Maure sets out his stall as a writer of fictional narratives. What really matters to Benoît, as a *romancier*, and to his audience, as consumers of fiction, is the *how* and the *why* of the Trojan War, not the *when* and the *how long* (Glasser, p. 23). Other shifts and transpositions have left their mark in less obvious modifications of the representation of time in the sources. The objective time of Dares is replaced by affective time, which, through the creation of detailed micro-chronologies for individual episodes, functions as a foregrounding device, ultimately conditioning audience response to significant events in the narrative. The impact of these clusters of references to time is reinforced by the temporal parataxis inherent in traditional episodic construction, which, as we have seen, is preferred to the prototype interlace of Book VI of Dictys, even at the expense of a certain narrative coherence.

19 On the links with the *chansons de geste*, see Aimé Petit, *Naissances du roman: les techniques littéraires dans les romans antiques du XIIe siècle* (Paris: Champion; Geneva: Slatkine, 1985), pp. 287–96. The technique of alternating battle scenes with subplots (notably love stories), which Petit describes on p. 318 as 'un procédé qui fait penser à celui de l'entrelacement', is never used for the narration of simultaneous actions.

Transposing the Enterprise of Adventure: Malory's 'Take the Adventure' and French Tradition

JOY WALLACE

THE QUESTION OF the development and use of Malory's expression 'take the adventure' is of more than purely semantic interest as it impinges also upon technical, conceptual, structural and ethical aspects of the study of the *Morte Darthur*.[1] In terms of technique, Malory's treatment of the motif reveals a feature of his transmission and transposition of what he is pleased to call the 'Freynshe book': the body of thirteenth-century French prose Arthurian romances which, together with English romances and chronicles, formed the chief sources of the *Morte Darthur*.

1 There is a growing scholarly interest in the concept of *aventure* in medieval literature, reflected in the XVth Annual International Arthurian Congress held at Leuven in 1987, where *aventure* formed one of the topics for discussion; see *Arturus Rex 2: Acta Conventus Lovaniensis 1987*, ed. by W. Van Hoecke, G. Tournoy, W. Verbeke (Leuven: Leuven University Press, 1991). Important studies of some aspect or aspects of *aventure* prior to this conference include E. Eberwein, *Zur Deutung mittelalterlicher Existenz* (Bonn and Cologne: Roehrscheid, 1933), esp. pp. 29–32; R. Locatelli, 'L'avventura nei romanzi di Chrétien de Troyes e nei suoi imitatori', *Acme, Annali della Facoltà di Filosofia e Lettere dell'Università Statale di Milano*, 4 (1951), 3–23; E. Köhler, *Ideal und Wirchlichkeit in der höfischen Epik*, 2nd edn (Tübingen: Niemeyer, 1970), trans. by E. Kaufholz as *L'Aventure chevaleresque, idéal et réalité dans le roman courtois* (Paris: Gallimard, 1974); G. Burgess, *Contribution à l'étude du vocabulaire pré-courtois* (Geneva: Droz, 1970), pp. 44–55; W. R. J. Barron, 'The Ambivalence of Adventure: Verbal Ambiguity in *Sir Gawain and the Green Knight*, Fitt I', in *The Legend of Arthur in the Middle Ages, Studies Presented to* A. H. *Diverres by Colleagues, Pupils and Friends*, ed. by P. B. Grout, R. A. Lodge, C. E. Pickford and E. K. C. Varty (Cambridge: Brewer, 1983), pp. 28–40; D. H. Green, 'The Concept *Aventiure* in *Parzifal*', in *Approaches to Wolfram von Eschenbach: Five essays*, ed. by D. H. Green and L. P. Johnson (Bern: Lang, 1978), pp. 83–157. See also M. Whitaker, *Malory's Kingdom of Adventure* (Cambridge: Brewer, 1984); D. L. Hoffman, 'Malory's "Cinderella Knights" and the Notion of Adventure', *Philological Quarterly*, 67 (1988), 45–56.

The conceptual interest of the investigation has already been suggested by Jill Mann, who argued in an important essay that the expression 'take the adventure', when used by Malory's knights, indicates a transposition of French *emprendre l'aventure* by the English author.[2] In her opinion, Malory's rejection, in the 'Tale of King Arthur', of most of the metaphysical scheme imposed by the Grail adventures upon his chief source for the tale, the *Suite du Merlin*, opens the way for his expression 'take the adventure' to imply a negotiation with an 'autonomous and uncertainly organised world' (p. 89) which is not explicitly controlled, as is the world of his source, by God. 'Taking the adventure' in the *Morte Darthur* is then, in Professor Mann's interpretation, much less the constrained submission to the will of God that it is in the *Suite* than a willed submission to chance, the unknown and irrational element in life.[3] In the course of investigating the technical and conceptual aspects of Malory's transmission of the motif, we shall encroach upon the equally important questions of the structural principles, and the constructed ethics, of the *Morte Darthur*. In Part I, I address the conceptual aspect of the motif: the localization of and limitation to the irrational contained within its formation in French tradition and in Malory's transmission of that tradition. Basic to the argument of this section is a contention about Malory's technique of adaptation. In brief, a word-for-word comparison of the relationship between the *Morte Darthur* and its French sources needs to be informed by an awareness that Malory sometimes transposed words and phrases from a part of the *Freynshe book* other than the one he was ostensibly following. In Part II, I address the structural and ethical aspects, describing how Malory's transposition advances a critique of the motif which is original to the *Morte Darthur*.

FORMATION AND TRANSMISSION OF THE MOTIF

Malory's phrase 'take the adventure' is an Englishing of the French *emprendre l'aventure* and draws on a complex set of notions: mortal danger, justice, contractual rights and obligations, providence and

2 J. Mann, '"Taking the Adventure": Malory and the *Suite du Merlin*', in *Aspects of Malory*, ed. by T. Takamiya and D. Brewer (Cambridge: Brewer), 1981, pp. 71–91.

3 In the terms suggested by F. P. Pickering, Malory's use of 'take the adventure' would then signify the transposition of an Augustinian scheme into a Boethian one. The fullest statement of Pickering's theory is found in *Augustinus oder Boethius? Geschichtsschreibung und epische Dichtung im Mittelalter und in der Neuzeit*, 2 vols (Berlin: E. Schmidt, 1967 and 1976). See also his *Essays on Medieval German Literature and Iconography* (Cambridge: Cambridge University Press, 1980), especially 'Notes on Fate and Fortune', pp. 95–109 and 'The "fortune" of Hartmann's Erec', pp. 110–29; and his *Literature and Art in the Middle Ages* (London: Macmillan, 1970), pp. 168–222.

custom. I consider that the genesis of the motif may be found in Chrétien. While the phrase *emprendre l'aventure* itself is not found in his works, its constituent parts may be traced to three other phrases found in the *Chevalier de la Charrete*: *anprandre la bataille*; *se metre en aventure*; and *passer un passage/trespas*.[4] From the instances of these phrases it is possible to isolate a formal constraint upon the wilder connotations of chance and recklessness in the enterprise of adventure. God and feudal obligation underpin the semantic clusters which express the idea of putting oneself at risk by undertaking a battle, whilst the irrational and arbitrary can be said mainly to reside in the encounter with the *passage*. The contexts of the four instances of *se metre en aventure* in the *Charrete*,[5] seem to have given to the phrase *emprendre l'aventure* (which occurs later in the prose romance tradition) the connotation of a specific calculated risk which is to be taken at a particular place, or *passage*. The first instance of *se metre en aventure* is found in Lancelot's reply to the knight who has offered him an easy passage across a stretch of water – for a price. Lancelot replies that he has no intention of so risking his head (*Charrete*, 2636–39). He thus utters a specific response to a calculated risk which is located in a particular place.[6] *Aventure* here is 'risk' or 'mortal danger', rather than pure contingency. The *passage* in question is a crudely physical one; the tenor of the bargain proposed is that of reciprocity rather than justice; the arbitrary or irrational is located in the notion of a 'custom', the upholding of which imposes difficult tasks upon the knight who would engage with it.[7] Yet, as the *Charrete* also shows, it is the nature of *aventure* to go beyond specific trials in particular places and this opens up around Chrétien's use of *se metre en aventure* a space of the unknown into which God can be introduced. The damsel who tells Lancelot and Gauvain of the 'deus molt felons passages' (l. 655)[8] that

[4] References throughout this essay are to Chrétien de Troyes, *Le Chevalier de la Charrete* (*Lancelot*), ed. by M. Roques, Classiques Français du Moyen Age, 86 (Paris: Champion, 1958).

[5] See *Charrete*, ll. 2636–39; 3084–90; 3999; 4804–09, and M.-L. Ollier, *Lexique et concordance de Chrétien de Troyes* (Montreal: University of Montreal, and Paris: J. Vrin, 1986), pp. 262–64.

[6] Compare Thomas, *Les Fragments du Roman de Tristan*, ed. by B. H. Wind, 2nd edn, Textes Littéraires Français, 92 (Geneva: Droz and Paris: Minard, 1960), Frag. Douce, ll. 1172–73, where Caerdin's use of the expression indicates a general attitude to the possibility of danger of an unspecified kind.

[7] On custom, see E. Faral, *Recherches sur les sources latines des contes et romans courtois du moyen âge* (Paris: Champion, 1913), pp. 307–88; E. Köhler, 'Le Rôle de la coutume dans les romans de Chrétien de Troyes', *Romania*, 81 (1960), 386–97; L. Carasso-Bulow, *The Merveilleux in Chrétien de Troyes' Romances* (Geneva: Droz, 1976), p. 127.

[8] On the *passages* of the water and sword bridges, see R. S. Loomis, *Arthurian Tradition and Chrétien de Troyes* (New York and London: Columbia University Press, 1949), pp.

have to be crossed in order to reach Gorre adds 'mes il a assez antre deus/ avantures don je me tes' (ll. 666–67), which suggests that there is an element of the unknown beyond the dangers of the two *passages* which she does describe. As the next instance of the expression in the text indicates, God has a part to play in the notion of the dangerous *passage* (ll. 3084–90). Lancelot determines to undertake the trial of the bridge while at the same time submitting to the will of God (l. 3088). The folk-motif of the dangerous *passage* has become more complex than in ll. 2636–39; it is now a trial both of the hero's physical prowess and of his faith in God.

This adds a new dimension to the concept of *se metre en aventure* which is made more explicit in the subsequent use of the expression in the *Charrete*. It is developed in the prose romance tradition (particularly in the *Mort Artu*)[9] where Malory met it and informs the determination of his Balin and Launcelot to 'take the adventure that God woll ordayne for' or 'gyff' them.[10] Through this dimension the concept of *se metre en aventure* moves away from the mysterious implications of *passage* towards a context both legal and religious. In the *Charrete*, *se metre en aventure* is closely connected with another phrase, *anprandre la bataille* (ll. 4909; 4928–29; 4938) and thus locates the mysterious irrational aspect in the expression 'take the adventure' specifically in *passage*, for in *anprandre la bataille*, irrationality is replaced by notions of providential control, contract and obligation. Putting oneself *en aventure* by undertaking a battle on behalf of someone else is not an unstructured submission to chance: it occurs within the legal context of the judicial duel, which is posited on the notion of immanent justice.[11] As Beverly Kennedy explains (pp. 42–44), the perception of the element of chance incorporated in the duel was more than the kind of bookmakers' odds which might be calculated from the comparative strengths and weaknesses of the opponents. God had a role to play, although the precise nature and extent of His participation in the *aventure* of trial by combat was not universally agreed. We find evidence of what Kennedy terms the 'religious' attitude

222–27. For a more recent discussion of the motif, see J.-C. Lozachmeur, 'Le Motif du "passage périlleux" dans les romans arthuriens et dans la littérature orale bretonne', *Études Celtiques*, 15 (1976–77), 291–301.

9 See, for example *La Mort le roi Artu*, ed. by J. Frappier, Textes Littéraires Français, 58 (Geneva: Droz, 1964), 75.38; 76.18; 84.10; 119.25; 146.51.

10 See Sir Thomas Malory, *Morte Darthur*, in *The Works of Sir Thomas Malory*, ed. by E. Vinaver, rev. by P. J. C. Field, 3rd edn, 3 vols (Oxford: Oxford University Press, 1990), I, 64.12–13; 70.19–20, 89.4–5; II, 1066.17–18.

11 See R. Howard Bloch, *Medieval French Literature and Law* (Berkeley: California University Press, 1977), pp. 13–62; B. Kennedy, *Knighthood in the 'Morte Darthur'* (Cambridge: Brewer, 1985), pp. 39–47.

in the preliminaries to the second battle fought between Lancelot and Meleagant in the *Charrete* (ll. 4943–84).

In the context of a judicial duel the power of the irrational is limited not only by the role of God but also by the elements of contract and obligation. This aspect enhances our understanding of the term 'to take the adventure' which occurs later in Malory's 'Balin' narrative within a feudal structure requiring Balin to win back Arthur's favour. The knight's placing himself *en aventure* for someone other than himself gives him certain rights. In the legal context in which the battle for the queen in Gorre takes place in the *Charrete*, the simple contractual notion expressed before Lancelot crosses the sword-bridge (his faith in God will protect and strengthen him in the face of physical danger) becomes more complex. The expression *se metre en aventure* is used by Bademagu to Lancelot and by Meleagant to his father in both judicial duels fought by the two knights to decide who has the right to the queen. Bademagu is disturbed that the queen will not speak to Lancelot after the knight has put himself *en aventure* for her by fighting Meleagant (*Charrete*, l. 3999) and claims that 'ele a tort' (*Charrete*, l. 3997).[12] The implication is that Lancelot's conduct in putting himself at risk for the queen gives him the right to her favour; Meleagant makes such a right explicit in his own case (*Charrete*, ll. 4804–09). Because of the contractual notion underlying the practice of putting oneself *en aventure* for someone else, *aventure* becomes, in this context, a measure of obligation. Examples from the *Mort Artu* show that this has wider application than the judicial duel of the *Charrete*.[13]

Having extracted from the *Charrete* some formal constraints upon the wilder connotations of chance and recklessness in the enterprise of adventure, with concomitant implications for a reading of the motif in Malory, we find in the prose romance tradition (where the English author actually met the motif of 'taking the adventure') confirmation of Chrétien's constraints and the addition of new ones. In the Prose *Lancelot* and the Prose *Tristan*, the notions embodied in Chrétien's two expressions *se metre en aventure* and *anprandre la bataille* coalesce in the new expression *anprendre l'aventure*. In the *Lancelot*, the Lady of the Lake admonishes the young knight whom she has nurtured:

> 'Biax filz de roi, itant vos anseignerai au partir, qant plus avroiz achevees avantures felonesses et perilleuses, plus seürement anprenez

[12] The same idea is conveyed using an expression semantically close to *se metre en aventure: se metre en (tel/mortel) peril*, in *Charrete*, ll. 3334 and 3952–53.

[13] For example *Mort Artu*, 188.21 emphasizes Mordred's obligation to the hosts of men who have put themselves *en aventure* for him in the war against Arthur.

les aventures a achever, car la ou vos laroiz a achever les aventures par proesce que Dex ait mise en chevalier il n'est pas encores nez qui maint a chief celes que vos avroiz laissiees.'

(Prose *Lancelot*, 154.33–38)[14]

There are several features of this passage and its context which establish conventions for the motif against which later texts may be measured. The Lady of the Lake recommends an attitude to the undertaking of adventure which embeds a certain ethical justification into the structure of the motif: the more terrible the adventure the more ready Lancelot should be to undertake it, drawing confidence from his own incomparable *proesce* that only he *can* achieve it: *aventure* in this sense is 'destiny' rather than 'chance'. There is thus in the origins of the motif in the prose romances a formal constraint upon interpreting *aventure* as chance and the knight's attitude to its enterprise as reckless. Surplus is also structured into the motif: the achieving of one task should only lead to the undertaking of more (Prose *Lancelot*, 154.8–14). The context of the Lady of the Lake's admonishments to Lancelot reveals other aspects of the motif evident in later transmissions of it, in particular in Malory's 'Balin' narrative. It involves the undertaking of disparate and perhaps conflicting tasks, an aspect which gives heterogeneity to the ensuing adventures (Lancelot must avenge the wounded knight and also undertake the defence of a lady suffering at the hands of a predator); it is made up of parts, all of which must be completed (Prose *Lancelot*, 193.34–38); it is posited on the arbitrarily unnecessary (Arthur cannot understand why the wounded knight whose adventure Lancelot undertakes should need further avenging, as the knight himself killed the man who wounded him, Prose *Lancelot*, 150.27–28); the undertaking of the adventure will apparently earn the king's displeasure, introducing the element of conflict between knight and court into the motif (Prose *Lancelot*, 151.9–14); and the undertaking of the adventure makes of the knight a hapless homicide (Prose *Lancelot*, 258–60; 273–74).

The author of the Prose *Tristan*, characteristically influenced by the *Lancelot*, makes of *emprendre l'aventure* a leitmotif in the tale of 'Li Chevaliers a la Cote Mautaillee' (Brun le Noir).[15] It is here that I believe

[14] *Lancelot do Lac: The Non-cyclic Old French Prose Romance*, ed. by Elspeth Kennedy, 2 vols (Oxford: Clarendon Press, 1980). I am grateful to Elspeth Kennedy for drawing my attention to this passage.

[15] *Le Roman de Tristan en Prose*, ed. by Renée L. Curtis, 3 vols, I (Munich: Max Hueber, 1963); II (Leiden: E. J. Brill, 1976); III (Cambridge: Brewer, 1985). See E. Baumgartner, *Le 'Tristan en prose': Essai d'interprétation d'un roman médiéval* (Geneva: Droz, 1975), p. 327; E. Kennedy, 'Les Structures narratives et les allusions intertextuelles dans *Le Tristan*

Malory found the phrase, divining its importance to the extent that he attached it not only to his own Sir La Cote Male Tayle, but also to Balin, Gareth, Launcelot, Marhalt and Bors.[16] We thus address the technical aspect of this inquiry into Malory's transposition of the motif of 'taking the adventure'. It can be demonstrated, although I have not space to do it here, that his use of his *Freynshe book* was flexible: there are many instances of his transposing a translation of a French word or phrase to another part of the story he is retelling. This point, reinforced by Malory's well-attested taste for repetition of significant phrases and by the lack of certain knowledge as to the order of his reading and adapting of French romances, forms the basis of my contention that Malory transposed the motif of 'taking the adventure' from the Prose *Tristan*.[17] The phrase *emprendre l'aventure* or some variant of it is so common in the story of Brun in the Prose *Tristan* that, even given that Malory was following a version not identical to one of the extant redactions of the French romance, he must still have found a significant number of instances.[18] The verb *emprendre* is used of the young stranger's encounter with a lion which first wins him Arthur's approval (Prose *Tristan*, 641.18; 642.14).[19] Once the damsel bearing the shield arrives at court, the verb is used of the owner of the shield, the knight who was killed (Prose *Tristan*, 644.17) and then, emphatically, of Brun's relationship to the adventure of the shield. In particular there is dense lexical reiteration of the phrase *emprendre l'aventure* in paragraph 645. The phrase punctuates much of the narrative and can be seen to have attained the status of formula in its inclusion in the narrative switch which turns the tale back from Lancelot to Brun (Prose *Tristan*, 751.22–25).

As well as the mere fact of its repeated use, there are several features of

en prose', in *Nouvelles recherches sur 'Le Tristan en prose'*, ed. by J. Dufournet (Geneva: Slatkine, 1990), pp. 123–47.

16 For Marhalt, see *Works*, 173.2–175.9; for Bors, *Works*, 799.15. I have not space to expound on these two instances, which in any case are less important to my argument in that they both refer to a lodging place adventure and are not structured within the larger motif of 'taking the adventure' as are the acts of the four knights I do discuss.

17 A separate but relevant point is that while the exact relationship between the Prose *Tristan* and the *Roman du Graal*, of which the *Suite du Merlin* is a part, is disputed, influence of the *Tristan* on at least one part of the *Roman du Graal*, (the adventures of Gauvain, Yvain and Le Morholt in MS BN, f. fr. 112) may be discerned, so that there is the possibility that the French 'Balin' story was itself influenced by the Prose *Tristan*; the French Balin does say at one point 'ceste queste que je ai emprise'; cited by Vinaver, *Works*, n. 82.6–8 (p. 1314).

18 See Vinaver's discussion, *Works*, pp. 1466–67.

19 All references to the Prose *Tristan* are to the Curtis edition, as the Ménard edition does not publish the beginning of the 'Li Chevaliers a la Cote Mautaillee' story found in Curtis, II.637 – III.709.

the usage which have bearing upon the meaning of 'taking the adventure' in the *Morte Darthur*. Many of the formal limitations to the irrational are reproduced from the *Lancelot*, and thus were present to Malory in his source. The importance of God's role in the enterprise of adventure is apparent in Brun's speech at Prose *Tristan*, 649. Given Malory's characteristic compression of his French sources, it is even possible to see in this passage (or any version of it he may have found in his French book) the direct origin of Balin's and Launcelot's declaration 'I woll take the adventure that God woll ordayne for/gyff me'. There are in addition two passages which modify suggestions of recklessness in the undertaking of adventure, and thus ultimately influence our interpretation of Balin, who is often considered to be reckless. When Lancelot rebukes the *demoisele mesdisanz* for her insulting words to Brun, he explicates the notion which informs the taking of adventure in Malory's stories of Balin, Gareth and La Cote Male Tayle: that the very undertaking of a particular adventure is in itself dependent upon inner worth – worth which others are slow to acknowledge (Prose *Tristan*, 685.17–18). It is a private manifestation of the socially and legally constructed confidence in the triumph of virtue which is at the basis of the judicial duel. Also crucial to the implications of 'taking the adventure' is the exchange between Brun and his host before *les destroiz de Sorelois* (Prose *Tristan*, 693–97). The host's reply to the knight indicates that the element of surplus (the 'more than one bargained for' which so afflicts Balin) is integral to the enterprise of adventure: in Brun's case he has to take on *l'aventure de sis chevaliers*. This point may be developed with reference to Lancelot's questions to Plenorius in the closing stages of the 'Li Chevaliers a la Cote Mautaillee' story (Prose *Tristan*, 774), in which the notions of completion and propriety are foregrounded.[20] Lancelot's concern indicates the importance, in undertaking an adventure, of fulfilling all its elements, however heterogeneous they may be. The heterogeneity and the imperative to undertake successfully all the parts of the adventure provide the formal structure for the compulsiveness or recklessness which a psychological reading tends to find in Malory's 'Balin'.[21]

MALORY'S TRANSPOSITION AND CRITIQUE OF THE MOTIF

Until this point I have focused on the formation of the motif of 'taking the adventure' in French tradition and what Malory transmitted of this. Yet of course the motif looks very different in Malory's text from any of

[20] See *Le Roman de Tristan en Prose*, ed. by P. Ménard, 6 vols (Geneva: Droz, 1987–93), I, 72.

[21] Such as that made by Tennyson; see *Idylls of the King*, 'Balin and Balan'.

its manifestations in French romance. I consider that the reason for the profound differences is not that Malory introduced new emphasis on the irrational, allowing less space for God (see Mann), but rather that he made a vital change to the way the motif was positioned in French tradition in order to reposition it within his own structure and in so doing give to it a quite different ethical value. The implication of a reckless submission to chance hovers around Malory's takers of adventure, but is generally preempted by the features of the motif he inherited. Recklessness can definitely be said to exist only when some of these features are altered or at least skewed: it haunts the 'Balin' and emerges with disastrous clarity in the case of Launcelot, in the episode of the 'Fair Maid of Ascolat'.

The ultimate explanation for this ethical revaluation is to be found in an important structural alteration Malory makes to the motif. In addition to the elements of the motif of *emprendre l'aventure* transmitted from the Prose *Lancelot* to the Prose *Tristan* and thence to the *Morte Darthur*, there is a broader structural feature present in the French prose tradition which Malory altered, thus reconfiguring and revaluing the motif. In both the *Lancelot* and the *Tristan*, the motif is part of Lancelot's biography; in turn the association with Lancelot positions it within *les aventures dou reaume de Logres* (Prose *Tristan*, 693.16–17).[22] In the Prose *Tristan*, the adventure which Brun undertakes, and which Lancelot successfully completes, is one of the *aventures* of Logres.[23] It is the adventure of the *destroiz de Sorelois*, the dangerous passages guarding access to the land held by Galehot, where Lancelot lived for a time. The centrality of the notion of the *felons passages* (first found in the *Charrete*) to the concept of 'taking the adventure' is seen in the *Tristan* in the exchange between the host and Brun.[24] Here, for the first time since the arrival of the *demoisele mesdisanz* at Arthur's court, the *destroiz de Sorelois* are invoked, and, also for the first time, the young knight himself appropriates the phrase *emprendre l'aventure* (Prose *Tristan*, 695.22–3) after which it is echoed by

22 The author of the Prose *Tristan* expanded the motif, attached only to Lancelot in the Prose *Lancelot*, to include the supplementary Fair Unknown, Brun, but retained the importance of Lancelot to the overall structure of the motif; see Kennedy, 'Les Structures narratives', pp. 134–35.

23 Following Elspeth Kennedy's argument (*Lancelot and the Grail: A Study of the Prose 'Lancelot'* (Oxford: Clarendon Press, 1986), pp. 143–55) these would not be the adventures leading up to a Grail quest but rather part of the less explicitly Christianized marvels of Logres alluded to in the *Lancelot* before it was repositioned in the Lancelot-Grail Cycle.

24 E. Kennedy, *Lancelot and the Grail*, p. 86, notes that the *passages*, mentioned in the *Lancelot*, 357.7–14 (where the author of the Prose *Tristan* found them), allude to the *felons passages* of the *Charrete*, ll. 654–55.

the host (695.6). While Malory retains the centrality of the *passages* to the taking of adventure in his version of the 'La Cote Male Tayle' story, he detaches them and the motif of 'taking the adventure' from the *aventures* of Logres and from Lancelot's biography. In so confining the motif to 'La Cote Male Tayle', Malory embeds it exclusively in the Fair Unknown theme, thus contracting the expansion the author of the Prose *Tristan* had achieved (in comparison with the *Lancelot*) when he attached the motif to Lancelot as mature knight. In addition, Malory has his Sir Gareth of Orkney 'take the adventure', thus confirming within the middle sections of the *Morte Darthur* the identification of the motif with the Fair Unknown theme.[25]

This identification has consequences for his reconfiguration of the motif in the *Morte Darthur* as a whole. It establishes a convention for the taking of adventure as a stance appropriate to the young untried knight rather than to the one who has already established his reputation. In the structure of the *Morte Darthur*, the convention reaches backward to the story of Balin as well as forward to the account of Launcelot's acts in the last narrative section of the text,[26] and here I borrow the spatial terms Felicity Riddy suggests as appropriate to describe Malory's structural principles.[27] Adapting Riddy's visual analogy, it is possible to understand Malory's reconfiguration of the motif of 'taking the adventure' as a structure of inner and outer 'panels'. The inner panels contain the two narratives in which the motif is firmly located within the Fair Unknown theme, the 'Tale of Gareth' and the 'La Cote Male Tayle' story; the outer panels the tale of Balin, and the Launcelot material in the last section of the text. By means of this spatial analogy I intend to argue that the identification of 'taking the adventure' with the Fair Unknown theme, found in the inner panels, forms a standard of comparison for the Balin and Launcelot narratives in the outer panels and that Malory uses this standard to advance a critique of the motif. To this critique I now turn, explicating it in the order in which we read it in both Winchester and Caxton: 'Balin'; 'Gareth' and 'La Cote Male Tayle'; and finally, 'Launcelot'.

In the previous section I suggested that the motif of 'taking the adventure' in Malory's 'Balin' narrative contains many of the formal and structural constraints upon connotations of the irrational built into the

[25] See C. Luttrell, *The Creation of the First Arthurian Romance* (London: Edward Arnold, 1974), pp. 120–26; 264–68.

[26] Printed by Vinaver as two separate tales; I follow M. J. Evans, 'The Explicits and Narrative Division in the Winchester MS: A Critique of Vinaver's Malory', *Philological Quarterly*, 58 (1979), 263–81.

[27] F. Riddy, 'Structure and Meaning in Malory's "The Fair Maid of Astolat"', *Forum for Modern Language Studies*, 12 (1976), 354–66 (pp. 354–58).

formation of the motif in French tradition. Given their new position within Malory's structure, these constraints may be read as part of Malory's critique of taking the adventure. Balin's adventure must be seen in the context in which Malory presents it, having detached it from *les aventures dou reaume de Logres* and the biography of Lancelot: the temporary retreat of Arthur from the 'romance' forces of adventure, which had previously begun to claim him, back to a renewed preoccupation with the wider defence of the realm. The adventure begins at the court which Arthur has summoned in the face of the threat posed by King Royns (*Works*, 54.21–55.18; 56.3–7; 61.6–24). In such a context, the conflicting pressures on the knight may be seen to be expressed by the two strands of meaning which we have isolated in the expression 'take the adventure'. For Balin both responds to the conventional pressure exercised upon the Fair Unknown to undertake a mysterious adventure which will necessitate the conquering of difficult *passages*, and succumbs to the feudal exigency of trying to win back Arthur's favour by putting himself *en aventure* for his king (*Works*, 66.30–35). The damsel girt with the sword, harbinger of Balin's adventure, both disrupts Arthur's preoccupation with the defence of the realm against Royns and suggests to the court that victory over Royns may include more than military success. A moral imperative, only to be assuaged by the undertaking and achieving of an adventure, is also at stake (*Works*, 62.4–6). At the same time, pronounced formal intimations of the Fair Unknown theme occur. The description of Balin is that of a man whose lowly status conceals innate worth, who has a compulsion to prove himself, and a conviction that the adventure belongs to him alone (*Works*, 62.33–63.27).[28] The emissary who arrives at court is, as is common in the Fair Unknown pattern, a damsel encumbered with a hard adventure (*Works*, 61.31–62.2). It is these formal features which I believe suggested to Malory the appropriateness of borrowing from the 'Li Chevaliers a la Cote Mautaillee' episode in the Prose *Tristan*, the phrase 'take the adventure'. By choosing to place it within the 'Balin' story, with its interrogation of the tension between individual and collective values,[29] the expression also draws on the contractual notions we first observed in the expressions *se metre en aventure* and *anprandre la bataille* in the *Charrete*.

The motif, displaced and recontextualized as it is, thus draws on

28 Only Balin realizes that what is mooted does actually constitute an adventure (*Works*, 63.2–5).

29 In this Malory reproduced in his own fashion the conflictive values of his source, the *Suite du Merlin*; see R. Morris, *The Character of King Arthur in Medieval Literature* (Cambridge: Brewer, 1982), p. 59.

aspects of its other configurations in French tradition and in the *Morte Darthur* itself. When compared with the request and granting structure of the court scene in the 'Tale of Gareth' (*Works*, 297.11–15), the start of Balin's adventure shows an ominous variation on the conventional relationship between king, knight and adventure to be undertaken. Balin approaches the damsel directly and privately instead of the customary intercession by Arthur (*Works*, 63.8–15). Even when he has succeeded in withdrawing the sword and forced the court to accord it the status of an adventure, his achievement is perceived to have been made in opposition to the court rather than on its behalf (*Works*, 63.32–4). The theme of conflict between Balin and the court is maintained. Although Balin puts himself *en aventure* for his king and, with his brother, succeeds in killing Arthur's enemy Royns, the victory seems scarcely relevant to the unfolding of his tragic fate. For at the end of the tale Arthur restates his initial detachment from adventure, reappearing only to utter a brief lament for the two brothers slain by each other (*Works*, 92.13–15). The first court scene with its skewing of the Fair Unknown motif of 'taking the adventure' proves finally to have been prophetic: Balin's adventure, individualistic and dysfunctional, was not an adventure for Arthur's court. Yet within the convention of contract and obligation, which we have discerned at the heart of the motif of 'taking the adventure', the absence of any regal sanction for Balin's adventure is less than he could with justice have expected and, while Malory offers no explicit criticism, his exercises on the Fair Unknown theme in the 'Tale of Gareth' and in the 'La Cote Male Tayle' story pick up this concern.[30]

An ethical evaluation of the motif of taking the adventure may be discerned in the hero's attitude to the enterprise of adventure in the 'Tale of Gareth', specifically in the progression from *passages* to battle which structures the Fair Unknown section of the narrative (culminating in the hero's encounter with the Red Knight of the Red Lands). The early stubborn reiterations gradually give way to an emphasis on the contractual obligations at stake in undertaking an adventure for someone else. Gareth's adventure becomes dignified retrospectively as 'my batayle' (*Works*, 313.4) – a battle of which the irrational element was confined to the *passages* of the colour knights. For once the encounter with the Red Knight of the Red Lands is attained, the question of motivation is addressed and explicated. As in the case of Meleagant and Lancelot in the *Charrete*, the hero's opponent is no simple predator. The Red Knight of the Red Lands insists, as did Meleagant, 'for hir I have done many

30 For a different reading of the ethical evaluation of Balin's adventure, see B. Kennedy, *Knighthood in the 'Morte Darthur'*, pp. 218–30.

stronge batayles' (*Works*, 321.37). In Gareth's reflections on the enterprise (*Works*, 322.1–9; 13–21) there is an important statement of the contractual element in 'taking the adventure' once it passes from the overcoming of *passages* to the legal context of undertaking a battle. The element of chance and the concomitant notion of the recklessness of the knight who submits to it are tempered by exigencies and rewards of a structure which socializes and legalizes the enterprise of adventure so as to keep pace with the hero's gradual emancipation from an imposed and isolationist identity.[31]

So, while the 'Balin' story leaves open the question as to whether or not 'taking the adventure' is approved in the ethics of the *Morte Darthur*, the narratives of 'Gareth' and 'La Cote Male Tayle' reposition and, in so doing, revalue the motif. In both the later episodes, the preoccupation with the wider defence of the realm has receded; but in that very selectivity and in the manifest formal enfolding of the motif of 'taking the adventure' within the Fair Unknown theme we find a constructed ethics. 'Taking the adventure' is positioned as a function of immaturity (in the technical sense of the young unproved knight), of whom more will be required once the adventure has been completed. Yet there is also an important difference between the two narratives which opens the way for the final unmistakeable critique of the motif to be offered in the account of Launcelot in the 'Fair Maid of Ascolat' episode. The fragility of the contract at the heart of taking the adventure is exposed as the 'La Cote Male Tayle' story detaches the motif again from the socialized and legitimized structure in which the 'Gareth' embedded it, and makes explicit the criticism of the court's attitude implicit in 'Balin'. In Malory's 'La Cote Male Tayle' story, the revaluation, through transposition, of 'taking the adventure' is effected by the way Launcelot introduces himself into the structure with the express purpose, not of completing one of the adventures of Logres mysteriously assigned to him, but of succouring the young knight. Not only does Launcelot explicitly criticize the court for having allowed La Cote Male Tayle to undertake such a hard adventure (*Works*, 467.5–8)[32] but the criticism is reinforced by Malory's reminder at the end of the story (*Works*, 476.32–24) that this adventure of the

31 I have not space here to expound upon this point, but it can be demonstrated by a reading of the encounters with the colour knights that there is a gradual emancipation from absolute constraint and imprisonment within a given identity on the part of both Gareth and his opponents.

32 While in characteristic fashion Malory seems to respond to a hint given elsewhere in his source (the damsel's words to Arthur at the very beginning of the adventure, Prose *Tristan*, 648.7–18) he explicates it and does what it is inconceivable that any French author would do: puts the criticism into the mouth of Launcelot.

passages of Surluse was incidental to the young knight's main purpose of avenging the death of his father (the reason why he wears the rent coat which gives him his sobriquet).[33]

Nonetheless, those useful locales of extra-human, extra-social responsibility, the *passages*, remain in the 'La Cote Male Tayle' story to prevent the critique of 'taking the adventure' becoming urgent, just as they had earlier helped preempt a full-scale condemnation of Balin or the court. But in the last narrative section of the *Morte Darthur*, in which Launcelot 'takes the adventure', the *passages* of Chrétien no longer exist, and this and other alterations to the motif finally permit its overt revaluation. We find the motif attached to Launcelot in his conversation with Guinevere at the beginning of the story of the 'Fair Maid of Ascolat':[34]

> 'But wytte you well,' seyde sir Launcelot unto the quene, 'at that justys I woll be ayenste the kynge and ayenst all hys felyship.'
> 'Sir, ye may there do as ye lyste,' seyde the quene, 'but be my counceyle ye shall nat be ayenst youre kynge and your felyship, for there bene full many hardé knyghtes of youre bloode.'
> 'Madame,' seyde sir Launcelot, 'I shall take the adventure that God woll gyff me.' (*Works*, 1066.9–18)

While Malory borrows the basic situation of the conversation from the *Mort Artu*, he expands it, introducing the tenor of conflict between Launcelot and the queen, and the motif of 'taking the adventure'. His departure from his French source at this point makes his insertion of the motif a matter of some importance. Launcelot's declaration must be read in the context of the religious and legal notions at stake in putting the self *en aventure* which characterize this last section of the *Morte Darthur*: it belongs notionally to the series of judicial duels which structure the narrative.[35] Given Bloch's thesis about the role of legal models in explaining the passage between a set of courtly ideals and literary forms,[36] the use of 'take the adventure' in this context can be read as retrospective sanction of Launcelot's behaviour in terms of a specific legal code. He says that he will take the adventure 'that God woll gyff' him, thus

33 I thus interpret Malory's use of the motif as an aspect of his general critique of those values incompatible with his own which he found in the Prose *Tristan*; see Vinaver's Commentary, *Works*, pp. 1443–533.

34 On these 'connecting passages', see *Works*, pp. 1588–89.

35 Launcelot against, respectively, Mador, Mellegaunt, and Gawain (*Works*, 1055–59; 1133–40; 1215–21).

36 Bloch, *Medieval French Literature and Law*, pp. 198–99.

articulating the Providentialist viewpoint that God ordains the outcome of a joust undertaken to prove innocence or guilt. Given the context of the declaration (the accusations of adultery between Launcelot and Guinevere) it can be argued that Launcelot artificially constructs the jousts as judicial duels, and thus makes of them an opportunity, within a system of immanent justice, to make his disputed innocence manifest. The speciousness of this act, and Elaine's death, both indicate fissures in dependence on the Providentialist attitude to the outcome of the judicial duel, which are to widen in subsequent events. These fissures are underlined by Malory's inclusion (not from the *Mort Artu*, but from the *Lancelot*) of the 'Knight of the Cart' story with its extremely problematic account of Launcelot's battle with Mellegaunt to prove the queen's innocence of adultery (*Works*, p. 1592). Further, in Malory's version of the story, as in the prose adaptation of the *Charrete* in the *Lancelot*, there are no longer Chrétien's *passages* which, by creating a usefully elusive space of extra-human irrationality and arbitrariness, serve to absolve the dilemmas of human innocence and guilt, and of God's role in the exposure of the just. In this light, Launcelot's determination to 'take the adventure' this late in the scheme of things can be read as another element in the interrogation of the basis of the judicial duel made manifest in Malory's treatment of the battle between Gawain and Launcelot, in which he strips away the elaborate phraseology of the duel found in the *Mort Artu*.[37] In so doing he implicitly replaces the comparatively sophisticated notions of justice and obligation which *anprandre la bataille* acquires in the *Charrete* with the more primitive code of reciprocity informing the instances of *se metre en aventure* in Chrétien's poem. Malory's Gawain phrases his vows in the 'body for body' language of reciprocity and revenge (*Works*, 201.1–6; 1213.28–31; 1215.13–15; 1221.1–17; 1232.18–19). 'Taking the adventure' is thus positioned within a context of increasingly assertive and ethically difficult 'taking the battle' situations. This context, in the disastrous encounter between Gawain and Launcelot, is revealed as the 'body for body' reciprocity at the heart of the motif in its earliest appearance in Chrétien's *Charrete*.

Launcelot's determination to 'take the adventure' before the 'Fair Maid' episode also skews the convention of the Fair Unknown theme which enfolds the motif in the 'Gareth' and 'La Cote Male Tayle'

[37] This emphasis is not found in the *Mort Artu* which, while it presents various characters as criticizing Gawain for cloaking pure reciprocity and revenge beneath the framework of the judicial duel, still emphatically retains the elaborate machinery and phraseology of the duel.

narratives. In that the use of this expression echoes these young Fair Unknowns, and that now as never before he disguises himself in response to criticism, Launcelot places his achievements in the 'Fair Maid' episode as the compensatory ones of the untried and reviled young knight rather than as the surplus of proof indulged in by the already tested and mature knight. His use of the phrase 'take the adventure' can thus be read as an aspect of his increasingly anachronistic behaviour in the last narrative section. For knightly adventure is in general constructed as obsolete here.[38] Malory is reinterpreting in his own fashion what he found in the *Mort Artu*. In both French and English texts, the events take place in a post-Grail world in which the characters once more have to situate themselves within society and history. One of Malory's techniques for transposing the *Mort Artu*'s construction of the anachronistic nature of knightly adventure[39] is to restrict the way of adventure to Launcelot and the handful of knights – particularly Gareth and Urry – presented as closest in essence to the type of the *knyght aventures* of which Launcelot is, for Malory, the supreme exemplar. The anachronism of knightly adventure emerges strongly in the nostalgic use of verbs, which predicated the knightly relationship to adventure earlier in the *Morte Darthur*, in the context of the healing of Sir Urry (*Works*, 1151.26–29; 1146.25; 1147.21; 1151.22–23). Another technique is the careful placement of the words *adventure* and *adventures* within premonitions of what is to come after the exposure in Guinevere's chamber (*Works*, 1168.29; 1176.26). Gawain's prediction of the adventures which might happen when Guinevere is put to the stake shows how far adventure has gone beyond the conventional knightly encounter; the use of the word is an index of the widening pattern of fate which informs the narrative of the last events of Arthur's kingdom. The killing of Gareth is paradoxically both the most appalling adventure of the *Morte Darthur* and, together with the killing of the adder which precipitates the mortal combat between the forces of Arthur and Mordred, the most enmeshed in human responsibility – and thus least the product of chance. In such a context, Launcelot's decision to 'take the adventure' at the beginning of the 'Fair Maid' episode partakes of a general anachronism of knightly adventure in this last narrative section of the work. In its formal dislocation of the Fair Unknown convention of taking the adventure (the time of

38 Another aspect of the aesthetics of remembrance in the last tales, analyzed by Mark Lambert, *Style and Vision in 'Le Morte Darthur'* (New Haven and London: Yale University Press, 1975), pp. 124–221.

39 Evident, for example, at *Mort Artu* 3.39; 70.24; 174.2.

adventure now past and damsels no longer encumbered with swords and shields), Launcelot's behaviour is indeed 'reckless' when judged by the only standards against which we can measure this quality: the ethics constructed by prior use of the motif in Malory's own text.

Lancelot in Wales

CERIDWEN LLOYD-MORGAN

MANY OF THE Arthurian characters in twelfth- and thirteenth-century French romances have names which appear to be ultimately of Celtic origin, to the extent that in some cases Old French and Middle Welsh forms may be easily recognisable as related. The heated debates that once raged around the question of the supposed Celtic origins of Arthurian romance have now largely died away, but it may still be useful to clarify areas of uncertainty where in fact fairly clear-cut evidence does exist and it is possible to reach firm conclusions. The purpose of this paper is to examine the case of Lancelot in order to establish in precisely which Middle Welsh texts he appears, and to consider whether either the name or character were known to Welsh native tradition or whether Welsh knowledge of him was derived from French sources.[1]

The late R. S. Loomis was a particularly strong advocate of the theory of Celtic Arthurian origins in general, and he argued at length that the character Lancelot had his roots in Celtic tradition, despite the apparently French, non-Celtic form of his name.[2] According to Loomis's rather complex argument, Lancelot was descended from the Celtic God Lug, from whom he believed two characters mentioned in the Welsh Arthurian tale of *Culhwch ac Olwen*, Llwch Llawwynnyawc and Llenlleawc Wyddel, were also derived. Moreover he linked both the character and name of Lancelot to Lleu Llaw Gyffes, who appears in

1 An earlier form of this paper was delivered to the meeting of the British Branch of the International Arthurian Society held at Aberdeen, September 1991.

2 R. S. Loomis, *Celtic Myth and Arthurian Romance* (New York: Columbia University Press, 1927), pp. 90–98, *Arthurian Tradition and Chrétien de Troyes* (New York: Columbia University Press, 1949), pp. 187–95, *Wales and the Arthurian Legend* (Cardiff: University of Wales Press, 1956), pp. 161–63. See also *Trioedd Ynys Prydein*, ed. & trans. by Rachel Bromwich, 2nd edn (Cardiff: University of Wales Press, 1978), p. 415.

Welsh in the non-Arthurian context of *Pedeir Keinc y Mabinogi* (The Four Branches of the Mabinogi). I shall not deal in detail with the way in which Loomis reached this remarkable conclusion, but would simply stress at the outset that there is no surviving indigenous Welsh Lancelot story whatsoever, nor do we find any such story in Irish or other medieval Celtic vernacular sources. There is no extant translation or adaptation of any Lancelot text in Welsh, neither of Chrétien's *Chevalier de la Charrete* nor of any version of the *Prose Lancelot*. Nonetheless, Lancelot as a character does appear in certain Welsh texts based on French romances, and the treatment of his name by the Welsh redactors who adapted this foreign material for a new audience suggests that Lancelot was not recognised as a character of indigenous origin.

The usual practice of Welsh redactors, when adapting or translating French material, was to try to identify any proper names with possible Welsh counterparts. Sometimes the equivalents were obvious and easy to find: Owein for Yvain, Gwenhwyfar for Guenièvre, Kei for Keu or Ké, and so on. Sometimes the names were not very close morphologically, but the characters could still be identified, perhaps by their common attributes, or the similarity of the stories associated with them. Peredur and Perceval, Gwalchmei and Gauvain, Myrddin and Merlin are obvious examples. This happens as early as the thirteenth century with the three Welsh tales corresponding to Chrétien's *Conte del graal*, *Yvain* and *Erec*. Later, when *La Queste del Saint Graal* and *Perlesvaus* came to be translated into Welsh at the end of the fourteenth century in the text now known as *Y Seint Greal* or *Ystoryaeu Seint Graal*,[3] the translator succeeded in finding Welsh equivalents for a remarkable number of French personal names, even those for quite minor characters, such as Owein Vrych, corresponding to Yvains li Avoltres, and Llacheu for Loholt, Arthur's son. However, when Lancelot du Lac appears in these two French grail romances, the Welsh redactor simply adapts the name a little to accommodate the demands of Welsh phonology, and calls him Lawnslot or

3 The complete text was published in *Selections from the Hengwrt Manuscripts*, ed. by Rev. Robert Williams, 2 vols (London 1874–92), I: *Y Seint Greal*, whilst the first part, corresponding to the *Queste* has been recently re-edited, see *Ystoryaeu Seint Greal. Rhan I. Y Keis*, ed. by Thomas Jones and others (Cardiff: University of Wales Press, 1992); a second volume is in preparation. For a discussion of the text see Ceridwen Lloyd-Morgan, 'A Study of *Y Seint Greal* in Relation to *La Queste del Saint Graal* and *Perlesvaus*' (unpublished doctoral thesis, University of Oxford, 1978) and 'Perceval in Wales: Late Medieval Welsh Grail Traditions', in *The Changing Face of Arthurian Romance. Essays on Arthurian Prose Romances in Memory of Cedric E. Pickford*, ed. by Alison Adams, Armel H. Diverres, Karen Stern and Kenneth Varty (Cambridge: Brewer, 1986), pp. 78–91.

even Lawnslot dy lac. As this is the same procedure as he adopts for other personal names found in his French sources and for which no Welsh equivalent is known, we may conclude that for this particular translator at least the character called Lancelot in the French texts did not correspond to anyone known to him in native Welsh tradition. What is known of the circumstances of production of *Y Seint Greal* suggests that he was working in a milieu where a wide variety of texts could have been available to him, for the translation appears to have been commissioned by the Glamorganshire nobleman Hopcyn ap Thomas, one of the major patrons of Welsh literature at the end of the fourteenth century. It was for him that the Red Book of Hergest was compiled (now MS Jesus College 111 in the Bodleian Library, Oxford), one of the most important medieval compendia of Welsh poetry and prose, and the same scribe was responsible for both the earliest – probably the original – manuscript of *Y Seint Greal*, MS Peniarth 11 (National Library of Wales, Aberystwyth) and also for substantial portions of the Red Book. It is difficult to believe that the translator could not have found a native equivalent for the name of Lancelot had one existed.

Such evidence does indicate, therefore, that in the case of Lancelot we are dealing with a visitor from abroad, not a character of Celtic origin. Now in the case of *Y Seint Greal*, Lancelot plays an important role precisely because he is one of the major protagonists in *La Queste del Saint Graal* and *Perlesvaus*, the two romances on which the Welsh translation is based. But we must also consider in what other Welsh texts Lancelot appears, and what their sources were.

Apart from *Y Seint Greal*, the references to Lancelot in Middle Welsh written sources tend to be very brief, and very scattered. They occur mostly in non-narrative sources, although they may occasionally refer to a narrative context in which Lancelot appears. One important source is the Triads. Although some of the Triads appear to go back to very early times, Rachel Bromwich in her magisterial edition has pointed out that some of them appear to have been reworked at a later period, perhaps in response to changing literary fashions. One manuscript in particular, MS Peniarth 50, written in the first half of the fifteenth century, has some interesting examples where new Arthurian characters have been introduced, apparently in response to the vogue for Arthurian tales of French origin, or perhaps partly as a consequence of the new availability of such material (Bromwich, pp. xxxi–xxxiv). One of the Triads (*Trioedd Ynys Prydein* no. 86) is a brand new compilation, based on *Y Seint Greal*, as the redactor explicitly acknowledges. However, it is clear that he has used not *Y Seint Greal* alone, but that he has also had access to the *Prose Lancelot*. The Triad runs as follows:

Tri Marchawc o Lys Arthur a enillawd y Greal, ac eu duc y Nef:
Galaad vab Lawnslot y Lac,
a Pheredur vab Efrawc Iarll,
a Bort vab Brenhin Bort.

A'(r) ddeu gyntaf oeddynt wery o gyrff. A'(r) trydydd oedd ddiweir, am na wnaeth pechawt knawdawl ont unweith. A hynny drwy brovedigaeth yn yr amser y ennillawd ef [. . .] verch Brenyn Brangor, yr honn a vu Ymherodres yn Constinobyl, o'r honn y deuth y Genedlaeth vwyaf or byt; ag o'r genedlaeth Joseph o Arimathia y hanoedynt yll tri, ac o lin David brofwyt, mal y tystolaetha *Ystorya y Greal*.

(Three Knights of Arthur's Court who won the Graal, and it brought them to Heaven:
Galaad son of Lawnslot of the Lake,
and Peredur son of Earl Efrawg,
and Bort son of king Bort.

And the two first were virgin of body. And the third was chaste, for only once had he committed bodily sin; and that, through temptation, at the time he won [. . .] daughter of King Brangor, who was Empress in Constantinople, and from whom was descended the greatest race in the world. All three were sprung of the race of Joseph of Arimathea, and of the lineage of the Prophet David, as the History of the Graal testifies.) (Bromwich, p. 212)

Here the names of the three knights are taken from the first part of *Y Seint Greal*, based on *La Queste del Saint Graal*, but the note which follows and glosses the triad itself contains information not included there, for the detail concerning King Brangoire's daughter is found only in the *Prose Lancelot*.[4] Moreover, at this point in the *Prose Lancelot* the name of the king's daughter is not given, hence the Welsh scribe has left a gap in the manuscript (see Bromwich, p. 213).

Another, related text, *Pedwar Marchog ar Hugain Llys Arthur*, which is, in essence, a grouping of triads to form a list, includes the triad 'Tri Marchoc Gwyry oedd yn Llys Arthur: Bwrt ap Bwrt, brenhin Gwasgwin, a Phredur ap Efroc iarll, a Galath ap Lanslod Lak' (Three Virgin Knights were in Arthur's Court: Bwrt son of Bwrt King of Gascony, and Peredur son of Earl Efrog, and Galath son of Lanslod Lak).[5] The combination of three of the knights involved in the grail quest, all described in terms of sexual abstinence, together with the mention of Lancelot as Galaad's

4 *The Vulgate Version of the Arthurian Romances*, ed. by H. Oskar Sommer, 8 vols (Washington: Carnegie Institution, 1909–13), IV: *Le Livre de Lancelot del Lac*, pp. 269–70.

5 Bromwich, pp. 250–55, also pp. cxxxv–cxxxix, and Lloyd-Morgan, 'A Study of *Y Seint Greal*', p. 230.

father, shows that this group was probably based either on Triad 86 quoted above, or else directly on *Y Seint Greal*. The next triad in the *Pedwar Marchog ar Hugain* (Bromwich, pp. 250–52) lists 'Tri Chadvarchoc oedd yn Llys Arthur: Cadwr Iarll Kernyw, a Lanslod Lak, ac Ywain ap Urien Rreget' (Three Knights of Battle were in Arthur's Court: Cadwr Earl of Cornwall, and Lanslod Lak, and Ywain son of Urien Rheged). Here Lancelot is associated with characters from earlier tradition. Owein ab Urien appears in the earliest, pre-Geoffrey, Welsh poetry and prose tales,[6] whilst Cadwr appears in the *Brutiau*, the Welsh versions of Geoffrey of Monmouth's *Historia Regum Britanniae*, so that both were familiar names in Welsh storytelling (Bromwich, p. 297). Thus the context provides no particular clue as to the source of the reference to Lancelot. It may be that he was included because of his presence in the preceding triad; otherwise the fact that he is associated with non-French characters suggests that the triad may have been inspired by *Y Seint Greal*, where, in the second part of the text, based on the *Perlesvaus*, Lancelot is an important defender of Arthur's interests. It is significant that the gloss to this triad states: 'ac ni chavas Arthur erioed gywilydd mewn brwydr y dydd i gwelai eu hwynebeu yn y maes' (and Arthur was never shamed in battle on the day that he saw their faces in the field).

The second important area where references to Lancelot occur is poetry. References to Arthurian characters in Welsh poetry of the later Middle Ages are always somewhat frustrating, because they are usually couched in highly conventional terms. Normally such references occur in praise poetry, where the poet's patron, or a relative of his, is compared to heroes of history, myth, romance or story. Moreover, the demands of metre, rhyme and *cynghanedd*[7] limit or influence the ways in which such heroes are described or presented. Consequently, even where further details are given in addition to the character's name, as a rule these are not specific enough to enable us to pinpoint a source. This is a major disadvantage when we are dealing with a character like Lancelot who appears in a number of different texts. In his case, of course, apart from Chrétien's *Chevalier de la Charrete* and later the *Prose Lancelot*, in both of which he is the main protagonist, there are a number of other French texts where he plays a major role: other romances of the Vulgate Cycle, such as the *Queste del Saint Graal* and the *Mort Artu*, as well as independent romances such as the *Perlesvaus*. At times it can be impossible even to establish whether a given poet is using a French source or not.

6 For a list of sources see Bromwich, pp. 479–83 and 560–61.

7 A complex system of alliteration and assonance used in Welsh poetry, especially in the so-called 'strict metres'.

However, it is highly significant that, just as no references to Lancelot in the Triads can be shown to predate *Y Seint Greal*, and those Triads which refer to him seem to be derived ultimately from that same source, so too the references to Lancelot in the work of the Welsh poets all appear to postdate *Y Seint Greal*.

As Rachel Bromwich has noted (p. 415), Lancelot was not known to the *gogynfeirdd*, the court poets of the Welsh princes, who flourished in the twelfth and thirteenth centuries. Although his name appears frequently in the work of the *cywyddwyr*, the poets active from the fourteenth century on, he seems not to have been known to the earliest of them. The first example seems to be that in the poem 'I lys Gwilym ap Gruffudd o'r Penrhyn' by Rhys Goch Eryri (fl. 1385–1448), where the poet simply compares his subject to both Lancelot and his son Galaad: 'Gwilym Lawnslod ni 'mgilia,/Glewlwyth aer, ail Galath da' (Gwilym [like] Lancelot will not retreat,/Heir to a valiant family, a second good Galaad).[8] This poem later refers to Gwilym's second wife, Sioned or Jonet, a widow whose first husband was appointed Chamberlain of North Wales in 1399, and so it cannot have been composed before about 1400.[9] The combination of references to both Lancelot and Galaad suggests that the source was either the *Queste del Saint Graal* or, more probably, the Welsh version of it which forms the first part of *Y Seint Greal*. Since all the available evidence points to *Y Seint Greal* being produced at the end of the fourteenth century, it seems more than likely that Rhys Goch Eryri was one of the first poets to draw on its subject matter. References to Galaad imply knowledge of Lancelot as his father, since he is presented within the context of this relationship in *La Queste del Saint Graal*, where the son is first introduced as a character and future grail hero, and the earliest references to Galaad occur likewise in the work of Rhys Goch Eryri and in one of the last poems of his older contemporary, Iolo Goch (c.1320–98).[10]

The other poets who include references to Lancelot were all active in the mid or late fifteenth century, by which time *Y Seint Greal* was undoubtedly known to the poets, as witness, for example, the *cywydd* by

8 *Cywyddau Iolo Goch ac eraill*, ed. by Henry Lewis, Thomas Roberts & Ifor Williams, 2nd edn (Cardiff: University of Wales Press, 1937), p. 310, ll. 25–26.

9 Ibid., p. 313, l.6, and see notes, pp. 391–92.

10 Poem in praise of Sir Rosier (Roger) Mortimer: *Cywyddau Iolo Goch ac eraill*, p. 48, l. 11 and note, p. 347, and *Gwaith Iolo Goch*, ed. by Dafydd Johnston (Cardiff: University of Wales Press, 1988), p. 87, l. 111 and note, p. 292; on the basis of known events in the subject's life, the editors date this poem between 1394 or 1395 and 1398, so this is probably the first reference to Galaad in Welsh poetry and perhaps the very first instance of a poet drawing on *Y Seint Greal*. See also Lloyd-Morgan, 'A Study of *Y Seint Greal*', p. 238.

Guto'r Glyn (c.1435–c.1493), asking for the loan of the manuscript.[11] Guto'r Glyn himself describes a nobleman as 'un glod a Lawnslot di Lag' (as praiseworthy as Lancelot du Lac),[12] whilst Lewis Glyn Cothi (c.1420–89) also likens a subject to 'Lawnslod'.[13] Dafydd Nanmor (fl.1450–80) refers in a similar context to 'Lawnslod Dvlag',[14] and Tudur Aled (c.1465–c.1525) to 'Syr Lawnslod'.[15] These references to Lancelot provide little or no narrative context, but are included in order to bolster the poet's eulogy of his patron; this particular name is then no more than just one selected from the large pool of names taken from both native and continental sources that was used by the poets.[16]

A third major group of sources containing references to Arthurian characters consists of various disparate and composite texts, apparently compiled by scribes whose interests were primarily antiquarian. These include a group of Arthurian genealogies preserved in certain sixteenth- and seventeenth-century manuscripts.[17] In contrast to the poetry and Triads, these genealogies reveal consistent direct borrowing from the *Prose Lancelot*. They are clearly based on written rather than orally transmitted sources, and include many personal names derived from the romances of the French Vulgate Cycle. The most important French sources used are the *Estoire del Saint Graal*, the *Prose Merlin*, the *Prose Lancelot* and the *Livre d'Artus*, although sometimes it can be difficult, if not impossible, to establish whether the *Prose Merlin* or the *Prose Lancelot* was the precise source. Nevertheless, some cases are quite unambiguous, notably Brenin Brangor (Brangoire roi d'Estrangoire), mentioned in the *Prose Lancelot* as the father of the girl who was the cause of Bohort losing his virginity.[18] The difficulty of pinpointing whether the

11 Lloyd-Morgan, 'A Study of *Y Seint Greal*', pp. 47–50; Daniel Huws in *Ystoryaeu Seint Greal*, p. xiv.

12 *Gwaith Guto'r Glyn*, ed. by J. Llywelyn Williams & Ifor Williams (Cardiff: University of Wales Press, 1939), p. 4, l. 48.

13 *Gwaith Lewis Glyn Cothi*, ed. by Gwallter Mechain & Tegid (Oxford & Denbigh: Cymmrodorion Society, 1837–39), p. 425, l. 38.

14 *The Poetical Works of Dafydd Nanmor*, ed. by Thomas Roberts & Ifor Williams (Cardiff: University of Wales Press, 1923), p. 59, l. 58.

15 *Gwaith Tudur Aled*, ed. by T. Gwynn Jones (Cardiff, Wrexham & London, 1926), p. 65 and 182.

16 Ceridwen Lloyd-Morgan, '*Breuddwyd Rhonabwy* and Later Arthurian Literature', in *Arthur of the Welsh*, ed. by Rachel Bromwich, A. O. H. Jarman & Brynley F. Roberts (Cardiff: University of Wales Press, 1991), pp. 183–208 (p. 204); David Geraint Lewis, 'Mynegai i'r enwau priod storïol yng ngwaith cyhoeddiedig y cywyddwyr' (unpublished master's thesis, University of Wales: Aberystwyth, 1968).

17 P. C. Bartrum, 'Arthuriana from the Genealogical Manuscripts', *National Library of Wales Journal*, 14 (1965), 242–45; Ceridwen Lloyd-Morgan, 'Nodiadau ychwanegol ar yr achau Arthuraidd a'u ffynonellau Ffrangeg', ibid., 21 (1980), 329–39.

18 Sommer, *Vulgate Version*, IV, 262–70.

Prose Merlin or *Prose Lancelot* was the source of a given proper name also arises with other late, composite texts, such as the fifteenth-century *Darogan yr Olew Bendigaid*, where the redactor has made extensive use of the French Vulgate Cycle, as well as sources in Welsh and Latin, to create a very composite semi-Arthurian narrative.[19] However, putting all these borrowings together, and allowing for redactors making use of *Y Seint Greal* with its translations of the *Queste* and *Perlesvaus*, there is still plenty of evidence that the *Estoire*, *Prose Merlin* and *Prose Lancelot*, as well as the *Queste*, were known in Wales. Whether the *Mort Artu* was also available is more difficult to establish, as there are other sources, such as the *Historia Regum Britanniae* and its vernacular versions, which would have provided accounts for this last chapter of Arthurian history, but since the other Vulgate texts were undoubtedly available we may conclude that at least one complete manuscript version of the Vulgate Cycle had reached Wales, certainly by the fifteenth century.

Such a manuscript may in fact have arrived earlier, however, for the redactor of *Y Seint Greal*, working in the closing years of the fourteenth century, undoubtedly had access to the *Prose Lancelot*, at least at one point. This is revealed in the section based on the *Queste*, when Peredur/Perceval's aunt foretells that three knights will succeed in the grail quest. In the French she says:

> 'si en seront li dui virge et li tierz chastes. Et de ces deus virges sera li chevaliers que vos querez li uns et vos li autres, et li tierz Boorz de Gaunes'.[20]

In *Y Seint Greal* this has been expanded:

> 'A'r deu a vyd marchogyon gwyry, heb wneuthur pechawt godineb o'e kyrff eiryoet na'e vedylyaw. Y trydyd a vyd diweir; kystal yw hynny ac na bu idaw wreic eiryoet onyt vn weith. A'r weith honno y kaffat arnaw som a phrofedigaeth, ac ny byd vyth idaw mwy; ac am hynny y gelwir ef yn diweir'
>
> (And the first two will be virgin knights, without ever having committed the sin of fornication either in body or thought. The third will be chaste, that is to say that he never had any woman as wife but once. And on that occasion deceit and temptation were put upon

19 R. Wallis Evans, '*Darogan yr Olew Bendigaid* a *Hystdori yr Olew Bendigaid*', *Llên Cymru*, 14 (1981–82), 86–91; Ceridwen Lloyd-Morgan, '*Darogan yr Olew Bendigaid*: Chwedl o'r bymthegfed ganrif', ibid., 64–85, and 'Prophecy and Welsh Nationhood in the Fifteenth Century', *Transactions of the Honourable Society of Cymmrodorion* (1985), 9–26.

20 *La Queste del Saint Graal*, ed. by Albert Pauphilet, Classiques Français du Moyen Age (Paris: Champion, repr. 1972), p. 73, ll. 12–14.

him, but that will not happen to him ever again, and for that reason he is called chaste.)[21]

The translator, therefore, knew more about the circumstances under which Bohort lost his virginity than he could have acquired from the *Queste* alone. His addition to the translation of a reference to the trick that had to be perpetrated on Bwrt/Bohort demonstrates that he had access to the *Prose Lancelot*, for only there is this detail found. The girl's old nurse gives Bohort a magic ring which makes him love the girl, and that night Helain li Blancs is conceived.[22] In the *Queste* the only reference to this event does not include the detail of the magic ring or refer to the trick: it states only that a *preudom* with whom Bohort is staying confesses him and finds 'qu'il ne s'ert onques meffez en corruption de char, fors a cele hore qu'il engendra Elyan le Blanc'.[23]

If, then, the text of the *Prose Lancelot* was available in Wales, we might hope to find specific records of such manuscripts in other sources. So far, however, only one reference has come to my notice, namely a fragment in a copy made around 1400 of the C Version of *Piers Plowman*, which is now MS 212 in Trinity College, Dublin.[24] This fragment of the *Prose Lancelot* was once part of the cover of the volume, and the inclusion in the manuscript of annals relating to Wales, especially the southern border region, for the period 1293–1349, provides evidence that it had once been in hands west of Offa's Dyke.

The final question that we must consider is also, perhaps, the most difficult: why was no Lancelot romance ever adapted into Welsh? Since Chrétien's *Yvain*, *Erec* and *Perceval* gave rise to Welsh retellings, it might seem strange to ignore his *Chevalier de la Charrete*. We know that *La Queste del Saint Graal* was translated in full into Welsh, and parts of the *Prose Merlin* adapted into Welsh,[25] so why not the *Prose Lancelot*? After all, the evidence suggests that it was in fact available. Had there been an adaptation of Chrétien's *Chevalier de la Charrete* as a precedent, this might have prompted a fifteenth-century patron to commission a Welsh translation of the *Prose Lancelot*. The situation would have been analogous to that of the *Queste*, for it is clear that, as a grail romance, the *Queste* had affinities and narrative overlap with the Welsh tale of *Peredur*, itself corresponding to Chrétien's *Perceval*, and so could slip

21 *Ystoryaeu Seint Greal*, ll. 1583–87.
22 Sommer, *Vulgate Version*, IV, 267–70.
23 *La Queste del Saint Graal*, p. 166, ll. 23–25.
24 John Scattergood, 'An Unrecorded Fragment of the *Prose Lancelot* in Trinity College, Dublin, MS 212', *Medium Aevum*, 53 (1984), 301–06.
25 J. H. Davies, 'The Birth of Arthur', *Y Cymmrodor*, 24 (1913), 247–64.

easily into a pre-existing tradition. But the *Lancelot* had no such forerunner, and the story of Lancelot's development as a knight had no clear parallel in native Welsh tradition. Virtually the only Welsh redactor to make extensive use of the *Prose Lancelot* was Elis Gruffudd, who incorporated material from it in the Arthurian section of his Chronicle of the Six Ages, which he composed in the 1540s and 1550s.[26] His use of the *Prose Lancelot* is all the more striking in that he borrows not only proper names but also complete episodes, such as two dreams which Arthur has and his attempts to have them interpreted.[27] But Elis Gruffudd compiled his chronicle in Calais, where he had lived since 1530, and had access there to a far wider variety of written sources than his predecessors in Wales would have had. Moreover, his explicit intention was to make available in Welsh material from abroad that was not well known to his countrymen.[28]

I have suggested elsewhere that the absence in Wales of any fully-fledged Tristan tale or romance may be partly due to unease at what may have been perceived as a rather equivocal attitude to an adulterous relationship which cuckolds the king.[29] The story of the love of Lancelot and Guinevere is in many ways analogous to the Tristan legend, and it is worth considering whether in both cases the theme of adultery involving the king's wife prevented these stories from being cast in their entirety into a literary form in Welsh, and prevented them from achieving the prominence accorded to traditions attached to other Arthurian characters. A further – perhaps complementary – possibility is that the Welsh redactors, their patrons and audience, preferred stories of military exploits to those of lovers' meetings. Certainly there is no indigenous Welsh tradition bearing any resemblance to *fin'amors* or *courtoisie* in Welsh. In the early prose tales, such as the Four Branches of the Mabinogi, there is little talk of love, and the emphasis is on the dynastic and political purposes of any formalised sexual union; even in *Culhwch ac Olwen* Culhwch's marriage to Olwen, with whom he has been fated to

26 The Chronicle occupies four volumes of a unique holograph manuscript; the Arthurian section is contained in NLW MS 5276D, part II. On Elis Gruffudd, see Thomas Jones, 'A Welsh Chronicler in Tudor England', *Welsh History Review*, 1 (1960), 1–17, and Prys Morgan, 'Elis Gruffudd of Gronant – Tudor Chronicler Extraordinary', *Proceedings of the Flintshire Historical Society*, 25 (1971–72), 9–20.

27 NLW MS 5276D, ff. 329v–332v; see Sommer, *Vulgate Version*, III, pp. 200–02 and 220–23, and *Lancelot do Lac*, ed. by Elspeth Kennedy, 2 vols (Oxford: Clarendon Press, 1980), I, 260–62 and 289–92.

28 See the prologue to the second part of his Chronicle, NLW MS 3054D (National Library of Wales, Aberystwyth), f. 2v.

29 Ceridwen Lloyd-Morgan, 'Tristan et Iseut au Pays de Galles', *Pris-ma*, 7 (1991), 89–98, and 'Trystan ac Esyllt: y ddau draddodiad', *Ysgrifau Beirniadol*, 18 (1992), 43–54.

fall in love, is primarily a narrative device, and a means of acquiring property along with a wife. Moreover, the redactor of *Y Seint Greal*, in translating the *Queste* in particular, often heavily abridges passages of discussion, whether of Lancelot's love for Guinevere or of theology, whilst retaining, even embroidering, scenes of military activity. If this redactor is typical, his procedure indicates that the idea of chivalry in the service of one's lord was easier to accommodate than that of love service.

Not only does the surviving evidence suggest that both the name and the character of Lancelot had developed in France rather than in Wales, it also indicates that transplanting him to Wales, at a period when French romance was fashionable and being adapted into Welsh, raised a number of difficulties. The fact that Lancelot makes an appearance at all in Welsh would seem to be due to his important role in the grail romances. In both the *Queste del Saint Graal* and *Perlesvaus* he is presented as the lover of Guinevere, albeit in rather different ways, and in the *Queste*, additionally, he is the father of Galaad and has his own part in the grail quest. His role in both romances is sufficiently integral to the narrative that it would have been well nigh impossible for the Welsh redactor of *Y Seint Greal* to have excluded him altogether when preparing his translation of these two romances. Once this Welsh version was available, other writers were able to quarry it and may even have been inspired by it to look further afield and turn to original French sources such as the *Prose Lancelot* or *Mort Artu*. But it is significant that no Welsh redactor, either before or after the production of *Y Seint Graal*, was ever inspired, or commissioned by a patron, to produce a Welsh version of any complete Lancelot story. Lancelot may be better described as a visitor to Wales rather than as a returning emigrant.

Translation as Reception: *La Danse macabré*

JANE H. M. TAYLOR

THE STUDY OF the medieval reception of the medieval text is arguably one of the major current critical preoccupations of the community of medievalists. Illumination, marginalia, rubrication, marginal notations, compilation, adaptation[1] are all pressed into service as contemporary authentic material providing evidence which, properly interpreted, permits the sort of reconstruction of contemporary response which might, *a priori*, have seemed an impossibility for a readership so chronologically remote and so critically inarticulate. In the present paper, I propose to address a further category of evidence: the evidence of the translation. This is not of course a new field: it is perfectly commonplace to locate twelfth-century reader-response to Virgil's *Aeneid*, say, in the modifications and transformations imposed on it on the level of content by the author of the *Roman d'Eneas*.[2] What I intend to argue here, however, is

[1] This is in response to calls like that of Daniel Poirion for 'une critique sémiologique décrivant la transformation des textes par des pratiques comme la traduction, la reproduction globale ou partielle, le résumé, l'interpolation' ('Ecriture et réécriture au moyen âge', in *Intertextualités médiévales*, *Littérature*, 41 (1981), 109–18 (p. 109)). The bibliography on these topics is now unencompassable; for some initial suggestions, see Sarah Kay, 'Continuation as Criticism: the Case of Jaufré Rudel', *Medium Aevum*, 56 (1987), 46–64; Sylvia Huot, 'Authors, Scribes, Remanieurs: A Note on the Textual History of the *Romance of the Rose*', in *Rethinking the* Romance of the Rose: *Text, Image, Reception*, ed. by Kevin Brownlee and Sylvia Huot, Middle Ages Series (Philadelphia: University of Pennsylvania Press, 1992), pp. 203–233; Sylvia Huot, 'Vignettes marginales comme glose marginale dans un manuscrit du *Roman de la Rose* au quatorzième siècle', in *La Présentation du livre: Actes du Colloque de Paris X-Nanterre (déc. 4–6, 1985)*, ed. by E. Baumgartner and N. Boulestreau, Littérales: Cahiers du Département de Français, 2 (Nanterre: Centre de Recherche du Département de Français de Paris X, 1987), pp. 173–86.

[2] See among others R. J. Cormier, *One Heart, One Mind: The Rebirth of Virgil's Hero in Medieval French Romance*, Romance Monographs, 3 (Mississippi: University of Mississippi

that it is also legitimate to read response into quite minor lexical choices which the translator necessarily makes during his transposition of his source text, hereafter ST. I take as my material a translation of the early fifteenth-century *Danse macabré*, done into English by John Lydgate. In the space at my disposal, I shall confine myself to just one lexeme, *dance*, and show how an interesting convergence of translational choice may provide evidence for a particular reading of the ST.

A poem known as the *Danse macabré* may well have existed before 1376,[3] but the earliest date attested is 1424–25 when, according to the so-called Bourgeois de Paris,[4] the verses were painted below a fresco along an arcade in the Innocents' cemetery in Paris. Text and verses were a remarkable success: the mere fact that this artistic production alone is mentioned by the Bourgeois in his journal, the fact that before long the *Danse macabré* constituted a landmark and tourist attraction in Paris, the fact that copies and near copies were made all over France is evidence of their impact[5] – as indeed is the fact that even if the fresco was destroyed in the seventeenth century, copies of the verses had been made in manuscript, and were published by Guyot Marchant in 1485,[6] along with a set of superb engravings. Additional evidence of the popularity of the verses is furnished by the proliferation of manuscripts and editions, and by the three separate translations of the text which were made in the course of the fifteenth century alone.[7]

Of these translations, the one which concerns us here was done by the

Press, 1973), and D. Poirion, 'De l'Éneide à l'Énée: mythologies et moralisations', *Cahiers de Civilisation Médiévale*, 19 (1976), 213–29.

3 The phrase is used by Jean Lefèvre in his *Respit de la mort*, ed. by Geneviève Hasenohr-Esnos, SATF (Paris: Picard, 1969), ll. 3078–81: 'Je fis de Macabré la dance/ Qui toutes gens maine a sa tresche/ Et a la fosse les adresche,/ Qui est leur derraine maison'. The meaning of these lines is much disputed; for a brief overview of the issues, see the editor's note on pp. 195–97.

4 *Journal d'un Bourgeois de Paris de 1405–1449*, ed. by Colette Beaune, Lettres Gothiques (Paris: Le Livre de Poche, 1990), p. 220.

5 The fullest studies remain those of James M. Clark, *The Dance of Death*, Glasgow University Publications, 86 (Glasgow: Jackson, Son and Co., 1953), and for the history of the Dance in general, Stephan Cosacchi, *Makabertanz: der Totentanz in Kunst, Poesie und Brauchtum des Mittelalters* (Meisenheim am Glan: A. Hain, 1965).

6 Two manuscripts, B.N. f. fr. 25550 and f. lat. 14904, claim to have copied the verses directly from the Innocents. Guyot Marchant's *editio princeps* of 1485 survives in only one copy in the Bibliothèque Municipale in Grenoble (Catalogue Maignien, no. 234).

7 As well as Lydgate's translation, which is the main focus of this paper, a translation into Latin was made by Pierre Desrey and published by Guyot Marchant in 1490 (there is no modern edition; I hope to provide one in a forthcoming study on the *Danse macabré*), and another into Spanish; see *Danza general de la muerte*, ed. by Haydée Bermejo Hurtado and Dinko Cvitamovic (Bahia Blanca: Cuardernos del Sur – 2 – Testos comentados, 1966), the editors seeing the translation as made or adapted from the French text (see pp. 10–11).

prolific John Lydgate, who certainly saw the verses *in situ*, as it were, in the graveyard. Between 1426 and 1429 he was attached to the administrative staff of the Duke of Bedford in Paris, and more particularly to the Earl of Warwick.[8] During this period he produced a number of translations from French, ranging from the relatively slight *Devowte Invocacioun to Sainte Denys* to the vast if somewhat pedestrian *Pilgrimage of the Life of Man*.[9] His *Dance of Death* – perhaps one of the more artistically successful of his translations – was done, he says, at the instigation of 'Frensshe clerkis',[10] after 'machabres daunce' which he had seen 'depict oones in a wal':

> The whiche daunce at seint Innocentis
> Portreied is with al the surplusage
> To schewe this worlde is but a pilgrimage. (35–37)

Like many late medieval translators, Lydgate is reflective: he intervenes in his authorial voice to comment on the very process of translation. His French is, he says, shaky:[11] 'Rude of langage y was not borne yn fraunce [. . .] Of her tunge I haue no suffisaunce' (ll. 669–71). Fortunately, however, he has been able to count on the interpretative help ('sterynge', which Warren glosses as 'guidance', and 'mocioune', 'encouragement') of the French clerks who suggested the undertaking:

8 According to Walter F. Schirmer, *John Lydgate: A Study in the Culture of the Fifteenth Century*, trans. by Ann E. Keep (London: Methuen, 1961), p. 116, he 'occupied a senior post on Bedford's administrative staff as some sort of liaison officer.'

9 On Lydgate's reputation and on his expertise as a translator, see Derek Pearsall, *John Lydgate* (London: Routledge and Kegan Paul, 1970). An extensive bibliography of recent work on Lydgate will be found in Alain Renoir and C. David Benson, 'John Lydgate', in *A Manual of Writings in Middle English*, ed. by Albert E. Hartung (Hamden, Ct: Archon Books/The Shoestring Press for the Cornell Academy of Arts and Sciences, 1980), VI, 1809–920, 2071–175.

10 I propose to cite from the A-version of the poem contained in the edition of the Ellesmere manuscript done by Florence Warren, EETS o.s. 181 (London: Humphrey Milford for the Oxford University Press, 1931); line numbers will be cited from that edition in the text. I make no judgement as to its primacy (indeed, it seems difficult to determine the priority of the two versions, and it is virtually certain that Lydgate himself revised his text). On the textual history of Lydgate's *Dance of Death*, and in particular on the two versions, 'Ellesmere' and 'Lansdowne', see Beatrice White's introduction to Warren's edition of the text, pp. xxiv–xxxi, and a useful article by Derek Pearsall, 'Signs of Life in Lydgate's *Danse Macabre*', in *Zeit, Tod und Ewigkeit in der Renaissance Literatur*, ed. by James Hogg (Salzburg: Institut für Anglistik und Amerikanistik, 1987), III, 58–71.

11 This must surely be a flagrant humility topos, given the quantity and accuracy of Lydgate's translations; see Schirmer, pp. 120–29.

Of frensshe clerkes takyng acqueyntaunce
I toke on me to translaten al
Owte of the frensshe Macabrees daunce.

Bi whos a-vyse and cownseille atte leste
Thurh her steryng and her mocioune
I obeyed vnto her requeste
Therrof to make a pleyne translacioun
In Inglisshe tunge. (21–29)

Even so, he says, his translation has no claim to word-for-word accuracy: simply, it represents the substance and sentiment of the original: 'Owte of the frensshe I drowe hit of entent/ Not worde be worde but folwyng the substaunce' (ll. 665–66). None of this, of course, is especially original. The anonymous English translator of Coudrette's *Mélusine*,[12] working towards the end of the fourteenth century, had similarly recognised that while translation necessarily implies compromise with the original text:

As of latin ho-so will fourge uers
Wourdes most he change sondry & diuerse

the translator's role is to preserve the essence of his ST:

Preseruing, I trust, mater and sentence
Vnwemmed, vnhurt, for any excesse,
Or by menusing don by violence
Warded and kepte haue to intelligens,
That will vnderstande.[13]

Lydgate's disclaimer, in other words, is pretty conventional.[14] But its

12 *The Romans of Partenay, or of Lusignen; Otherwise Known as the Tale of Melusine. Translated from the French of La Coudrette (before 1500 A.D.)*, ed. by the Rev. Walter W. Skeat, EETS (London: N. Trübner and Co, 1866), ll. 6558 ff.

13 Further information on the techniques of translation into English will be found for the Wycliffites in Sven Frisholt, *The Wycliffe Bible* (Stockholm: Bröderna Lagerström Bodtryckare and Almqvist & Wiksell, 1953–73); for Trevisa in Traugott Lawler, 'On the Properties of John Trevisa's Major Translations', *Viator*, 14 (1983), 266–88; for Chaucer in Tim William Machan, *Techniques of Translation: Chaucer's Boece* (Norman, Oklahoma: Pilgrim Books, 1985). On medieval translation into English in general, see the valuable article by R. Ellis, 'The Choices of the Translator in the Late Middle English Period', in *The Medieval Mystical Tradition in England*, ed. by Marion Glasscoe (Cambridge: Brewer, 1982), pp. 18–46.

14 For further examples and commentary on this topic, see Claude Buridant, 'Translatio medievalis: Théorie et pratique de la traduction médiévale', *Université de Strasbourg, Centre de philologie et de littératures romanes: Travaux de linguistique et de littérature*, 21 (1983), 81–136. There are some very valuable comments also on translation strategies

conventionality should not blind us to the fact that it postulates an unsystematic but particular model for translation: an interpretative strategy which allows the translator to distinguish what is essential in his ST from what is contingent. This model is distantly a precursor of much more recent models of the process of literary translation, and because these models directly relate the translation to the question of reception of a given text, I propose to expand briefly on them.

Any translator knows that the unsophisticated model of the translation process which imagines direct and one-for-one equivalences for lexical items in the ST being transferred serially and unthinkingly to the target text (TT) is absurd even for the most referential of texts. Correspondences are generated, at the very least, at sentence level: the translator first subjects the ST to a process of analysis, or exegesis, which extracts from the sentence its 'kernel' of meaning, and it is this kernel which is transferred into the receptor language via a process of restructuring.[15] But of course even this oversimplifies: more useful models postulate concurrent processes which – at the risk still of some oversimplification – suppose the mobilisation of three different strategies which might be called *comprehension*, *interpretation* and *explicitation*.[16] The first and last of these are probably self-explanatory. *Comprehension* (is this where Lydgate needed his *frensshe clerkes*?) centres on the constitutive elements of the ST, and might be loosely described as serial: word by word, sentence by sentence, the translator deciphers the ST, becoming aware of the ranges of meaning potentially attached to a particular syntagm. The final phase, *explicitation*, proposes a translation which will necessarily involve a series of compromises: in the case of Lydgate's translation, for instance, the

for the medieval vernacular text in Rita Copeland, *Rhetoric, Hermeneutics and Translation: Academic Traditions and Vernacular Texts*, Cambridge Studies in Medieval Literature, 11 (Cambridge: University Press, 1991), ch. 7, 'Translation as Rhetorical Invention: Chaucer and Gower'. A suggestive study of a late-medieval French translator is Françoise Guichard-Tesson's, 'Le Métier de traducteur et de commentateur au XIVe siècle d'après Evrart de Conty', *Le Moyen français*, 24–25 (1989), 131–67.

15 I do not wish to claim that this model is itself modern. On the contrary, it is not dissimilar to that of St Jerome himself; see Rita Copeland, 'The Fortunes of "Non verbum pro verbo": or, Why Jerome is not a Ciceronian', in *The Medieval Translator: The Theory and Practice of Translation in the Middle Ages*, ed. by Roger Ellis (Cambridge: Brewer, 1989), pp. 15–35. For more recent theorists, see for instance Eugene Nida, *Towards a Theory of Translating, with Special Reference to the Principles and Procedures Involved in Bible Translating* (Leiden: Brill, 1964) and his 'Science of Translating', *Language*, 45 (1969), 483–98.

16 The terms are borrowed from an article by Josef Čermák, 'La Traduction du point de vue de l'interprétation', in *The Nature of Translation: Essays on the Theory and Practice of Literary Translation*, ed. by James S. Holmes (The Hague/Paris: Mouton, 1970), pp. 23–42.

constraints imposed by his decision to re-express the ST in verse will limit his choice of rhyme words, or impose certain rhythmical patterns. But from the point of view of reader-response, it is the central, *interpretation* phase that is the important one. It is during this phase that the translator moves from the virtual to the actual, operating a series of choices between potential meanings. The criteria to permit this will involve not just comprehension, but some perception of the function and message of the text, and this will be related to all sorts of extraneous information: linguistic codes and literary conventions in the source language and their equivalences in the target language, social and cultural factors at play in the ST, an assessment of the intended audience for both ST and TT. Given these, the translator can develop what James S. Holmes calls a 'mental map' of the source text, which can then be used 'as a kind of general criterion against which to test each sentence during the formulation of the new, translated text,'[17] this being, as de Beaugrande expresses it, 'not the original text, but rather the representation of the text that is originally generated in the translator's mind.'[18]

This process, whereby the translator elicits in the ST its communicative function, is clearly akin to the critical process. In both cases, the primary stimulus is the ST, and it is the translator's duty to elicit and as far as possible preserve its *invariant core*,[19] the sense which must remain inviolate. But in the translation of a poem particularly, the translator's exegetical and interpretative skills play a part at least as important as his comprehension skills. To balance sense against sound, rhythm against rhyme, stanzaic pattern against sentence-structure, convention against originality, all demands a process of critical assessment:

> As much as the critic, the translator is obliged to analyse the poem. He is, however, not allowed to kill it in the process. On the contrary, it is his task to resurrect the poem after dissection, and to offer it again to the reader, *enriched by his criticism and commentary which are necessarily, if imperceptibly, built into the translation* (my italics).[20]

17 See his 'Describing Literary Translations: Models and Methods', in *Translated! Papers on Literary Translation and Translation Studies*, ed. by James S. Holmes (Amsterdam: Rodopi, 1988), pp. 81–91 (pp. 82–83).

18 Robert de Beaugrande, 'Factors in a Theory of Poetic Translating', *Approaches to Translation Studies*, 5 (Assen: Van Gorcum, 1978), p. 25.

19 The term is used by Anton Popovic, *A Dictionary for the Analysis of Literary Translation* (Edmonton, Alberta: Department of Comparative Literature, University of Alberta, 1976); see also his 'Aspects of Metatext', *Canadian Review of Comparative Literature*, 3 (1976), 225–35.

20 André Lefevere, 'The Study of Literary Translation and the Study of Comparative Literature', *Babel*, 17 (1971), 13–15 (p. 15).

What this implies, of course, is that even if the casual reader is unaware of the critical and explicatory processes which subtend the selected translation, the critic is able to use the evidence of the TT, the translated text, in conjunction with and set against the source text, to resurrect at least some of the translator's processes of criticism and commentary. As Lefevere says, the translation

> constitutes *an eminently testable act of reception*, which can be studied independently of its actual production in time (my italics).[21]

In pursuit of this act of reception, the critic can perform a mapping process which parallels that of the translator. The latter uses interpretative and exegetical skills to build a map of the ST. The critic having available ST and TT is able to map not only the ST but the TT, looking in both for distinctive features that seem significant and deserving of comparative analysis. Once the two descriptive processes are complete, the critic can confront and correlate the two maps, and use the match or divergence of the two to make a tentative reconstruction of the translator's reading of the ST. Such a reading, ideally, covers the broadest spectrum of questions: what part of the meaning potential of the ST has the translator judged must be preserved? What rearrangement strategies have been deployed? What rhetorical devices have been judged indispensable to underline and develop the message of the ST? What evaluation strategies have been applied to each of the constituent elements of the ST (by which I mean not only the lexicon, but also syntax, coherence, prosody . . .)? But of course a study on this scale would exceed the limits of the present paper; I shall confine myself therefore to a brief study of the translation of just one particular lexeme, *danse[r]*, in the translation of which a coherent pattern can, I consider, be discerned, a pattern from which can be inferred a distinct and individual reading.

The French ST of 1424[22] – unsurprisingly – makes extensive use of the lexeme *danse[r]*, which appears some 22 times in its 532 lines. The collocations vary: often, when used by the *Morts*, the verb is couched in the future (l. 19) or in the imperative (ll. 134, 230, 585), or, when used by the living, it is combined with verbs such as *falloir* (l. 494), in

21 André Lefevere, 'Programmatic Second Thoughts on "Literary" and "Translation" ', *Poetics Today*, 2 (1981), 39–50.

22 Neither of the two modern editions of the French text is critical. Warren publishes a partially edited transcript of the text on pp. 79–96. I use the unsatisfactory text published by Edward F. Chaney, *La Danse Macabré des Charniers des Saints Innocents à Paris* (Manchester: Manchester University Press, 1945), which transcribes and only partially edits the text of Guyot Marchant's edition of 1486.

questions such as 'Fault il que la dance mainne?' (l. 57). Generally, the lexeme is indeed unqualified: only in one couplet does one victim, the King, elaborate on the nature of this particular dance:

> Je n'ay point apris a danser
> A danse et note si sauvaige. (105–06)

a couplet which suggests, as I have argued elsewhere,[23] a dance defined as threatening because undisciplined and unchoreographed.

On the simplest distributional level, by comparison with his exemplar, Lydgate multiplies occurrences of the lexeme *dance*. In a translation which, with some additions, numbers 672 lines, the word *daunce* recurs some 41 times, and this from a translator who shows considerable philological ingenuity in matching lexicon, syntax and prosody. These raw figures, however, conceal certain distinct and coherent patterns of insertion and expansion which are relevant to the present discussion. The most basic category of occurrences is, of course, simple substitution where for a neutral verb, commonly *suivre* or *mourir* (the latter neutral here in the sense that it constitutes the *topic* for which *danser* is the *vehicle*),[24] the translator substitutes the lexeme *daunce*, thus reinforcing the underlying textual metaphor as the following examples show:

1. Cardinal! Sus legerement!
   Suivons les autres tous ensemble. (82–83)

   But yit for-thi ȝe *folow* shul yn dede
   With other folke my *daunce* for to lere. (91–92)

2. Il convient que la mort *suivez*,
   Combien que moult l'avez haye. (243–44)

   ȝe mote come *daunce* thowȝ ȝe be nothing light (236)

3. Prenés cy consolation.
   Pour toute retribution,
   Mourir vous convient sans demeure. (308–10)

   For ther is now no consolacioun
   But *daunce* with vs for al ȝowre hye renoun. (316–17)

[23] 'Que signifiait danse au quinzième siècle? Danser la Danse macabré', *Fifteenth-Century Studies*, 18 (1991), 259–77.

[24] I borrow this terminology from Eva Feder Kittay, *Metaphor: Its Cognitive Form and Linguistic Structure* (Oxford: Clarendon Press, 1987), in preference to the more hermetic *tenor* and *vehicle* of I. A. Richards, *The Philosophy of Rhetoric* (London: Oxford University Press, 1936).

4. Vecy vostre dernier marchié,
Il convient que par cy passez. (325–26)

hauyng moste rewarde
To lucre & wynnynge as I vndurstonde
But now to *daunce* ȝe mote ȝeue me ȝowre honde. (331–33)

This consistent reinforcement of the metaphor should perhaps be linked to another phenomenon. Lydgate adds to his ST a small additional number of living respondents, including three women: the *Lady of gret astate* (ll. 185–200), the *Abbesse* (ll. 249–64), the *Gentilwoman amoraus* (ll. 449–64), the *Joroure* (ll. 353–496), and finally the *Tregetoure* (ll. 513–28). In the verses which he devises for his supplementary figures, and which are remarkable calques of the content, metre and lexicon of those he derived from his French original, only one dancer, the *Juroure*, is not associated with the word *daunce*. Indeed the lexeme sometimes achieves an interesting and emphatic effect of counterpoint: thus *Dethe* addresses the *Lady of gret astate*:

Come forth a-noon my lady & Princesse
ȝe most al-so go vp-on this daunce. (185–86)

to which she replies:

Allas I see ther is noon other bote
Dethe hath yn erthe no ladi ne maiestresse
And on his daunce ȝitte moste I nedes fote.
(192–94; see also ll. 253, 453, 517)

In Lydgate's judgement of what constitutes congruous interpolation, in other words, the sort of seamless continuity which he engineers seems to demand what amounts to systematic reiteration of the dominant metaphor of the ST.

It also demands – or at least invites – a 'personalisation' of dance, its appropriation by the figures of the dead. Interestingly, since his ST seems to have envisaged a dialogue not between an abstraction *death* and the living, but rather between the living and the individual dead, each of whom speaks as *Le Mort*,[25] Lydgate baptises his protagonist, consistently, *Dethe*. In the ST, in conformity perhaps with the possibility that the dead

[25] Chaney's edition adopts the *Le Mort* of Guyot Marchant's *editio princeps*; the manuscripts alternate between *la mort* and *le mort*, but also prefer the latter. For the dead as *Doppelgänger* of the living, see my 'Un miroer salutaire', in *Dies Illa: Death in the Middle Ages*, ed. by Jane H. M. Taylor, Vinaver Studies in French, 1 (Liverpool: Francis Cairns, 1984), pp. 29–43.

are *sosies* or counterparts of the living, the dead seem to present themselves to the living as fellow victims subordinated as the living will shortly be to the rhythms of the dance, subsuming them into the category *nous*. Lydgate's *Dethe*, on the other hand, strongly individualised, becomes himself the orchestrator of the dance, which in turn he appropriates: thus the Pope identifies this as *Dethe's* own dance:

> But for al that deth I mai not flee
> On *his* daunce with other for to trace. (69–70)

and *Dethe* himself addresses the Emperor:

> Be-hinde leue ȝowre tresowre & richesse
> And with other to *my* daunce obeie. (77–78)

Dance becomes all the more threatening in that it is associated with a figure of power who exercises an inexorable authority over the living dancers, rather than an activity from some unidentified source to which all participants, dead and living, submit in a spirit of solidarity.

The reinforcement of the metaphor is however operated most substantially at one particular point in the poem. I quoted above that single couplet where one of the living comments on – I am tempted to say 'glosses' – the notion of *dance* fundamental to this poem:

> Je n'ay point apris a danser
> A danse et note si sauvaige. (105–06)

Lydgate's translation of this passage involves a degree of interesting syntactic and lexical manipulation, but it retains, as well as the lexeme *danse*, certain direct borrowings, here italicised:

> I haue not *lerned* here-a-forne to daunce
> No daunce in sothe of fotynge so *sauage*. (113–14)

Simply, the translation exchanges the lexeme *note* (privileging music), with the term *fotynge*, 'step', both, of course, syntagmatically associated with the term *dance*. This makes all the more startling a second 'gloss' which Lydgate provides in ll. 505–09. What he does is to capitalise on the presence of the Minstrel to offer a contextually apposite expansion of his ST, minimally prompted no doubt by the first line of the French original and perhaps by the insistence on music:

> De *danser* ainsi n'eusse cure;
> Certes, tres enviz je m'en mesle,
> Car de mort n'est painne plus dure.

J'ay mis sous le banc ma *vielle*;
Plus ne *corneray sauterelle*
N'autre danse; mort m'en retient. (497–502)

Lydgate's version, however, is remarkably inventive:

This *new* daunce is to me so *straunge*
Wonder *dyuerse* and passyngli *contrarie*
The *dredful fotyng* dothe so ofte *chaunge*
And the *mesures* so ofte sithes *varie*. (505–08)

The words and expressions italicised here have no semantic equivalent in the ST, and yet in a sense they objectify the vehicle *dance* by first isolating two of its syntagmatically related features (*fotyng* again, and *mesures*), and then fixing them in terms of two paradigmatic sets: one, *straunge*, *dyuerse*, *contrarie*, which foregrounds the dance's alienness, the other, *chaunge*, *varie*, which foregrounds its irregularity.[26] I should emphasise that nothing in the ST at this point in the text authorises this extension of the metaphor, but also that nothing in the ST as a whole displays this degree of elaboration: alienness and irregularity are not associated in the ST with the dance. We must assume therefore that they can only derive from the poet's individual reading of his ST, and are based on similarity discovered *post factum* between topic and vehicle; the conceptual 'map' of Lydgate's *Dance* is thus made significantly different from that of his ST.

It is of course important not to over-rationalise by making inflated claims to trace the processes whereby ST is transformed into TT. But that Lydgate chooses so systematically to exploit and extend a metaphor relatively undetermined in the ST is, I think, best explained by assuming that the translational process takes place against a reading which takes account of both textual and iconographic systems – a reading that at the Innocents' cemetery was inevitable.[27] The lexeme dance is overdetermined in Lydgate's translation in ways that precisely fit the 'map' provided by the frescoes. That the *Morts* should become *Dethe*, for instance, seems best explained by the fact that the individual and plural *Morts* of the Innocents were probably, as they are in all the painted Dances, virtually identical in appearance: similar cheerful rictus, similar types of

[26] The term is adopted from Jiri Levy, *Die literarische Übersetzung: Theorie einer Kunstgattung*, trans. by W. Schamschula (Frankfurt: Athenäum, 1969); see especially pp. 35–37.

[27] For other studies of this dual signifying system, see my 'Danse macabré and bande dessinée: A Question of Reading', *Forum for Modern Language Studies*, 25 (1989), 356–69, and 'La Danse Macabré, une relecture', in *Fins de siècle: Colloque de Tours, 4–6 juin 1985*, ed. by Pierre Citti (Bordeaux: Presses Universitaires, 1990), pp. 99–110.

movement, similar state of decay, to the extent that the *Morts* can be differentiated only by different attributes such as spade, or pick-axe, or shroud. It is not therefore implausible that the *iconographic* images of the dead overlay the relatively unobvious linguistic signs represented only by a minor change in definite article (*le* rather than *la*). Similarly, that the translation should choose to isolate and play out the particular features syntagmatically associated with the lexeme *dance* that we have described above is perhaps also best explained by contact with the signifying systems both of the text and of the frescoes. We have of course no accredited copy of the frescoes,[28] but it is characteristic of all the illustrations of the poem, wall-paintings, panel-paintings, engravings, that they should accentuate the athleticism of the dead: energetic, cartoon-like figures at La Chaise-Dieu, grotesque stances and animal masks at Kermaria-en-Isquit, contorted limbs in Guyot Marchant's engravings.[29] The frescoes at the Innocents, in all probability, figured the anomalous movements and wrenched limbs, the unidentifiable and contradictory dance-steps, the incompatibility between static living and acrobatic dead that would authorise Lydgate's emphasis on 'alienness' and 'irregularity'.

What I suggest, therefore, is that Lydgate's 'map' of the text he translates is coloured by a reading that, influenced by the simultaneous reading of text and image, perceives characteristics within the vehicle which have interesting and functional analogues with those of the topic. If the metaphor remains undeveloped, for instance, then the reluctance of the living to dance can be comprehended only on the level of the topic. Lydgate, ingeniously, develops the metaphor so that their reluctance is motivated also on the level of the vehicle: hence the emphasis on the strangeness and incomprehensibility of the dance, such that the living find it impossible to join in. We are, in other words, seeing an enrichment of the metaphor, an enrichment to which, presumably, other readers, other viewers, are susceptible – and which may do much to explain why, so soon after its painting in 1424–25, the *Danse macabré* became both tourist attraction and point of literary and linguistic reference.

28 It is impossible to substantiate the commonly argued thesis that Guyot Marchant's engraver has copied the Innocents' frescoes; for the arguments adduced, however, see a useful summary in Pierre Vaillant, 'La Danse macabre de 1485 et les fresques du Charnier des Innocents', in *La Mort au Moyen Age: Colloque de la Société des Historiens Médiévistes de l'Enseignement Supérieur* (Strasburg, 1977), pp. 81–86.

29 A range of reproductions is given by S. Cosacchi (see note 5).

Tabula Gratulatoria

Ms Flora Alexander
Dr Elizabeth Andersen
Dr Elizabeth Archibald
Dr Ray Barron
Prof. Jeanette Beer
Dr Philip Bennett
Dr Bart Besamusca
Ms Madeleine Blaess
Dr David Blamires
Dr Frank Brandsma
Dr Geoffrey Bromiley
Dr Leslie Brook
Mrs Hilda Brown
Dr Glyn Burgess
Dr Carleton Carroll
Dr Carol Chase
Mr Sidney Close
Dr Anne Cobby
Dr Helen Cooper
M. Robert Deschaux
Prof. Armel Diverres
Dr Jennifer Fellows
Ms Melanie J. Florence
Ms Linda Gowans
Mr Andrew Hamer
Dr Ruth Harvey
Dr Christine M. Hill
Mr Fred Hodcroft
Ms Karen Hodder
Prof. David Hook
Prof. A. Hudson
Dr Tony Hunt
Mr Nicolas Jacobs
Dr Harry Jackson
Dr Sarah Kay
Prof. Douglas Kelly
Prof. Norris Lacy
Dr Pat Lewis
Dr Claude Luttrell
Profs Donald Maddox and Sara Sturm-Maddox
Prof. Nicholas Mann
Dr Peggy McCracken
Prof. Philippe Ménard
Prof. Ian Michael
Drs Roger and Margaret Middleton
Prof. Maldwyn Mills
Mr and Mrs Moynihan
Dr Evelyn Mullally
Dr D.G. Pattison
Valda Pinder
Prof. Alan W. Raitt
Mrs Joyce Reid
Prof. Felicity Riddy
Dr Christina Roaf
Dr Gillian Rogers
Prof. Peter Russell
Ms Olive Sayce
Prof. Harvey Sharrer
Prof. Ian Short
Bernadette Smelik
Dr and Mrs C.R. Sneddon
Prof. Mary Speer
Dr Jane H.M. Taylor
Mrs F.R.E. Turner
Prof. Wolfgang van Emden
Prof. Kenneth Varty
Mrs Carole Weinberg
Dr J.E. Weiss
Mrs Andrea M.L. Williams
Dr Anne Wilson
Ms Jocelyn Wogan-Browne
Prof. Friedrich Wolfzettel

Institutional Libraries
The Brotherton, Leeds
Edinburgh University
The John Rylands, Manchester
Royal Holloway College, London
King's College, London
Rijksuniversiteit Utrecht
Taylor Institution, Oxford
University of Warwick

Index